The Civil War Bookshelf

THE CIVIL WAR BOOKSHELF

50 Must-Read Books About the War Between the States

ROBERT WOOSTER

CITADEL PRESS
Kensington Publishing Corp.
www.kensingtonbooks.com

CITADEL PRESS
books are published by

Kensington Publishing Corp.
850 Third Avenue
New York, NY 10022

All Kensington titles, imprints, and distributed lines are available at special quantity discounts for bulk purchases for sales promotions, premiums, fund-raising, educational, or institutional use. Special book excerpts or customized printings can also be created to fit specific needs. For details, write or phone the office of the Kensington special sales manager: Kensington Publishing Corp., 850 Third Avenue, New York, NY 10022, attn: Special Sales Department, phone 1-800-221-2647.

First Citadel printing October 2001

10 9 8 7 6 5 4 3 2 1

Printed in the United States of America

ISBN 0-8065-2188-0

Library of Congress Number: 2001091882

To Catherine

CONTENTS

ACKNOWLEDGMENTS

An author's most pleasant task comes in thanking those who have helped see a book to completion. As is always the case, I wish I knew how to more eloquently acknowledge those who have contributed to this work. But after spending a good deal of time thinking about, writing, and correcting what I had hoped would be a more suitable expression of thanks, I've decided to scrap those early drafts in favor of a simpler, more direct series of acknowledgments.

The idea for this book came from the staff at Citadel Press, and I'm grateful for the opportunity to have done it. It has given me the excuse to read and reread a number of great books about the American Civil War. Trying to explain these books in a manner suitable to a general readership has been a daunting challenge. Mike Lewis, my editor at Citadel, patiently endured my delays and missed deadlines, for which I'm appreciative. As the first draft of this manuscript wound its way through the usual editorial circles in mid-1999, Citadel Press filed for bankruptcy, and the rights were acquired by Kensington Publishing. This delayed publication for two years, but did have the happy (if unforeseen) result of allowing me to incorporate several recent works about the Civil War into my book.

I wrote this book during a three-year stint (1997–2000) as chair of the Department of Humanities at Texas A&M University–Corpus Christi. I owe a great debt of gratitude to several people who helped with my administrative chores. Pain Hain, dean of the College of Arts and Humanities, has always been a friend and supporter and has listened to my various complaints with unfailingly good cheer. The same can be said for David Mead, then assistant dean of the college. It was also an honor to work with my friends and fellow chairs during this period, Mark Anderson (Department of Visual and Performing Arts) and David Billeaux (Department of Social Sciences). And I was proud to represent a splendid department faculty. Our Humanities secretaries, Noemi Ybarra and Sonya Witherspoon, helped to cover for many of my mistakes in judgment and memory, for which I am extremely grateful. In my private employ, Sonya has also been of invaluable service in helping prepare this manuscript—typing, collating, editing, formatting, and checking the text through multiple revisions. She deserves special thanks.

I'm also blessed with a wonderful family. My parents, Edna and Ralph Wooster, have seen me through good and bad times, never wavering in their love and encouragement. My wife, Catherine Cox, has been incredibly supportive of this and all my other professional endeavors. As usual she has been a perceptive critic and editor, taking time away from her own work as professor of English to save me from countless errors. Someday I hope to be able to repay her. Maybe dedicating this book to her is a start.

INTRODUCTION

Over a decade ago it was estimated that fifty thousand books had been written about the American Civil War. That number has obviously increased since then, sparked in part by the popularity of Ken Burns's nine-part documentary, *The Civil War*. When it was first aired by the Public Broadcasting System in September 1990, approximately forty million viewers watched all or parts of the eleven-hour series. Countless others have seen it on reruns or videotape since then. Its popularity reflects not only the high quality of the series, but also Americans' longstanding fascination with their nation's bloodiest conflict.

The Civil War has drawn the attention of many of our most talented historians, novelists, and poets, and dozens of Pulitzer Prizes and National Book Awards have been bestowed upon works about the nation's terrible civil conflict. Personal diaries and reminiscences, biographies, battle histories, social and economic analyses, atlases, dictionaries, narratives, philosophical forays, novels, and poems have enlightened and entertained us. *The Civil War Bookshelf* attempts to describe and rank the best, most influential, and most readable of these books in a form that layman and specialist alike will find instructive, entertaining, and provocative.

This book is intended for those interested in the Civil War, and is hopefully written in a manner that will satisfy a broad audience. I have attempted to explain the books without using jargon or making unnecessary references to obscure events that might be unfamiliar to general readers. However, I have tried to avoid oversimplifying complex issues. I owe it to readers, as well as the historical figures who struggled so mightily with the problems of mid-nineteenth century America, to deal with complicated themes in a serious fashion.

For my own interpretations of the war, I encourage readers to see the introductory essay in my *Civil War 100: A Ranking of the Most Influential People in the War Between the States* (Citadel Press, 1998). Rather than repeating a similar tract here, an annotated chronology (see page 251) guides readers through the war's major events. That chronology has been keyed to events and people mentioned in *The Civil War Bookshelf.* I've also included appendices (see page 241) consisting of several tables and charts: one outlining the presidential elections between 1848 and 1876, one depicting slaveholding patterns, and several comparing Northern and Southern resources in 1860. All are designed to provide readers with supplemental information on important issues raised in the text.

In selecting the books, I set out several general parameters, some of which I followed more closely than others. Since *The Civil War Bookshelf* is aimed at a diverse general audience, I decided to exclude all multi-volume works. Rather than overwhelm readers, I preferred to give them a broader taste of shorter accounts. Those seeking more information can look within the essays for direction or to the bibliography (see For Further Study, page 235). I admit that I wavered on this issue several times. How could I not include classic multi-volume accounts such as Bruce Catton's moving trilogy about the main Union army on the eastern front, *The Army of the Potomac* (1951–53), or Shelby Foote's mammoth study, *The Civil War* (1958–74), or Douglas Southall Freeman's pioneering analysis of Confederate generals, *Lee's Lieutenants* (1942–44)?

I suppose I cheated a bit on this issue. Concerning trilogies by Catton and Foote, I included my favorite individual volume from each set (*A Stillness at Appomattox* [2] and *The Civil War: A Narrative; Fredericksburg to Meridian* [17], respectively). As for Freeman's masterwork, I was saved by Stephen Sears's remarkably good abridgement of the original three volumes (*Lee's Lieutenants: A Study in Command* [4]), which was published while I was working on the first drafts of *The Civil War Bookshelf.*

I couldn't find a way to work in several of the other great multi-volume books about the Civil War; they deserve at least a mention. Some will surely criticize my omission of Allan Nevins's classics: the two-volume *Ordeal of the Union* (1947), which covers 1847 to 1857; the two-volume *Emergence of Lincoln* (1950), which covers 1857 to 1861; and the four-volume *War for the Union* (1959–1971). My determination not to include multi-volume sets was a factor in my decision not to include other notable contributions such as Virgil Carrington Jones's trilogy, *The Civil War at Sea* (1960–62); Kenneth Williams's thorough five-volume study, *Lincoln Finds a General: A Military Study of the Civil War* (1949–59), which follows the war through the end of 1863; and James G. Randall's four-volume biography, *Lincoln the President* (the last volume completed by Richard Current in 1954–55).

In order to expose readers to a diversity of styles, arguments, and approaches, I had initially intended to include only one of each author's books. Rather early in the project, however, I decided to make a couple of exceptions to this general rule. Because they are so important to our understanding of the Civil War, I included two books by James M. McPherson: *Battle Cry of Freedom: The Civil War Era* [1] and *For Cause and Comrades: Why Men Fought in the Civil War* [7]. McPherson's *Battle Cry of Freedom* is by far the best survey of the period, and *For Cause and Comrades* explains why nearly three million Americans fought against one another for four long years. McPherson also contributed an essay to Gabor S. Boritt's anthology *Lincoln, the War President: The Gettysburg Lectures* [37].

I also selected two of Kenneth M. Stampp's classics: *The Era of Reconstruction, 1865–1877* [11], along with *And the War Came: The North and the Secession Crisis* [19]. In my view there is still no better introductory survey to reconstruction than Stampp's, and his *And the War Came* is such a lucid and important analysis of the months immediately preceding the war that I deemed it a necessary read. An essay by Stampp also appears in *Lincoln, the War President* [37].

In a slightly different category, David Herbert Donald edited and wrote one essay in the anthology *Why the North Won the Civil War* [3], as well as writing the brilliant biography *Lincoln* [6].

Professor Donald also coauthored *The Civil War and Reconstruction* [34]. Archer Jones was coauthor of two books on my list: *The Politics of Command: Factions and Ideas in Confederate Strategy* [25] and *Why the South Lost the Civil War* [29]. Four writers whose books I included also contributed essays to *Ken Burns's* The Civil War: *Historians Respond* [43]: Gary Gallagher, author of *The Confederate War* [5]; Gabor S. Boritt, editor of *Lincoln, the War President* [37]; Leon Litwack, *Been in the Storm So Long: The Aftermath of Slavery* [26]; and C. Vann Woodward, editor of *Mary Chestnut's Civil War* [44]. Finally, Robert V. Bruce wrote an essay published in *Lincoln, the War President* [37], as well as his full-length study of the North's attempts to develop new military ordnance, *Lincoln and the Tools of War* [32].

This may seem to be a long list of exceptions, but I otherwise adhered to my one book per author rule. What books did this guideline lead me to exclude that I otherwise might have included? I'm a great fan of Bruce Catton, but since I selected the last volume in his *Army of the Potomac* trilogy, *A Stillness at Appomattox* [2], I could not pick any of the three volumes in his *Centennial History of the Civil War.* My inclusion of Emory M. Thomas's *Robert E. Lee: A Biography* [9] worked against my also including his fine survey of the Confederacy, *The Confederate Nation, 1861–1865* (1979), or his briefer analysis, *The Confederacy as a Revolutionary Experience* (1971). Similarly, my decision to include Joseph Glatthaar's *March to the Sea and Beyond: Sherman's Troops in the Savannah and Carolinas Campaigns* [22] mitigated against my selecting his excellent *Forged in Battle: The Civil War Alliance of Black Soldiers and White Officers* (1990).

I made my selections with a definite bias in favor of readability and accessibility. As a consequence, I included none of the old nineteenth- and early-twentieth-century classics, such as James Ford Rhodes's eight-volume *History of the United States From the Compromise of 1850 to the McKinley-Bryan Campaign of 1896* (1892–1919). Further, I relegated the very fine recent work, *Religion and the Civil War* (ed. Randall M. Miller, Harry S. Stout, and Charles Reagan Wilson, 1998), to my "Honorable Mention" category. The book fills an important historical void, but I feared that its seventeen individual essays might be disconcerting to nonspecialists. I also shied away from accounts written by participants in the war, a decision sure to be questioned by some experts. These primary sources are invaluable to historians, but I've never had much luck getting general readers (including my students) to actually read them. I did cover two classics from this genre: *Mary Chestnut's Civil War*, edited by C. Vann Woodward [44] and James A. Fremantle's *The Fremantle Diary: Three Months in the Southern States* [33]. Mary Chestnut's diaries and journals about the Confederacy, though not always easy to read, are such an essential part of Civil War scholarship that anyone interested in the period needs to be familiar with them. And Fremantle, an officer on leave from the British army, writes in such an engaging and revealing manner that modern readers will find his diary quite accessible. Ulysses S. Grant's *Memoirs and Selected Letters* (1990) are also described in the "Honorable Mentions" section.

I selected none of the general histories written in the nineteenth century. Often compiled by participants, these books, such as Jefferson Davis's two-volume *Rise and Fall of the Confederate Government* (1881), are interesting, but reveal more about the bias of the author than about the realities of the wartime years. As a university professor who often teaches undergraduate and graduate courses on the Civil War, I've also learned that modern readers usually find nineteenth-century prose florid and unmanageable.

I assembled *The Civil War Bookshelf* with an eye toward covering the entire Civil War era, which I define broadly as the period between 1848, when the United States ended its war against Mexico, and 1877, when the federal government ended its involvement in reconstruction. However, given my self-imposed restriction to limit my list to fifty books, I tried to remain focused on the war itself. The majority of books covered deal with the period between the firing on Fort Sumter by the Confederates in April 1861, to the surrender of Confederate armies in the field in spring and summer, 1865.

The Civil War Bookshelf includes three broad surveys of the war years. James McPherson's *Battle Cry of Freedom* [1] is the best starting point for anyone interested in the Civil War. His elegant, comprehensive survey covers the period between 1848 and 1865. Even at eight hundred pages, it is well worth every reader's thorough investigation. This brilliant book, published in 1988, replaced an older volume by James G. Randall and David Herbert Donald, *The Civil War and Reconstruction* (1961) as the best overall survey of the war. Still, a revised version of the Randall and Donald book, now written by Donald, Jean H. Baker, and Michael Holt [35], remains a highly useful account of the period, and has the virtue of also covering reconstruction. Finally, I've included the beautifully illustrated book which accompanied the Ken Burns PBS documentary: *The Civil War: An Illustrated History* [42], by Geoffrey C. Ward, with Ric and Ken Burns. A fourth, Russell Weigley's *Great Civil War: A Military and Political History, 1861–1865* (2000) is briefly described in the "Honorable Mentions" section.

Despite my decision to emphasize the war years, I believe readers cannot truly understand why the war came and what the war meant without knowing something about the decades immediately before and after the conflict. I've included several books which deal with the prewar period. David Potter's *Impending Crisis, 1848–1861* [12] is a magisterial discussion of the political events of the 1850s. For analysis of affairs in the North, I've selected Eric Foner's *Free Soil, Free Labor, Free Men: The Ideology of the Republican Party Before the Civil War* [31], and Kenneth Stampp's *And the War Came: The North and the Secession Crisis, 1860–61* [19]. William L. Barney studies the secession movement from the Southern perspective in *The Secessionist Impulse: Alabama and Mississippi in 1860* [40].

Similarly, I've included a sampling of the best books about the period immediately following the war. It was during these years that Americans figured out what the results of the war would be; Northerners had not agreed upon a plan for restoring the Union before the fighting ended. Kenneth Stampp's *Era of Reconstruction, 1865–1877* [11] remains an insightful and accessible overview of the controversies associated with the restoration of the Union. Leon Litwack's *Been in the Storm So Long: The Aftermath of*

Slavery [26] is a masterly description of emancipation. *Lee's Tarnished Lieutenant: James Longstreet and His Place in Southern History* by William Garrett Piston [47] is an intriguing discussion of how postwar political rivalries badly tarnished the reputation of one of the Confederacy's most capable generals.

I also selected books with an eye toward avoiding duplication of subject matter. Of course, it was not always possible, or desirable, to stick rigidly to this principle. Readers will find several books that deal with the two presidents, Abraham Lincoln and Jefferson Davis. In addition to David Herbert Donald's magnificent biography, *Lincoln* [6], I've included T. Harry Williams's lively analysis, *Lincoln and His Generals* [8]; Mark E. Neely, Jr.'s Pulitzer Prize–winning study, *The Fate of Liberty: Abraham Lincoln and Civil Liberties* [28]; Robert V. Bruce's classic tale of the president's attempts to foster innovative technologies, *Lincoln and the Tools of War* [32]; and an anthology, *Lincoln, the War President: The Gettysburg Lectures* [37], which contains essays by five Pulitzer Prize winners. The list is also a long one when it comes to Davis. The best overall biography is William C. Davis's *Jefferson Davis: The Man and His Hour* [16]. I've also included several other books that give substantial coverage to the Confederate president: *Jefferson Davis and His Generals: The Failure of Confederate Command in the West*, by Steven E. Woodworth [24]; *The Politics of Command: Factions and Ideas in Confederate Strategy*, by Thomas L. Connelly and Archer Jones [25]; and *Rebel Brass: The Confederate Command System*, by Frank E. Vandiver [48].

I acknowledge that this emphasis on the two presidents forced me to deemphasize some of the literature about social, cultural, and intellectual trends during the Civil War. My defense is twofold. First, these men were the duly elected presidents of their respective countries. Even acknowledging the realities of mid-nineteenth-century politics, in which all women and most black men were excluded from the ballot box, the elections of Davis and Lincoln profoundly affected the course of the war. Second, the literature about both presidents is not only of splendid quality, it holds some of the keys to why the war was won or lost. Did the

Confederacy lose because of Davis's mistakes, or some other cause—internal disunity or insufficient material resources, for example? By contrast, was Lincoln's leadership key to Union success, or could the North have won with another man at the helm?

I like biographies, so I've included biographical accounts of Robert E. Lee [9], Ulysses S. Grant [35], and James Longstreet [47]. My selection is a bit skewed toward two of the war's most intriguing personalities—Thomas J. "Stonewall" Jackson and William Tecumseh Sherman. A deeply religious Virginian whose brilliant exploits at the First Battle of Bull Run and in the Shenandoah Valley campaign vaulted him to national prominence, Stonewall Jackson is the center of many legends and a good deal of scholarly debate. His quirky, occasionally erratic behavior makes him a fascinating figure. I've included not only a comprehensive biography, *Stonewall Jackson: The Man, the Soldier, the Legend*, by James I. Robertson, Jr. [20], but also a broader-based study by Charles Royster—*The Destructive War: William Tecumseh Sherman, Stonewall Jackson, and the Americans* [21]. Jackson is also dealt with extensively in John Waugh's interesting collective biography, *The Class of 1846, From West Point to Appomattox: Stonewall Jackson, George McClellan, and Their Brothers* [27].

I've followed a similar line of reasoning on Union general William T. Sherman. Dubbed mentally unstable by some at the beginning of the war, Sherman proved a sturdy fighter at the Battle of Shiloh, and a fine corps commander under Ulysses S. Grant. His subsequent campaigns against Atlanta, Savannah, and the Carolinas rank among the war's most controversial. He is discussed not only in Royster's book [21], but in a full-length biography, *Sherman: A Soldier's Passion for Order* [38], by John F. Marszalek. Less biographical, but certainly closely related to the subject of Sherman, is Joseph Glatthaar's *March to the Sea and Beyond* [22].

Although I have tried to cast my net wide by considering the Civil War as an era, rather than simply four years of warfare, my bias remains firm toward military events. I like the reasoning used by Gary Gallagher, author of *The Confederate War* [5], in his essay for *Ken Burns's* The Civil War: *Historians Respond* [43]. Gallagher disagrees with critics who charged that Burns's documentary overemphasized military events, leaving out too many civilian issues in the process. As Gallagher explains, "I believe it important to remember that the subject of Burns's documentary was a mammoth *war*" (p. 41).

Readers will quickly recognize that *The Civil War Bookshelf* includes several books about strategy and broad military operations. By contrast, only one book about a specific campaign, Stephen W. Sears's *Landscape Turned Red: The Battle of Antietam* [14], made my list. Another book about a single campaign, Donald E. Sutherland's *Fredericksburg and Chancellorsville: The Dare Mark Campaign* (1998) is on my list of honorable mentions. This emphasis reflects my belief that Civil War enthusiasts sometimes become too engrossed in detail and trivia and miss the bigger picture. I'm not sure, for example, that general readers need to know that a certain regiment took a certain road to reach a particular hill at two o'clock on a specific afternoon. I've instead directed readers to broader, more analytical studies, hoping that those seeking additional details will consult the For Further Study section (see page 235) for additional titles.

The Civil War Bookshelf devotes less attention to naval affairs than to ground operations. There are some good books available on naval warfare, but most are rather narrowly focused. Of the one-volume surveys, my favorite is *Under Two Flags: The American Navy in the Civil War*, by William M. Fowler, Jr. [39]. *Under Two Flags* is suitable for general readers, and Fowler maintains an objective stance when dealing with rivalries between army and navy. Slightly more focused is Raimondo Luraghi, *A History of the Confederate Navy* [46], an exciting examination of Confederate naval strategy and operations. I've also included Robert M. Browning, Jr., *From Cape Charles to Cape Fear: The North Atlantic Blockading Squadron During the Civil War* (1993) in my "Honorable Mentions" category.

I've also included several books about events behind the lines. In the North the war years brought a number of "firsts"—the first income tax, the funding for the first transcontinental railroad, and the first major federal higher-education program. Allan G. Bogue,

The Congressman's Civil War [49], is a fascinating analysis of the workings of Congress. Phillip Shaw Paludan's *"A People's Contest": The Union and Civil War, 1861–1865* [13] is an exceptionally good analysis of the North. *The Civil War Bookshelf* doesn't include a similar survey of the Confederacy, although *Why the South Lost the Civil War* [29] devotes a good deal of attention to the Confederate home front, as do several essays in David Herbert Donald's anthology, *Why the North Won the Civil War* [3]. The latter book includes a fascinating essay on diplomacy; for a broader assessment of wartime relations between the United States and Great Britain, readers can see *The Union in Peril: The Crisis Over British Intervention in the Civil War,* by Howard Jones [30].

Although a historian by trade, I have recognized that fiction can help modern readers to understand the Civil War, especially at an emotional level. My favorite novel about the war is Michael Shaara's *Killer Angels* [10], a brilliant fictional account of the Battle of Gettysburg. More critical of Robert E. Lee's generalship than I would like, Shaara nonetheless captures the essence of this titanic struggle between the Union Army of the Potomac and the Confederate Army of Northern Virginia better than any historian. I suspect that few readers will be surprised by the inclusion of Stephen Crane's classic novel about a boy coming of age on the battlefield (loosely centered upon the historical Battle of Chancellorsville), *The Red Badge of Courage* [45]. Finally, I've included one epic poem—*John Brown's Body* [50], by Stephen Vincent Benét.

Ranking these great books was maddeningly difficult and sure to generate controversy. Believing that history and literature are more art than science, I did not even attempt to develop a numerical weighting system. Instead, I tried to balance the importance of a book's subject matter, its readability and suitability for general audiences, its influence on our understanding of the Civil War, and its success in getting across some fundamental point about the conflict. Thus James McPherson's *Battle Cry of Freedom* [1], by virtue of its immense scope, insightful analyses, and brilliant prose, ranked first. But the middle volume of Shelby Foote's huge trilogy, *The Civil War: A Narrative; Fredericksburg to Meridian*

[17], though a graceful and interesting book, ranked lower. This was because its subject matter is somewhat narrower, its great length might be intimidating to some readers, and its analysis is less influential on Civil War scholarship. I ranked *Lee's Lieutenants* [3], by Douglas Southall Freeman, very high, basing my decision on Freeman's magnificent style and huge influence upon subsequent writers.

If I thought books on the same subject were of roughly similar quality, I tried to rank them next to one another so as to improve the flow of the text. For example, I placed Gary Gallagher's *The Confederate War* [5] immediately after *Lee's Lieutenants* [4], as both deal eloquently with Confederate military leaders. Likewise, I clustered the two books directly related to the Ken Burns documentary together: the book that accompanied the PBS series, *The Civil War: An Illustrated History*, by Geoffrey C. Ward, with Ric Burns and Ken Burns [42], immediately precedes *Ken Burns's* The Civil War: *Historians Respond* edited by Robert Brent Toplin [43].

Writing this book has been a humbling experience. When I began this project, I must admit I didn't fully understand just how many and how *good* the best books about the Civil War were. Because of the criteria I've discussed above, as well as the large number of works written about our nation's greatest conflict, I've had to leave out a number of very fine books that many Civil War enthusiasts will undoubtedly miss. Let me assure those who did not find a particular favorite that cutting the list to fifty wasn't easy. Others will undoubtedly disagree with my selections and rankings. Hopefully, however, I've written a readable, accessible, and thoughtful guide to the best and most important books about America's largest and most important war.

The Civil War Bookshelf

1.

Battle Cry of Freedom: The Civil War Era

by James M. McPherson

James M. McPherson's *Battle Cry of Freedom* (1988) ranks among the world's greatest books. Elegant in style and measured yet forceful in its judgments, this survey of the Civil War era is suitable for a broad audience and serves as an excellent introduction to the period. Its author, a prolific and thoughtful member of the history faculty at Princeton University since 1962, had already established an excellent reputation in the field through his well-received books about blacks and the Civil War, as well as a fine survey, *Ordeal by Fire: The Civil War and Reconstruction* (1981). But *Battle Cry of Freedom,* part of the Oxford History of the United States series, soared to new heights with its magisterial assessment of the period.

The Civil War, argues McPherson, was a result of the North's rebellion against the South's traditional dominance of the United States. For years Southern demands for a limited federal government and strong protections for slaveholders had reigned supreme. In the Supreme Court Southern-born justices were always the majority until 1861, when Abraham Lincoln took office. Two-thirds of the time the Speaker of the House and president pro tem of the Senate were Southerners. Every president, except John Adams and his son, John Quincy Adams, had been either a Southerner or a Southern sympathizer.

McPherson also makes a compelling case for slavery's key role in dividing North from South. During the late 1840s the United States acquisition of Texas and the Southwest from Mexico and the settlement of Oregon's boundary with Britain had reopened an old question: What would be the fate of slavery in the newly acquired lands? Heated debates about the "peculiar institution" exacerbated other issues dividing North from South, such as the constitutionality and wisdom of federally sponsored railroads, tariffs, and the banking system. These conflicts highlighted the cultural and intellectual differences between Northerners and Southerners, who no longer attended the same types of churches or read the same books. By the mid-1850s the political parties reflected this sectionalism; Southern interests took control of the Democratic Party and Northerners dominated the newly formed Republican Party.

North-South tensions came to a head in May1860, McPherson claims, when the Republicans nominated Abraham Lincoln for president. Lincoln supported a broad platform of federally sponsored internal improvements (including railroads), advocated programs designed to assist the development of free-labor capitalism (including a higher tariff and banking reforms), vowed to clean up the corruption which had stained the previous Democratic administration, and promised to prevent the expansion of slavery into any new territories. To summarize, Lincoln advocated a more active federal government than Americans had ever seen. His electoral triumph in November represented a true political *revolution,* in McPherson's opinion, and meant that the North, not the South, had diverted from tradition. The secession of eleven Southern states thereafter thus represented a *counterrevolution*. "Union victory in the war destroyed the southern vision of America and ensured that the northern vision would become the American vision," McPherson posits. "From the war sprang the great flood that caused the stream of American history to surge into a new channel and transferred the burden of exceptionalism from North to South" (pp. 861–62).

Battle Cry of Freedom also offers a provocative analysis of the

war's outcome. Northern victory, McPherson insists, was not inevitable. Disagreeing with those who attribute the South's defeat to a loss of will, a scarcity of resources, or inadequate leadership, he puts forth what has come to be known as the "contingency" thesis to explain the war's result. He argues that the outcome could have been altered in "the contingency that hung over every battle, every election, every decision during the war" (p. 858). Confederate battlefield losses caused declining morale at home—not vice versa, he adds.

McPherson identifies four critical points that suggest the war's outcome could have been different. The first came in the summer of 1862, when Confederate counteroffensives shattered Union hopes of a quick victory. A second occurred that fall, when Confederate armies had advanced into Maryland and Kentucky. European mediation seemed a realistic possibility. Southerners abandoned this hope, however, after Confederate defeats at Antietam, Maryland, and Perryville, Kentucky. A third critical point came in mid to late 1863 when the North was victorious at Gettysburg, Vicksburg, and Chattanooga—all grievous blows to the South. Even so, the Confederacy came close to reversing the tide in the summer of 1864, when enormous Union casualties in Virginia and the army's slow progress toward Atlanta nearly ruined Lincoln's chances for reelection. In McPherson's view, changes at any of these important junctures could have led the South to win the war.

This keen sense of drama characterizes McPherson's work. *Battle Cry of Freedom* opens with a vivid description of U. S. troops accepting the surrender of Mexico City at the close of the war against Mexico (1848) and concludes with a summary of President Lincoln's speech concerning peace and reconstruction delivered from a White House balcony just two days after Robert E. Lee's surrender at Appomattox on May 1865. Southern sympathizer John Wilkes Booth, a member of the audience who had been planning to assassinate the president or take him hostage, delivers the final, disturbing words: " 'Now, by God, I'll put him through,' muttered Booth. 'That is the last speech he will ever make' " (p. 852).

Not all Civil War scholars have accepted McPherson's analysis of the war, especially his controversial contingency thesis. Reviewers of the book also have noted his lack of attention to intellectual, cultural, and economic affairs. A few have pointed out that McPherson sometimes fails to acknowledge the divisions within the North or South which make any broader generalizations about the two regions extremely hazardous. But even McPherson's critics generally acknowledge that *Battle Cry of Freedom* represents the best one-volume survey of the period. This readable and cogently argued work reflects a respected scholar's decades-long study of this terrible conflict. It should be the starting point for anyone who wants to understand the American Civil War.

2.

A Stillness at Appomattox

by Bruce Catton

A professional writer and editor rather than an academic, Bruce Catton (1899–1978) was the most widely read Civil War author of the twentieth century. He was born in Michigan and joined the navy during World War I. After the war he went into the newspaper business, working for the government before becoming a freelance writer and later editor of the highly regarded popular history magazine *American Heritage.* Catton was a magnificent stylist who combined materials from official records, regimental histories, and soldiers' diaries with the war stories he had heard as a youth to convey his message effectively if unobtrusively to his readers. His most powerful writing dealt with the Union Army of the Potomac, whose values seemed to mirror those of his own boyhood in Benzonia, Michigan (population 350). His first work in a trilogy about this army, *Mr. Lincoln's Army,* was published in 1951; *Glory Road,* the second, appeared the following year. In 1953 *A Stillness at Appomattox,* the final volume, won the National Book Award and the Pulitzer Prize in History.

In this last segment of his Army of the Potomac trilogy, which opens in the spring of 1864, Catton describes the army's transformation from a noble, if flawed, instrument into a ruthless war machine capable of victory on the eastern front. In the past volunteers had filled this magnificent army, but after three years of war, many of its veterans were gone, dead or maimed in the fighting, or back home after refusing to reenlist. Conscripts and bounty men took their place. To fill their draft quotas, individuals and communities often paid hundreds of dollars to anyone willing to flesh out the ranks. By and large the newcomers had neither the patriotism nor the character of their more experienced volunteer cousins, according to Catton. As theft, shirking duty, and desertion mounted, harsh discipline rather than ideological commitment became the primary means of keeping the army strong.

The Army of the Potomac also had a new commander. Ulysses S. Grant, leader of the successful Vicksburg campaign and victor at the battles of Fort Henry and Fort Donelson, Shiloh, and Chattanooga in Tennessee, had come east to Virginia, where he was appointed general-in-chief in March, 1864. Although known as a brilliant horseman who deeply loved his wife, the unassuming Grant hardly looked the savior. He was rumored to be an alcoholic and had failed at virtually every job he had tried during the 1850s. However, Grant was responsible for appointing the combative Phil Sheridan to command the cavalry, stripping rear garrisons in order to bring more troops to the front, and implementing General George Meade's plan for consolidating the army's five infantry corps into three, bringing not fanfare but competence to his new role.

The road south would not be an easy one. Ahead lay the lean but deadly Confederate Army of Northern Virginia, commanded by the brilliant Robert E. Lee, "the one soldier in whom most of the higher officers of the Army of the Potomac had complete, undiluted confidence," quips Catton (p. 43). From mid-May through July hardly a day passed without a major battle or horrific skirmish. The Federals were parried at the Wilderness, Spotsylvania, Cold Harbor, and Petersburg. Their casualties averaged more than two thousand men per day and poor generalship and sloppy staff work still plagued them. Winfield Scott Hancock's promising attacks in the Battle of the Wilderness and against the Rebel salient at the Battle of Spotsylvania (the Bloody Angle), had not been supported. A twenty-four-hour delay and subsequent failure to reconnoiter the ground at Cold Harbor had led to mass slaughter. The Army of the Potomac squandered another oppor-

A typical Union army mess tent for enlisted men.
NATIONAL ARCHIVES

tunity at Petersburg when Lee was given time to reinforce that strategic railroad junction with his entire army. A final chance was lost during the Crater assault, ruined by a division commander's decision to station himself in a protective bombproof shelter with a bottle of rum while his men were being annihilated by Confederate troops.

Still, Grant kept relentless pressure on Lee's forces, transforming the Union army's mission in the process, claims Catton. No longer would the Army of the Potomac retreat after a single battle; no longer would it focus upon the capture of Richmond. Instead it would fight and keep on fighting until one side was forced to give in. In addition, the soldiers would bring the war directly to the people of Virginia as never before. In the Shenandoah Valley and northern Virginia the conflict became total. Anything that might aid the Confederate cause was destroyed. War is never glorious, and the Union armies in the east concerted their efforts to ensure that every Southerner knew it.

Catton is at his literary best when he uses the dramatic end to the military career of Maj. Gen. Governor Kemble Warren to capture this new attitude, which included a growing intolerance for the mistakes and excuses of the past. Although he was considered a hero of the Battle of Gettysburg for having recognized the military importance of Little Round Top's high ground, Warren had, as corps commander, repeatedly been late in getting his men into position. Fearing that Warren's delays might result in yet another missed opportunity to crush the enemy at Five Forks, Sheridan summarily fired him on the spot. Catton's opinion of this decision, and the army's new attitude, is clear: "Sheridan had been cruel and unjust—and if that cruel and unjust insistence on driving, aggressive promptness had been the rule in this army from the beginning, the war probably would have been won two years earlier" (p. 358).

A Stillness at Appomattox is written from the viewpoint of the men who served in the Army of the Potomac. Through this technique Catton brings the war to life for the reader, who suffers with the dying and wounded, grows hungry with those who have marched all night and missed their breakfasts, and waits anxiously for the onset of the next battle. He does more than chronicle the soldiers' journey as they begin the spring 1864 campaign by crossing the Rapidan River. He transforms their experience into poetry through the dark, foreboding image of "a forest with the shadow of death under its low branches" intertwined with the hopeful springtime image of "dogwood blossoms . . . floating in the air like lost flecks of sunlight, as if life was as important as death" (p. 55). In a single magnificent sentence the reader is invited to share in the soldiers' emotional response to the war.

A Stillness at Appomattox goes on to capture the fears, dark humor, tragedies, and finally triumph of a Civil War army. Victory came at a little hamlet known as Appomattox Court House. "It was Palm Sunday, and they would all live to see Easter, and with the guns quieted it might be easier to comprehend the mystery and the promise of that day," writes Catton. "Yet the fact of peace and no more killing and an open road home seems to have been too big to grasp, right at the moment, and in the enormous silence that lay upon the field men remembered that they had marched far and were very tired, and they wondered when the wagon trains would come up with rations" (p. 379).

No other historian has ever written so eloquently about the experience of an army fighting in the American Civil War; *A Stillness at Appomattox* is the work of an author at the very peak of his narrative powers.

3.

Why the North Won the Civil War

edited by David Herbert Donald

Why the North Won the Civil War (1960) is a superb introduction to the most common explanations historians have offered for the North's victory in the American Civil War. The foundation of the book was a 1958 conference sponsored by Gettysburg College in which five leading scholars were asked to reexamine five different explanations for the war's outcome. The resultant essays were collected and edited by David Herbert Donald, a Pulitzer Prize winner whose biography of Abraham Lincoln [6] and contributions to *Civil War and Reconstruction* [34] are included in *The Civil War Bookshelf.* In just over one hundred pages, readers gain not only the insights of several prominent historians, but knowledge of the principal theories about why the North emerged victorious.

Two basic questions are reoccurring themes. First, was Northern victory guaranteed? Richard Current's essay, "God and the Strongest Battalions," makes a strong case for the "all but inevitable" (p. 29) Federal triumph. He points out that when the war began, the Union had a 5–2 edge in population, a 3–1 advantage in property value, a 10–1 lead in manufacturing, and a virtual monopoly over registered shipping. For the Confederacy to have compensated for these numerical imbalances, "the civilians of the South would have had to be several times as able, man for man, as those of the North" (p. 26). Current does, however, offer two caveats to the inevitability of Northern victory. One was the possi-

View of a massive Union supply base, 1864.
NATIONAL ARCHIVES

bility of foreign intervention in support of the Confederacy. The other was an early Union military disaster.

Current's essay thus poses the second major issue dominating *Why the North Won:* If Northern victory was not inevitable, what could the Confederacy have done differently in order to win? T. Harry Williams, author of *Lincoln and His Generals* [8], blames Southern generalship. Confederate generals never understood "the vital relationship between war and statecraft" (pp. 48–49), claims Williams in "The Military Leadership of North and South." They concentrated too heavily upon their immediate geographic areas and failed to grasp the importance of broader social, economic, and psychological factors. With the military development of Lincoln and generals Ulysses S. Grant and William T. Sherman, the Union enjoyed a tremendous advantage in military leadership.

David Potter, whose *Impending Crisis, 1848–1861* [12] remains the best single-volume study of the 1850s, focuses on the failures of the Confederate president, Jefferson Davis. In "Jefferson Davis and the Political Factors in Confederate Defeat," Potter points out that Davis appointed a weak cabinet, had too high an opinion of his own military abilities, and intervened too frequently in affairs better left to his subordinates. Instead of thinking about possibilities for success, Davis spent too much of his energy "proving he was right" (p. 104). Most important, argues Potter, the Confederate president never developed into the revolutionary leader his cause required, providing neither the inspiration nor the innovations demanded by the increasingly desperate situation.

Norman A. Graebner, who studies the history of diplomacy, seizes upon another alternative: Even limited European intervention could have tipped the scales in favor of the Confederacy. Britain, the world's strongest naval and economic power, threatened some form of intervention on several occasions before the autumn of 1862, when Union victory at Antietam and Lincoln's emancipation proclamation effectively ended any realistic possibility of its direct involvement. Each time, however, the Union's secretary of state William Seward interceded, rejecting the right of any European nation to interfere in American domestic affairs and warning that Britain's involvement in the war would threaten its flourishing trade with the Union. "Whatever the North's diplomatic advantages," Graebner concludes, Seward "understood them and exploited them with astonishing effectiveness" (p. 76).

In his own essay, "Died of Democracy," David Donald counters that the superiority of Northern political or diplomatic leadership was less relevant to its ultimate success than problems inherent to the Confederacy itself. Southerners insisted on maintaining all of their democratic liberties, he claims, despite the fact that a war was going on. Rebel soldiers frequently disobeyed orders from their officers and tossed aside irreplaceable camping equipment while on the march. Faced with such undisciplined behavior, the Confederate government was too hesitant to infringe upon civil liberties, even when the war effort demanded it. Martial law was extremely rare in the South. President Davis even refused to intervene in politics in order to secure the passage of legislation he believed was needed to win the war. The Confederacy, argues Donald, "died of democracy" (p. 79).

The frustrated reader might ask, "Why *did* the North win the Civil War?" My answer, if pressed, is that James McPherson's "contingency" thesis, which holds that the war's outcome could have been changed had there been different outcomes to several key battles, elections, or decisions *(Battle Cry of Freedom* [1]), presents a more sophisticated and satisfying response than any offered in these essays. Still, this little volume remains an excellent introduction to the literature of the Civil War.

4.

Lee's Lieutenants: A Study in Command

by Douglas Southall Freeman

(abridged in one volume by Stephen W. Sears, 1998)

Steeped in Confederate tradition, the writings of Douglas Southall Freeman have profoundly influenced our understanding of the American Civil War.

Freeman was born at Lynchburg, Virginia, in 1886, the son of a veteran of the Confederate Army of Northern Virginia. His family lived down the street from Jubal A. Early, one of that army's greatest fighting generals, and later moved to Richmond, the former capital of the Confederacy. After receiving his doctorate in history from Johns Hopkins University in 1908, Freeman left academia to become a journalist, and was named editor of the *Richmond News Leader* at the age of twenty-nine. He never lost his passion for history, however. An acquaintance gave him two leather-bound volumes containing Gen. Robert E. Lee's confidential wartime messages to President Jefferson Davis, long believed to have been lost. Freeman edited and published the work as *Lee's Confidential Dispatches* in 1915 and established himself as a leading historian of the Confederacy.

Publisher Charles Scribner's Sons quickly commissioned this promising author to write a 75,000 word biography of Lee. Freeman believed he could write it in two years; in fact, it took him nearly two decades. What was to have been a short biography turned into a four-volume masterpiece, *R. E. Lee,* which received a Pulitzer Prize in 1935. Freeman then turned his attention to

George Washington, but Lee's Army of Northern Virginia still haunted Freeman's thoughts, and in 1936 he set aside his work on Washington to further explore Lee and his officers. In 1942 the first volume of his classic work *Lee's Lieutenants: A Study in Command* was published, followed by two additional volumes over the next two years. By the time this history was finished Freeman had written approximately two million words about Lee and his generals and set standards of scholarship, style, and analysis which subsequent authors have often emulated but rarely matched.

The three volumes of *Lee's Lieutenants* (1942–44), like those of Freeman's earlier *R. E. Lee,* have long been staple reading for Civil War specialists, but their great length put off more casual readers. In 1998 Stephen W. Sears, whose own *Landscape Turned Red: The Battle of Antietam* [14] has won high regard, reduced *Lee's Lieutenants* to a single volume. He updates the sources and cuts the fourteen appendices and much of the detail in the battle accounts but retains the essence of the original work: Freeman's priceless interpretations of the general officers that served in Lee's army. The resultant one-volume masterpiece is accessible to a broad audience.

At the war's outset the Army of Northern Virginia was blessed with a fine cadre of promising general officers, Freeman argues. These included a wealth of graduates of the U.S. Military Academy, the Virginia Military Institute, and the South Carolina Military Academy (now the Citadel). Lee assumed command of the army in early June, 1862, after Joseph E. Johnston was wounded in the fighting at Seven Pines, Virginia. But organizational defects plagued the army throughout the Seven Days' Battles that followed in late June, the lack of coordination among division commanders robbing the Confederates of a decisive victory. To fix the structural problems Lee divided the army into two commands led by his best subordinates, James Longstreet and Thomas J. "Stonewall" Jackson.

The new system proved its worth during the Second Battle of Bull Run and the Battle of Antietam. But the heavy attrition of the fighting had left gaping holes in leadership positions. Major generals, for example, were supposed to command each of the army's

John Bell Hood: "At heart he is an executive officer, not a strategist."—Douglas Southall Freeman.
LIBRARY OF CONGRESS

nine divisions, but only four of the positions were filled. To resolve the crisis the Confederate Congress allowed President Jefferson Davis to appoint and assign twenty new general officers. Stonewall Jackson's death in 1863 (he died from complications after his own men accidentally wounded him during the Battle of Chancellorsville) necessitated another major reorganization. Rather than trying to replace Jackson, Lee carved the army into three corps to be led by Longstreet, Richard Ewell, and A. P. Hill.

This basic command structure would serve for the rest of the war. But the Army of Northern Virginia had run out of qualified general officers again. The Confederacy had made no systematic effort to develop new leaders, instead assuming that they would emerge from the lower ranks during combat. "The school of combat," insists Freeman, "did not graduate men enough to make good the casualties of instruction" (p. 22). After the second year of war only two men—John B. Gordon and William Mahone—"added materially to the vigor of the high command," he continued (p. 22). Others whom Freeman describes as promising, such as Dorsey Pender, Stephen Dodson Ramseur, and Robert Rodes, were killed before fulfilling their potential.

The Confederate army's shortage of officers became more pronounced as the war continued. After the Battle of Gettysburg, only five of the thirty-eight infantry brigades were led by men who had held the rank of brigadier general for one year or more. Twenty-two of the fifty-eight men who served as general officers from May 4 through June 3, 1864, fell during the costly Battle of the Wilderness and Spotsylvania campaign. Freeman points out the terrible effect of this attrition: Men were needlessly sacrificed by generals who were inexperienced or simply incapable of mastering the complexities of Civil War command. Even Lee's genius could not compensate for the Confederacy's material disadvantages and the deteriorating quality of subordinate officers.

A son of the South who recognizes that the Confederacy lost the war, Freeman is coolly objective about its leaders without becoming bitter or derogatory. His style is elegant, even courtly: Longstreet is "blunt and roughly bantering . . . slightly deaf, but a dignified, impressive man, known to his soldiers as 'Old Pete.' If he is not brilliant in strategy or in conversation, he is solid and systematic. Ambitious he is, but not disposed to pick quarrels. The secret of his power is his incredible nervous control. He never gets tired. Unfortunately," concludes Freeman, "he is beguiled by circumstances into thinking himself a strategist as well as an executive officer" (p. 30–31). Or take the heroic John Bell Hood, who "stood six feet, two inches and had a powerful chest and a giant's shoulders. His hair and beard were a light brown, almost blond; his penetrating, expressive, kindly eyes were blue. When he spoke it was with a booming, musical richness of tone. . . . By the autumn of 1862 he was to be one of the most magnificent men in Confederate service. For the admiration of the lettered he might have stepped out of the pages of Malory; to the untutored boy in the ranks, Hood was what every hero-worshipping lad wished his big brother to be" (p. 121). Alas, Hood lost a leg and the use of an arm from battlefield wounds; subsequent appointments to command of the Army of Tennessee proved "beyond the resources of a crippled general. . . . Perhaps he should never had been assigned an army. At heart he is an executive officer, not a strategist" (p. 38).

Douglas Southall Freeman remains a giant among Civil War historians nearly half a century after his death. Some critics have even suggested that his enormous influence led subsequent scholars to focus too much of their energy on the war's eastern front. *Lee's Lieutenants* is his best work, ranking even above his biography of Lee, which is sometimes too favorable to its subject. For insight into Lee I recommend works by Emory M. Thomas (*Robert E. Lee* [9]) and Gary W. Gallagher (*The Confederate War* [5]). But *Lee's Lieutenants,* abridged in one volume by Sears, remains the classic study of Civil War generalship.

5.

The Confederate War

by Gary W. Gallagher

Since the publication of the groundbreaking anthology *Why the North Won the Civil War* in 1960 [3], historians have continued to debate the reasons for the Confederacy's defeat. Some have focused on the home front, contending that Southerners had few unifying bonds save their fear of a society without slavery. Others have stressed the role of class and gender divisions. Planters and yeoman farmers had different goals and aspirations, and deteriorating conditions led many women to challenge the existing patriarchal system. Conscription laws, taxes, and the impressment of slaves further eroded Confederate loyalties. Other historians suggest that nagging doubts about the morality of slavery worked upon the consciences of some Southerners and prevented them from fully supporting the conflict against the North.

On the military front some scholars have challenged the abilities of Confederate generals, including the venerated Robert E. Lee. Thomas L. Connelly joined forces with Archer Jones to write the provocative *Politics of Command: Factions and Ideas in Confederate Strategy* [25], which contends that Lee was too focused on defending Virginia, to the detriment of the rest of the Confederacy. Another shot across the bow came from Grady McWhiney and Perry D. Jamieson, coauthors of *Attack and Die: Civil War Military Tactics and the Southern Heritage* (1982). Mc-

Whiney and Jamieson contend that Confederate generals, Lee included, were far too wedded to offensive tactics, which produced needlessly heavy casualties and bled the South dry of manpower.

Gary Gallagher takes all of these revisionists to task in *The Confederate War* (1997). The book, which stems from presentations Gallagher made at the University of Texas at Austin's Littlefield lecture series, represents the most ambitious and enthusiastic defense of General Lee and the notion of Confederate nationhood in print. The author of a respected biography of one of Lee's subordinates Stephen Dodson Ramseur, Gallagher is also a prodigious editor who has compiled anthologies on the campaigns in the Shenandoah Valley, Antietam, Fredericksburg, Chancellorsville, Spotsylvania, and the Wilderness, as well as one volume for each of the three days of the Battle of Gettysburg. None of these efforts, however, match the vigor, originality, and depth of the arguments set forth in his *Confederate War.*

Gallagher structures this work around several key points, each buttressed with solid logic and an array of examples. Many historians focus too much on domestic affairs, he contends: "Defeat in the military sphere, rather than dissolution behind the lines, brought the collapse of the Confederacy" (p. 11). Rather than demoralizing Southerners, physical privations, the loss of loved ones, and advancing enemy armies strengthened their loyalty to the Confederacy—but only so long as that nation's armies remained unbeaten.

In fact, Gallagher argues, Confederates fought very hard indeed, paying a higher price in blood during this war than any other group of white Americans in history. Roughly 800,000 Confederates saw military service, a figure representing about three quarters of its white population of draft age. Of these, more than 36 percent (290,000) were killed or wounded in battle. In contrast, only about half of those eligible to do so served in the Union army; just 17.5 percent of the Federal soldiers were killed or wounded in combat. Another 164,000 Confederates and 250,000 Yankees died from accident or disease. Confederate casualties (and Union ones as well) far exceeded those of other

Robert E. Lee.
LIBRARY OF CONGRESS

American wars, the next bloodiest being the Vietnam War (7.7 percent American casualties) and the Second World War (5.4 percent).

Gallagher refutes suggestions that Confederates lacked a sense of nationalism, pointing to an influential group of slaveholders as an example. "Reared among the sectional controversies of the late 1840s and 1850s, they harbored few if any doubts about the institution of slavery," he argues, "attributed base motives to northerners in general and Republicans in particular, often spoke of a distinct cultural identity for the South, and supported secession and united southern action when the crisis broke in the winter of 1860–61" (pp. 96–97). Admittedly some Southerners lost hope, but the vast majority did not, at least not until their armies were defeated. Gallagher acknowledges that Confederate citizens found much in their central government to criticize, but demonstrates that they found the success of their armies a point of tremendous national pride. He claims, "Robert E. Lee and his Army of Northern Virginia eventually became the most important national institution" (p. 8).

Gallagher goes on to mount an aggressive defense of Lee. Southerners found much in Lee's "honorable, gallant, and audacious" personality to admire (p. 86). But his appeal went much deeper. His army's stunning successes in Virginia at the Seven Days' Battle, the Second Battle of Bull Run, and the Fredericksburg and Chancellorsville campaigns created an aura of invincibility that would not be shattered until very late in the war. Lee's aggressiveness stirred nationalist pride and depressed Northern morale, notes Gallagher. His combative strategy was indeed a bloody one, but it nearly defeated Union armies on three separate occasions—during the late summer of 1862, the late spring of 1863, and the summer of 1864.

The alternatives to Lee's aggressive posture were dubious at best, according to Gallagher. In the wake of the Vietnam War a few writers have suggested that the Confederacy's failure to adopt guerrilla tactics demonstrated the citizenry's lack of commitment to the cause. Others have argued that the Confederacy should have adopted a more passive, defensive posture, trading territory in order to save lives. Nonsense, retorts Gallagher, who points out that "the overwhelming imperative of maintaining white control in a slave-based society" (p. 127) rendered these alternatives unacceptable. Civilians in a democratic republic could not have been expected to support a government or an army which passively accepted the loss of their land and property. He also reminds us that when Confederates did adopt a defensive posture, as in north central Tennessee in the spring of 1862 and in Mississippi in 1863, they were eventually besieged (at Forts Henry and Donelson and in Vicksburg, respectively) and forced to surrender.

Revisionists will find much in *The Confederate War* to criticize, and the debate over why the Confederacy lost will continue. However, Gallagher offers a cogent and readable account of "how popular will, nationalism, and military strategy could not stave off defeat," to quote the book's dust jacket. He also raises an alternative question for his fellow historians. Rather than analyzing the reasons for Confederate defeat, why not investigate why the Confederacy fought for so long against such heavy odds?

6.

LINCOLN

by David Herbert Donald

Historians generally regard Abraham Lincoln as the greatest American president. Not surprisingly, legions of biographers have attempted to capture this remarkable man's life. David Herbert Donald's *Lincoln* (1995) is easily the best and most readable of these efforts. Given his earlier work this achievement is hardly surprising. Donald won a Pulitzer Prize in 1961 for the biography *Charles Sumner and the Coming of the Civil War* and earned a second one in 1988 for *Look Homeward: A Life of Thomas Wolfe,* a study of the great twentieth-century literary figure. Donald also helped produce two other books featured in *The Civil War Bookshelf,* serving as editor of *Why the North Won the Civil War* [3] and as coauthor, with Jean H. Baker and Michael F. Holt, of *The Civil War and Reconstruction* [34].

Many of the best Lincoln biographers, including James G. Randall and Carl Sandburg, have written sweeping, multi-volume accounts that covered not only the president's life, but his times. Donald, on the other hand, has "stuck close to Lincoln" (p. 14) in this one-volume study, focusing exclusively on Lincoln, the man. An image of an engaging, likable, and imperfect person emerges. One of Donald's major humanizing themes concerns Lincoln's intense personal ambition. From an early age the young Lincoln wanted to get away from his father, Thomas, and the grueling work of the family farm on Pigeon Creek, Indiana. "He was will-

Lincoln and his son Tad.
NATIONAL ARCHIVES

ing to try anything," explains Donald, "so long as it was not his father's occupations of farming and carpentry" (p. 37). Through hard work and intense study, Lincoln moved into increasingly profitable and influential positions—from store clerk to postmaster to surveyor to lawyer to state legislator.

Donald takes a close look at Lincoln's experiences in his law practice and his "tempestuous married life" (p. 14) with Mary Todd. Through intense, "brain-numbing labor" Lincoln built up his firm in Springfield, Illinois. The long hours prepared him well for the demands of the executive office. He truly deserved the political sobriquet Honest Abe, and his fairness and scrupulous honesty later proved a refreshing change from the scandal-ridden administration of his Democratic predecessor, James Buchanan.

Donald's biography also provides a genuine sense of Lincoln as a faithful but absent-minded husband and father. The reader shares Mary's frustrations with her inattentive husband who, after a long day at work, liked nothing more than to sit quietly and read; once, after he failed to acknowledge her third request that he stoke the fire, she whacked him across the nose with a piece of firewood. Readers of *Lincoln* also share in her intense pride in his accomplishments.

Donald reminds us of the repeated political defeats Lincoln endured before he won the presidency and points out his enormous capacity for growth as a human being. Lincoln lost his first race for the Illinois state legislature in 1832. He lost bids for the U.S. Senate in 1854 and again in 1858, the latter following momentous debates over slavery with rival Stephen A. Douglas. In 1856, he failed to gain nomination as the first vice-presidential candidate of the new Republican Party. But just as the long hours Lincoln worked as a lawyer prepared him for the physical demands of the presidency, Donald claims these character-building setbacks gave him the inner strength he would need to handle the long string of defeats later suffered by his generals in the Civil War. He also retained the intellectual flexibility to revise his own views about race. He recognized the need for emancipation and, in the very last speech of his life (April 11, 1865), became the first sitting American president to call for black suffrage, albeit on a limited scale. This capacity for immense personal growth served him well indeed, for few presidents have had so little formal education or national political experience as he did.

The key to understanding Lincoln, Donald argues, lies in recognizing "the essential passivity of his nature" (p. 14). Reluctant to take the initiative or make bold plans, Lincoln "preferred to respond to the actions of others" (p. 15). Hard decisions came only after lengthy deliberation. His moderate views proved the key to his winning the Republican nomination for president in 1860, but also helped to explain "his ineffectual leadership" (p. 293) during the Fort Sumter crisis, which reinforced public fears about his ability to hold office. At times his hesitancy verged on paralysis, as was the case in the months preceding the Chancellorsville campaign, when he failed to pay sufficient attention to influencing public opinion or guiding his generals with disastrous results. Donald also reveals a brooding, dark side to Lincoln. Nightmares haunted him frequently (including a vision of his own death), and he could only master his internal fears and misgivings with the greatest of effort. Lincoln believed that some higher force controlled his destiny, and he adopted a somewhat fatalistic but pragmatic Calvinism, Donald concludes. If one solution to a problem did not work, Lincoln believed that another needed to be tried. From this fatalism, however, came his endearing personal traits, such as his compassion and patient tolerance for others.

Lincoln has not received the critical acclaim of many of Professor Donald's earlier works. Critics have focused many of their attacks on Donald's determination to write the biography from Lincoln's point of view. Rather than judging his subject, Donald seeks to explain Lincoln's actions. This approach has undoubtedly disappointed those readers anticipating the judgments and analysis of a key historical figure by a prominent scholar. But what emerges is a brilliant portrayal of a very human figure. It was Lincoln's basic humanity that allowed him to become not only an effective war leader, but a great president. Although Lincoln's availability to White House visitors is scoffed at by the more bureaucratically minded, Donald's description of it captures the essence of Lincoln's greatness: "Remarkably, the President's systematic lack of system seemed to work. Stories of his accessibility to even the humblest petitioner, his patience, and his humanity spread throughout the North. For the first time in American history citizens began to feel that the occupant of the White House was their representative" (p. 311).

One cannot understand the Civil War without understanding Abraham Lincoln. A well-paced and thoroughly researched account by a preeminent historian, *Lincoln* is the place to begin.

7.

For Cause and Comrades: Why Men Fought in the Civil War

by James McPherson

Three million Americans took up arms against one another during the Civil War. What motivated them to fight their fellow Americans, and to continue their epic struggle for four years? Traditionally, soldiers either have been lured into combat by the prospect of economic gain—good pay or plunder—or have been coerced into military service. Once in the army, men have been motivated to fight by training, discipline, and leadership. But few of these incentives were present during the Civil War. Pay was low. Both the Confederate and Federal governments enacted conscription laws, but less than ten percent of men who saw military service were actually drafted. In an age characterized by individualism and self-reliance, the soldier's training was poor and discipline notoriously lax. The conflict was fought by amateurs and leadership, especially during the early years of the war, was erratic.

In the absence of traditional motivations, what led men to fight, and to keep on fighting? Bell Irvin Wiley, whose *Life of Billy Yank* (1951) and *Life of Johnny Reb* [18] remain classic accounts of the lives of Civil War soldiers, believes that the volunteers of the 1860s were no more motivated by ideology than the draftees of the Second World War. But James McPherson reaches a different conclusion. He outlines it in earlier works, including his magnificent *Battle Cry of Freedom* [1] and his short book of essays, *What They Fought For* (1994). His most compelling case is made in *For Cause and Comrades: Why Men Fought in the Civil War* (1997), which is a brilliant refutation of the argument that Civil War soldiers were unaffected by ideology.

In the absence of scientific samples or polling data earlier historians scoured letters, diaries, memoirs, and reminiscences of Civil War soldiers for evidence of why these men fought in the war. But however thorough their searches, they used examples in an anecdotal fashion. *For Cause and Comrades* takes a more systematic approach. McPherson has analyzed the letters and diaries of 1,076 soldiers (647 Union and 429 Confederate); he excluded works that were written after the war's end for publication or as memoirs. "What really counted," he concludes, after careful review of this evidence about soldiers' motivations, "were not social institutions, but one's own virtue, will, convictions of duty and honor, religious faith—in a word, one's character" (p. 61).

Some scholars have dismissed the seriousness of the language used by Civil War soldiers, who frequently spoke about honor, courage, glory, and their willingness to die for their country. McPherson, however, insists that these men meant what they said. "In this post-Freudian age these phrases strike many as mawkish posturing, romantic sentimentalism, hollow platitudes," he admits. "But these words were written in the 1860s, not today. . . . Our cynicism about the genuineness of such sentiments is more our problem than theirs, a temporal/cultural barrier we must transcend if we are to understand why they fought" (p. 100). McPherson's evidence seems overwhelming: the letters and diaries affirmed that more than two-thirds of their authors were motivated by patriotism.

Further analysis of these findings, at least in part, reaffirms the importance of class and region in the South. While class or regional differences found among Northern soldiers were small, in the Confederate army soldiers from slaveholding families were almost twice as likely to express patriotic sentiments as nonslaveholders. A similar pattern distinguished the lower and upper South. Eighty-four percent of South Carolinians spoke of patriotism, for example, while only 46 percent of those from North Carolina used the term or similar language.

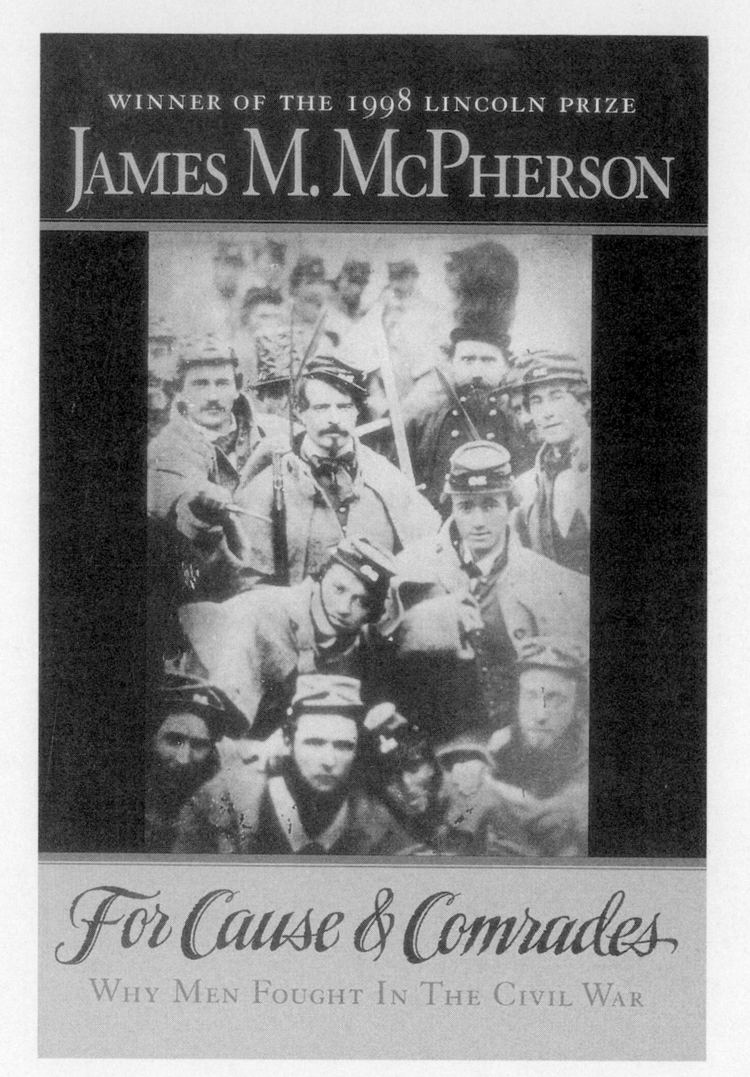

Both Northerners and Southerners insisted that they were the heirs to the revolutionary legacy of 1776. " 'I do feel that the liberty of the world is placed in our hands to defend,' " wrote one Massachusetts private, " 'and if we are overcome then farewell to freedom' " (p. 112). A significant percentage—42 percent of the Confederates and 40 percent of the Federals—discussed in some depth ideological issues like liberty, republicanism, resistance to tyranny, the Constitution, and self-government. Once again McPherson found that class played a major role in explaining differences among Confederates. Southerners from slaveowning families (47 percent) were much more likely to address these issues than were those from nonslaveholding families (28 percent).

If they did not fight this war, insisted the majority of soldiers, life would not be worth living to any honorable man. A man's honor was inextricably related to his actions on the battlefield. In part this attitude reflected the values of the societies the soldiers represented, McPherson claims. Men feared the effects of being deemed cowards even more than the dangers of battle. Since volunteers from a community typically joined the same company, word of their deeds would be reported to the folks back home.

McPherson finds little evidence that the soldiers' concepts of honor and courage changed over time. Here he disagrees with Gerald Linderman, whose *Embattled Courage: The Experience of Combat in the American Civil War* (1987) was the best book previously written on the subject. Linderman argues that veterans became increasingly skeptical about these values as the war went on. McPherson concludes otherwise. He cites a January 1865 letter, for example, in which an Illinois veteran of three and a half years of fighting used the word "duty" five times in a single sentence. He argues that the patriotism of both Union and Confederate soldiers was reinforced by a growing desire for revenge against the enemy, and by the impulse among many soldiers to link their sense of self-worth to the success of the army in which they served.

These men were truly fighting for cause and comrades. They could not dishonor themselves or let down their fellow soldiers. " 'I went in for the ware [war],' declared one Alabama private in March 1864, 'and I do expect to fite [fight] till the last for freedom' " (p. 170). And he did: two months later, during the Battle of the Wilderness this soldier was killed.

8.

LINCOLN AND HIS GENERALS

by T. Harry Williams

T. Harry Williams, professor of history at Louisiana State University from 1941 until his death in 1979, wrote several important books. His 1969 biography of the colorful Louisiana New Deal politician Huey Long won a Pulitzer Prize and the National Book Award. But most of Williams's scholarship dealt with the Civil War. His best work on the subject, *Lincoln and His Generals* (1952), is an elegant account of President Abraham Lincoln's attempts to develop a cohesive military strategy and to find generals who were capable of implementing it.

Before this book was published most Civil War historians had criticized Lincoln's handling of military affairs. Some portrayed the president as too willing to interfere in matters best left to professional soldiers; those with a more favorable opinion of Lincoln's performance argued that the president chose to remove himself from the decision-making process once Ulysses S. Grant emerged as a leadership force. Williams demonstrates that Lincoln not only taught himself to be an excellent military strategist, but continued to influence Grant's thinking through the war's end.

Lincoln and His Generals focuses on the president's growth as a war leader and his agonizingly long search for capable generals. As such, it is weighted more heavily to the war's first three years, during which time Lincoln experimented with but found wanting a platoon of candidates. In assuming an active role in planning and implementing national strategy, Williams points out, Lincoln was simply doing what previous wartime presidents, James Madison and James K. Polk, had done. The president soon came to understand that victory would be secured not by occupying enemy territory, but by defeating the Confederate armies in battle. In other words the president, Williams explains, recognized that "the army must be officered by fighting men" (p. 178).

To Lincoln's immense frustration, most of the professional soldiers he put in charge failed to grasp this fundamental concept. Winfield Scott, general in chief at the war's outset, was too old and enfeebled to energize Union forces. Scott's replacement, George McClellan, cut a dashing figure and proved a brilliant organizer, but was too cautious, conservative, and patronizing toward the president to guide the Union war effort successfully. Henry Halleck assumed the job in July 1862. Although he was a decent technician and administrator, Halleck, who was known as Old Brains for his theoretical expertise, habitually assumed the position of passive advisor rather than active leader.

Frustrated in his quest to find an effective supreme commander, Lincoln also found his generals in the field wanting. Matters in Virginia were especially perplexing in 1861 and 1862. Political pressures had forced Gen. Irvin McDowell to attack before his army was ready. McClellan, creator of the Army of the Potomac, wildly overestimated the size of enemy forces arrayed against him and never translated his abilities as an organizer into battlefield victories. John Pope, who was humiliated at the Second Battle of Bull Run, was obviously unsuited for high command. The bewhiskered Ambrose Burnside had been reluctant to replace McClellan and promptly demonstrated the wisdom of these self-doubts in his inept handling of the Battle of Fredericksburg. Joseph Hooker lost his nerve during the Battle of Chancellorsville. Lincoln finally found a competent, if uninspired, general in George Meade, who could at least avoid disaster at the hands of Robert E. Lee. But Meade seemed unwilling to assume the offensive, even in the wake of his splendid victory at Gettysburg in 1863.

President Abraham Lincoln visits Gen. George McClellan and the Army of the Potomac, 1862.
NATIONAL ARCHIVES

Events in the west also tested Lincoln's patience. The famous explorer John C. Frémont was his initial choice to take charge of Missouri's army, but the Great Pathfinder proved to be a boy trying to do a man's job, according to Williams. In Tennessee the slow-moving Don Carlos Buell was merely "a McClellan without charm or glamor" (p. 48). William Rosecrans, if anything even slower than Buell, nearly lost his army at the Battle of Chickamauga. Fortunately for the president, a scruffy-looking, unpretentious leader named Ulysses S. Grant was coming to the fore. Grant could fight. He forced the surrender of Forts Henry and Donelson, laying open Nashville, a strategic site, to Union occupation. Although he was initially surprised by a Confederate attack at Shiloh, Grant recovered in time to win. The president stood by his man despite allegations of his intemperance and incompetence, and was rewarded by Grant's capture of Vicksburg, and subsequent victories around Chattanooga.

In March 1864 Lincoln brought Grant east and named him general in chief. Still, as *Lincoln and His Generals* attests, the president remained involved in military affairs. Grant's strategy of hammering against the enemy simultaneously on all fronts (Williams labels this "Operation Crusher") bore a clear resemblance to moves Lincoln had advocated two and a half years earlier. And when Lincoln doubted the wisdom of Grant's efforts to remove George Thomas, the president "again . . . had been more right than Grant" (p. 345). Thomas promptly won a great victory at Nashville.

Williams recognizes that Lincoln was not infallible. In late January 1862 the president issued his General War Order No. 1, which naively declared that a general movement of all major Union field armies was to begin on February 22. The order—given without regard to the lengthy period it would take to organize and supply such a massive offensive or to the moves the enemy might make in the meantime—demonstrated Lincoln's intense frustration with the pace of the conflict. The president's willingness to support the independent action championed by John A. McClernand in the midst of Grant's Vicksburg campaign represented another serious error in judgment. Lincoln employed other political generals—notably Nathaniel P. Banks and Ben Butler—who cost the lives of thousands of Union soldiers. Williams notes such patronage at least enabled the president to form an effective political coalition.

Williams takes his research seriously, but it is the stylistic elegance of *Lincoln and His Generals* which sets it apart. "While Grant was becoming the joy of Lincoln's heart because he fought hard and did not shriek for reinforcements," explains Williams, "Rosecrans fought little and shrieked loudly" (p. 275). The surly Halleck "had the misfortune to look plain and act ordinary" (p. 137); Ben Butler "looked like a cross-eyed cuttlefish" (p. 214), Williams quips.

Written nearly half a century ago, *Lincoln and His Generals* has been criticized for its assertions that "a modern command system" (p. 291) emerged from the North's military victory and that in fostering this development Lincoln made "a large and permanent contribution to the organization of the American military system" (p. 14). Such claims go too far. The War Department of the postbellum years was outmoded, and it was Secretary Elihu Root (1899–1904) who established the Army War College, abolished the post of commanding general, and created the position of chief of staff. But Williams's brilliant characterizations of Lincoln's relationships with his generals and his establishment of the president as a central figure in the North's military victory makes *Lincoln and His Generals* a Civil War classic, suitable for specialist and nonspecialist alike.

9.

ROBERT E. LEE: A BIOGRAPHY

by Emory M. Thomas

Douglas Southall Freeman's *R. E. Lee: A Biography,* published in four volumes, remains the standard by which all biographies of Robert E. Lee are measured. Some readers, however, may be put off by Freeman's unabashedly favorable portrayal of his subject, or are daunted by the enormous length (over 2,400 pages) of this important work. Emory M. Thomas's *Robert E. Lee* (1995) serves as an excellent, and more economical alternative. Whereas Freeman focused largely on the Civil War years, Thomas balances his coverage of Lee's life (providing 190 pages on the period before the war, 176 pages on the war, and 50 pages on the postbellum years) in order to present a broader portrait of Lee the man.

Thomas's biography is most valuable for its explanations of the factors that motivated the Confederacy's most important general. Lee was shaped by the actions of his father, the Revolutionary War hero, Henry "Light Horse Harry" Lee III. Whereas his father had been a profligate spender who drove his family into debt and eventually abandoned them to live in Barbados, Robert was determined to maintain his honor and self-control. The younger Lee's self-discipline reflected his desire to avoid the constraints his father's irresponsible actions had forced upon him, Thomas claims. Robert, whose father once threw a chain across his door in hopes of keeping away his creditors, emerged from the U.S. Military Academy unblemished by a single demerit.

Duty dominated Lee's life, enabling him to balance the internal tension between his desire to control events and his personal search for freedom. Because his family's finances had been ruined by his father, Lee's life was filled with uncertainty. He owned no home of his own, which made him dependent upon the generosity of family and friends. Poor health rendered his wife a virtual invalid. But, as Thomas so convincingly demonstrates, Lee developed a tremendous ability to cope with the trials of life. Rather than focus on his own troubles, he made the best of bad situations, adopting a healthy if somewhat fatalistic attitude.

Thomas takes a fairly traditional approach toward Lee's Civil War leadership, stressing his contributions to the Confederate cause, and praising his performance as commander of the Army of Northern Virginia, which Thomas considered splendid. Critics of Lee, most notably Thomas L. Connelly and Archer Jones in *The Politics of Command* [25], contend that the Virginian did not concern himself enough with western affairs and unnecessarily wasted manpower in hopeless frontal assaults. In Thomas's view Lee learned much from his Mexican War service under Gen. Winfield Scott. By seizing the initiative, maneuvering swiftly, taking calculated risks, and acting decisively, Scott had overcome his numerical disadvantage and captured Mexico City. From this experience—and conscious of the North's considerable advantages in resources—Lee concluded that he could win the Civil War only by making a decisive stroke. Otherwise the Confederacy would be overwhelmed. Lee's decisions to fight at Antietam and Gettysburg were, in Thomas's opinion, straightforward: "he believed he could win" (p. 261). Indeed, Lee's strategy helped the Confederacy overcome the threats to Richmond in the spring of 1862 and continue the war for three more years.

Thomas admires Robert E. Lee, and presents him as a graceful, unselfish man who assumed responsibility for his own actions and believed in the notion of personal redemption. While most biographers concentrate almost entirely on Lee's performance during the Civil War years, Thomas recognizes Lee's postwar contributions, such as his innovative as leadership as president of Wash-

Robert E. Lee after the war.
LIBRARY OF CONGRESS

ington College (later renamed Washington and Lee University). Even in his discussions of Lee's military career, Thomas approaches his subject as a human being, with human shortcomings, not as a myth. Seeking to avoid personal confrontation even as army commander, Lee transferred subordinates he found wanting to different theaters rather than dismissing them outright. Of course, by avoiding a direct confrontation, he was passing off the problem to someone else. Although Lee developed a strong friendship with Thomas J. "Stonewall" Jackson, he failed to find the time to visit Jackson after the latter was mortally wounded at the Battle of Chancellorsville. More important, Thomas blames Lee for the catastrophic Confederate losses at Gettysburg, a defeat that he claims stemmed from "who Lee was" (p. 303). Preferring to lead by suggestion rather than direct order, Lee "insisted upon making possible for others the freedom of thought and action he sought for himself." Allowing his subordinates great flexibility had proved effective in the past. At Gettysburg, however, it had disastrous consequences: J. E. B. Stuart's critical absence during the first stages of the battle, Richard Ewell's fateful decision not to take Culp's Hill, and James Longstreet's interminable delays in striking the Federal left flank on the second day.

But this very humanity—the understandable errors, the struggles to overcome selfish desires, and the continual attempts to seek redemption—made Lee a great man, not a marble statue, argues Thomas. Thomas's Robert E. Lee emerges as a satisfyingly complex figure, a man who cherished and defended his personal freedoms, often by immersing himself in his duty. He frequently voiced his concerns about slavery and manumitted the 170-odd slaves bequeathed to him by his father-in-law three days before Lincoln's Emancipation Proclamation went into effect, even though he fought for a nation whose very essence revolved around the right to own slaves. Lee was a Christian who did not regularly attend church. He could be a tender parent and husband but was usually away from home, and he found his inabilities to control the lives of his wife and siblings frustrating, claims Thomas. As a professional soldier, Lee spent most of his time around other men but much preferred the company of women, especially young and pretty ones.

Readers will find Thomas's book an excellent, balanced biography. Written by a mature, thoughtful historian who has devoted most of his academic life to understanding the American Civil War, *Robert E. Lee: A Biography* emerges as the most objective, readable, and convincing one-volume account of the Confederacy's greatest warrior and most respected man.

10.

The Killer Angels
by Michael Shaara

The Killer Angels (1974) is the best fictional account of the Civil War, overshadowing even Stephen Crane's powerful *Red Badge of Courage* [45] and Stephen Vincent Bénet's moving *John Brown's Body* [50]. Awarded the Pulitzer Prize in fiction in 1975, Michael Shaara's novel describes the three-day Battle of Gettysburg, (July 1–3, 1863) during which George Meade's Army of the Potomac defeated Robert E. Lee's Army of Northern Virginia. Shaara uses historical characters to present his interpretation of this brutal engagement, which claimed more than 50,000 casualties.

By mixing historical events with fictional dialogue, Shaara captures the human drama of the Civil War. As would James McPherson in *For Cause and Comrades* [7] nearly two decades later, novelist Shaara suggests that soldiers of both sides were motivated to fight largely out of a sense of duty to friends, families, and comrades, as well as their respective causes. Southerners believed the war necessary to preserve their individual liberties against the federal government's unwarranted intrusions. Northerners had come to recognize that the war had to be fought not only to preserve the Union, but also to end slavery.

Shaara's key Confederate characters include generals Robert E. Lee and James Longstreet. Lee is depicted as tired, sluggish, and unimaginative, overcome by the burdens of defending the Confederacy. To Shaara Lee remained a prisoner of the past who

Joshua L. Chamberlain, hero of The Killer Angels.
NATIONAL ARCHIVES

failed to grasp the advantages that new rifled weapons and entrenchments provided to defenders on the Civil War battlefield. Longstreet, on the other hand, emerges as Lee's dependable warhorse, a man whose loyalty to his chief outweighed his better judgment—that the Confederates should remain on the tactical defensive. Rather than assaulting well-prepared Union positions, Longstreet believed, Lee should take up a strategic position that would force the enemy to attack. Such had been the case seven months earlier at the Battle of Fredericksburg, when the Confederates had thrown back Federal assaults with heavy losses. Ever the good soldier, Shaara's Longstreet nonetheless carried out Lee's attacks faithfully at Gettysburg.

Maj. Gen. John Buford and Col. Joshua Chamberlain are the central Union protagonists in *The Killer Angels*. Buford was a hard-bitten cavalryman who grasped the proper role of mounted troops on the Civil War battlefield. Instead of launching direct assaults, they harassed the enemy's rear, gathered information, and, fighting dismounted, slowed enemy progress. Recognizing the strategic value of the road junctions at Gettysburg, Buford delayed Confederate advances long enough to allow Union infantry to occupy excellent defensive positions south of the hamlet. Joshua Chamberlain, a former college professor, upstages even Buford in Shaara's account. Chamberlain's outnumbered regiment threw back repeated Confederate assaults on the Union's extreme left flank at Little Round Top, a site that was key to the Union's entire defensive position.

Shaara employs the best of both fiction and history. He uses historical evidence to tell a realistic story, and exercises the literary license to create the kind of dialogue no historian could ethically create. However, readers should be aware that the historical figures did not always measure up to the characters who emerge in *The Killer Angels*. Eager to hold an independent command, Longstreet finally got his chance in late 1863 during the Knoxville campaign. Here, however, he proved a mediocre leader, and returned to Lee's command in the spring of 1864. Likewise Shaara overestimates Chamberlain's importance to the defense of strategic Little Round Top. Although Chamberlain was later awarded the Medal of Honor for good reason, in the process of lionizing Chamberlain, Shaara neglects to discuss the actions of Gouverneur K. Warren, chief engineer of the Army of the Potomac. Warren was dispatched by Meade on the second day of the battle to ascertain what was happening at Little Round Top and quickly recognized the importance of the position. Finding the hill unoccupied, Warren ordered the reinforcements that made Chamberlain's stand possible.

Turner Home Entertainment based its movie *Gettysburg* (1993) on Shaara's novel. Although the photography is stunning and its depictions of battle scenes are generally well regarded, at four hours the film seems too slow and Martin Sheen appears miscast as Robert E. Lee. But the book describes in an outstanding way Civil War action in terms suitable to the general reader. As an historian I find it an enjoyable, entertaining account of the entire Gettysburg campaign. As a teacher I treasure *The Killer Angels* because I've found it to be one of a distressingly small number of books students will actually finish.

A former paratrooper, Shaara worked as a policemen, merchant seaman, and boxer before finally taking a teaching job in the English department of Florida State University in 1961. He went on to win a teaching award and publish several minor fictional works before completing *The Killer Angels*. He was then severely injured in a motorcycle accident in Italy after which he wrote two more books, but these latter efforts received only polite reviews. He died in 1988 of a heart attack.

11.

The Era of Reconstruction, 1865–1877

by Kenneth M. Stampp

The decade after the Civil War ended was one of the most complex and controversial in American history. How would a nation torn apart by a bloody internal conflict reconstruct itself? How quickly should this be done? What would be the fate of the former slaves, whose bondage had been ended by that war? And who should determine the answers to these fundamental questions? Students of the Civil War need some familiarity with these issues if they hope to understand the consequences of the nation's bloodiest conflict.

For a century after Robert E. Lee's surrender at Appomattox, writers typically depicted reconstruction as one of the darkest periods in our nation's history. Claude Bowers's *Tragic Era* (1929), which focused on the public scandals and bitterness of the times, exemplified the traditional view: "The prevailing note was one of tragedy. . . . Never have American public men in responsible positions . . . been so brutal, hypocritical, and corrupt. . . . The southern people literally were put to the torture . . . [by] rugged conspirators . . . [who] assumed the pose of philanthropists and patriots" (p. 5). The brutal mistreatment of Southern whites by a vengeful Congress characterized the period in this interpretation. Radical Republicans, supported by angry blacks, manipulative Northern carpetbaggers (men who supposedly packed all their possessions in cheap bags and headed South to exploit helpless people), and traitorous Southern scalawags (Southerners who supported reconstruction) engaged in a systematic effort to plunder the South.

Kenneth Stampp's *Era of Reconstruction* (1965) offers a convincing counterpoint to this analysis. Stampp describes how a divided but Republican-dominated Congress gradually managed to assume control of the reconstruction process. To ensure that the goals of the victorious Union were implemented in the South, Congress was forced to intervene. State governments, created under congressional sponsorship, were sometimes guilty of extravagance and waste, raising taxes in the process. However, they also left a record of considerable accomplishment: they built railroads, increased public services, established public schools, and expanded democracy by including blacks in the political process.

The road toward reconstruction was a slow one. Stampp reminds us that President Abraham Lincoln had wanted to restore the former Confederate states to the Union as quickly as possible and with a minimum of federal interference. However, Lincoln and Congress clashed over not only the terms of reconstruction, but also about which branch of government should oversee the process. Because he was a practical politician whose views about blacks and slavery were constantly evolving, Lincoln might have been able to reach an agreement with Congress about reconstruction had he survived. This was not true of his successor, Andrew Johnson, who served as president from 1865 to 1869. A Tennesseean whose devotion to the Union was counterbalanced by his fanatical determination to respect states rights, Johnson expressed little sympathy for the freedmen. Under his loose guidelines white Southerners promptly reelected their traditional leaders, many of whom had led the secession movement. Every Southern state also enacted measures (known as the Black Codes) which reduced the freedmen to virtual slavery by limiting their rights to assemble, own property, or leave their jobs.

Congressional reconstruction was thus a reaction to events in the South, according to Stampp. Several factors, he argues, motivated the Radical Republicans' desire to take control of reconstruction. Some wanted to take vengeance upon the South, or

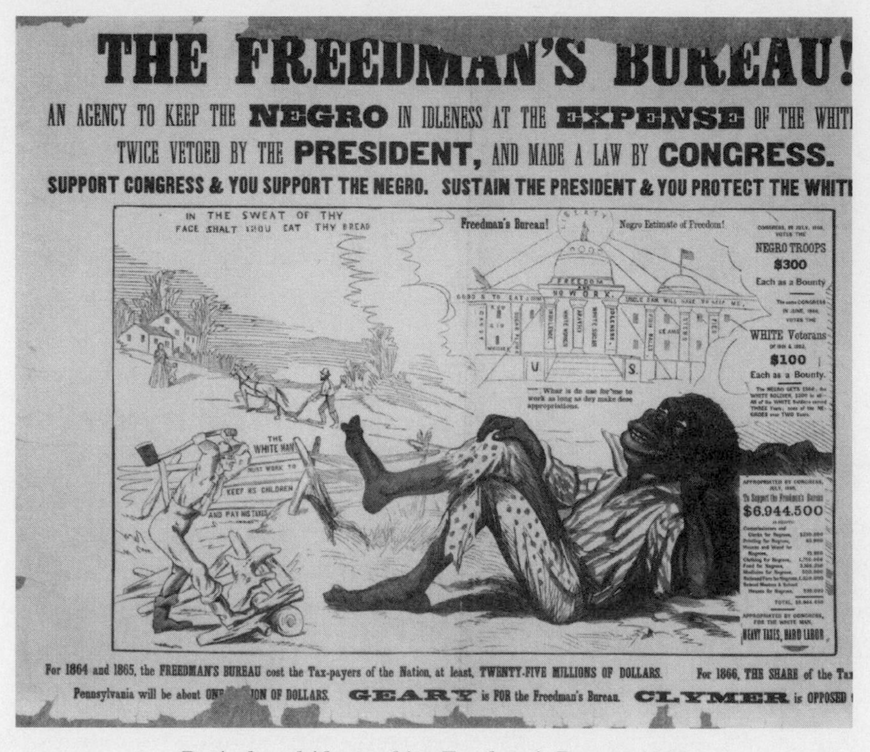

Racist broadside attacking Freedmen's Bureau, 1865.
LIBRARY OF CONGRESS

hoped to manipulate blacks into joining the Republican Party. Others sought to protect the interests of Northern businessmen. But many were also guided by a genuine concern for the welfare of the freedmen. Stampp points out that many Radical Republicans had been in the forefront of the reform movements of the 1850s. "Their pleas for justice for the Negro, their objection to the Johnson governments on the ground that the Black Codes were restoring a form of slavery, cannot be discounted as pure hypocrisy," he insists. "To the practical motives that the Radicals occasionally revealed must be added the moral idealism that they inherited from the abolitionists" (p. 102).

Contrary to the claims of traditional historians, radicals did not control Congress during reconstruction. Instead moderate Republicans held the balance of power. They were initially inclined to support President Johnson and to adopt measures which would quickly restore the Union, but they were shocked by the election of former Confederates to public office in the South. Ugly race riots in Memphis and New Orleans sparked further concern. Accusing Radical Republicans of treason, Johnson himself caused the final break by vetoing a bill that extended and enlarged the Freedmen's Bureau, a federal agency established to assist former slaves.

Motivated by what Stampp describes as "the genuine fear that President Johnson, through his southern governments, was going to lose the peace" (p. 118), Northern voters elected a veto-proof Republican majority in the congressional elections of 1866. In a series of measures passed in 1867 and 1868 over President Johnson's vetoes, Congress outlined its blueprint for reconstruction. The plan abolished the Johnson governments and divided the ten unreconstructed Southern states (Tennessee had already rejoined the Union) into five military districts. Civilian state governments were established under the army's supervision. Those persons who had violated a previous oath of allegiance to the U.S. Constitution by joining the Confederate cause were prohibited from participating in the political process. New state governments were required to ratify the Fourteenth Amendment (granting all male citizens due process) and submit their constitutions for congressional approval. Congress also passed the Tenure of Office Act, designed to prevent the intrusion of the still-obstructive President Johnson, and after several confrontations, the House impeached the president. Although the Senate failed to convict him (falling a single vote shy of the necessary two-thirds majority), the president's power was effectively broken, although he would serve through 1869.

Northerners eventually lost interest in this crusade, and conservative governments had regained control of every Southern state by the end of the 1870s. Blacks were relegated to second-class citizenship within American society. But despite these obvious failures of reconstruction, Stampp concludes that the Radical Republicans deserve a good deal of credit. He points out that in the Fourteenth and Fifteenth Amendments (which granted all male citizens the right to vote), "adopted only under the conditions of radical reconstruction," lay the foundation for the modern civil rights movement. "If it was worth four years of civil war to save the Union," reasons Stampp, "it was worth a few years of radical reconstruction" to give blacks the ultimate promise of equal rights (p. 215).

The Era of Reconstruction is a brilliant synthesis of revisionist interpretations of the decade that followed the end of the Civil War. Newer studies in scholarly circles have demonstrated that the period was even more complex than Stampp's book suggests. But for a general audience it remains the best and most accessible survey of reconstruction, and essential reading for anyone who wants to understand the Civil War era.

12.

THE IMPENDING CRISIS, 1848–1861

by David M. Potter

Few readers of popular history are familiar with the name David M. Potter (1910–71), but every serious student of the Civil War should know his work. Through his brilliant lectures, carefully crafted essays, and penetrating books, Potter influenced an entire generation of historians. His *People of Plenty: Economic Abundance and the American Character* (1954) was an original, innovative book which identified economic abundance as the key factor in shaping the American historical experience. Potter also wrote numerous essays on the South, the study of history, and freedom. But the majority of his writing concerned the coming of the Civil War, and *The Impending Crisis, 1848–1861* (1977), is a necessary foundation for anyone interested in the period.

Like all of Potter's works, *The Impending Crisis,* completed and edited by Don E. Fehrenbacher, is more analytical than descriptive. His writing is clear and precise, avoiding jargon and polemics. History, he believed, should be honest and fair, written to help others understand the past rather than to judge it. His background offered him a national perspective. He was born in the South but lived much of his adult life outside of it, teaching at Yale and later Stanford. *The Impending Crisis* captures the rich complexities and subtleties of the political events of the 1850s. Insisting that nothing was inevitable, Potter probes the alternatives to war that were available to Americans. He believed that slavery, which had "a polarizing effect upon the sections" (p. 42), was fundamental to understanding the sectional controversy. But the issue was more than a stark choice between two extremes. "The question," he explains, "was not a choice of alternatives—antislavery or proslavery—but a ranking of values" (p. 45). Northerners had to determine whether or not their fears of slavery outweighed their love for the Union, whereas Southerners had to weigh their national patriotism against their desire to protect slavery.

What follows is a brilliant analysis of the shifting political tides of the 1850s in which several themes emerge. One concerns the steady stream of tactical victories won by the South in Congress and the courts. As part of the Compromise of 1850, Southerners gained a fugitive slave law which authorized federal agents to actively seek out and return runaway slaves to their masters. In the Kansas-Nebraska Act of 1854, Southerners secured the repeal of the Missouri Compromise, which had prohibited slavery in territories north of the 36'30" parallel. This made possible the expansion of slavery into Kansas, or even Nebraska. In 1857 the Supreme Court issued the Dred Scott decision, a ringing endorsement of the Southern claim that Congress had no right to prevent slavery in the territories. In 1858 Southern Democrats tried to force the acceptance of a territorial government in Kansas through Congress under the distinctly proslavery Lecompton Constitution.

These apparent Southern victories, however, added to neither the area, influence, nor security of the Southern system. Northerners refused to abide by the Fugitive Slave Act of 1850. Despite the Kansas-Nebraska Act, relatively few Kansans cared very much about slavery, Potter argues, insisting that the average settler was far more concerned about land titles. The Dred Scott decision strengthened Northern beliefs in a slaveowners' conspiracy. And Kansas voters rejected the proslavery Lecompton Constitution, preferring to delay their statehood until the resignation of Southern congressmen resulting from secession allowed its acceptance as a free state in early 1861. According to Potter's analy-

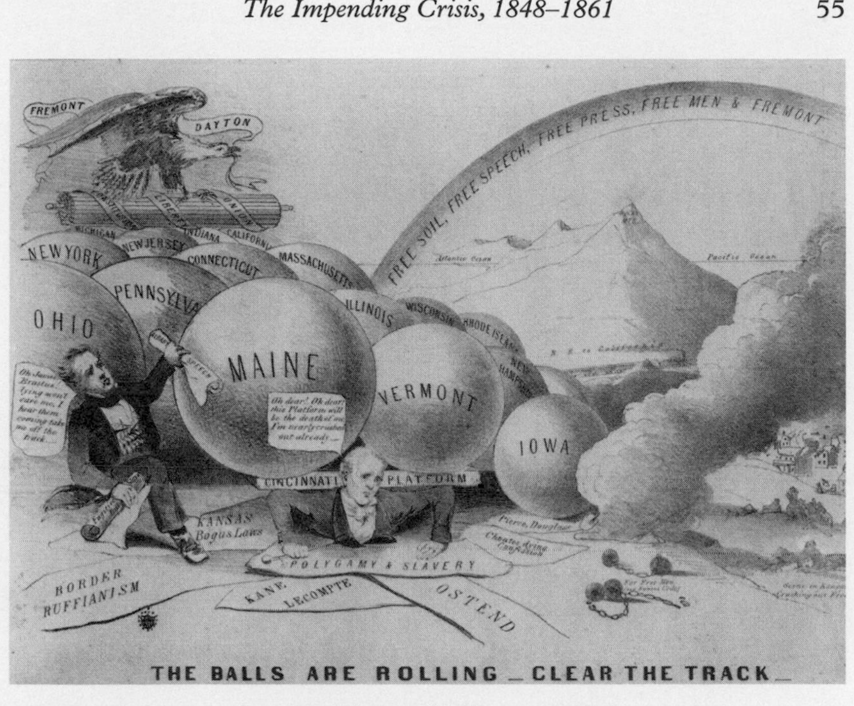

Pro-Republican political cartoon, 1856.
LIBRARY OF CONGRESS

sis, the South expended a tremendous amount of political capital but had little to show for its efforts.

He concludes that these empty Southern triumphs destroyed the one remaining "bulwark of bisectionalism, the Democratic Party, which alone stood between the South and sectional domination by the Republicans" (p. 326). In 1852 Democratic presidential candidate Franklin Pierce won the support of a majority of free as well as slave states. Neither section had imposed its will upon the other, either within the Democratic Party or in the national election. But controversies over the Kansas-Nebraska Act passed in 1854 shattered this sectional balance. The Whig Party was destroyed as a national institution. Out of its ashes came the Republican Party, which was entirely reliant upon Northern support. Southern interests came to dominate the Democratic Party. By 1860 the nation saw what amounted to two distinct elections for president. In the North the contest was between Abraham Lincoln (Republican) and Stephen A. Douglas (Northern Democrat); in the South, John C. Breckinridge (Southern Democrat) and John Bell (Constitutional Union Party). Lincoln won but his party had not even bothered to run tickets in ten Southern states.

Potter emphasizes the internal divisions within the South and the very narrow margin of support for the secession movement. "One is left with a feeling," he contends, "that the South did not want a separate destiny so much as it wanted recognition of the merits of southern society and security for the slave system" (p. 469). Southerners were united not by a sense of separate nationalism but by the fear that slavery was under attack, and by their insistence that Northerners "recognize not only their rights but also their status as perfectly decent, respectable human beings" (p. 478). Potter argues that the short campaign period (seven states seceded in less than three months), low voter turnout in elections of representatives to the secession conventions, and failure of most state conventions to submit their work to a popular vote all displayed that many Southerners lacked enthusiasm for the secession movement. A small political shift "might have tipped the balance the other way," he concludes. "In this situation, a relatively small number of resolute secessionists were able to guide a confused and excited electorate into a program for dissolving the Union" (p. 500).

Even after the lower South seceded, Potter believes, some form of peace still would have been possible if either side had really wanted it. But "the very familiarity of crisis—its chronic presence during three decades—had bred a contempt for it" (p. 516) by the winter of 1860 to 1861. On the Union side Lincoln consistently underestimated the strength of the secessionist movement in the South, and until very late saw the South's threats as bluffs by a section intent upon political blackmail, not disunion.

Astute observations such as these sparkle throughout *The Impending Crisis,* which is the culmination of David Potter's lifelong efforts to understand the origins of the Civil War. In fact, I don't believe anyone can truly understand the causes of America's most terrible conflict without reading this insightful volume. Sadly Potter did not get to see the manuscript come to fruition; he died of cancer in 1971 at age sixty-one before he had finished the book. At the time he was president of both of the nation's most prestigious historical organizations—the Organization of American Historians and the American Historical Association. Fortunately, Don E. Fehrenbacher, a colleague of Potters' from Stanford and a noted scholar in his own right, completed *The Impending Crisis,* which received the Pulitzer Prize in history in 1977.

13.

"A People's Contest": The Union and the Civil War, 1861-1865

by Phillip Shaw Paludan

One of life's genuine pleasures is rediscovering a great book. I had read Phillip Paludan's *"A People's Contest"* (1988) several years ago, and as I was assembling ideas for this book, naturally included it on my list of prospects. I had forgotten just how good it is, however. In a single volume Paludan explains why Northerners supported this long conflict, describes the Union war effort, and analyzes the effects of the struggle upon Northern society. Paludan points out that historians too often write about either the Civil War or industrialization, as if the events were entirely separate. Instead, he establishes the interrelationships between these two momentous occurrences.

The Civil War proved to be a stern test of Northern commitment to modernization and self-government, Paludan points out. Northerners realized that industrialization and changes in the means of production were bringing exciting new opportunities and riches; unfortunately, all were not sharing equally in this bounty. Many feared that amidst the race for riches, America would lose sight of its ideals. Likewise, Northerners entered the conflict with a deep faith in law and order, and a commitment to self-government fostered by their intense personal involvement in local government and political parties. The war would test, shape, and in the end validate the North's basic values and aspirations, Paludan argues. Voters now had a clear choice between the Republican modernizers—"a party of hope"—and the Democratic traditionalists—"a party of memory" (p. 102). This competition helped guarantee that the dialogue over values and aspirations continue in an orderly, constitutional manner. The debates over civil liberties had a similar effect in that they kept Northerners involved in and committed to the political process.

After Southerners left Congress and a Republican president took over the White House, the federal government accelerated the processes of industrialization and modernization, with mixed results. "In the name of patriotism" (p. 150), argues Paludan, Congress concentrated economic power in the hands of northeastern bankers and businessmen. They voted to subsidize railroads without regulating them, even though industrial workers experienced declining living standards as a result. Agriculture became increasingly specialized and mechanized, but the gap between rich and poor "narrowed hardly at all" (p. 197). Economic development was nonetheless booming, and the rewards seemed to justify Northerners' faith in the free labor system.

Despite this prosperity the path to victory was not easy. While Congress mobilized the North's economic resources, President Lincoln searched for military leaders capable of employing that awesome power. At first glance George McClellan's good looks, West Point education, and organizational skills—what Paludan describes as "modern talents" (p. 84)—seemed to embody the spirit of the era. McClellan wanted to fight a conservative war, however, a war that would not revolutionize society. Into the breach, eventually, stepped Ulysses S. Grant, whose unassuming appearance and "overwhelming commonality" better represented the continuing involvement of average Northerners in the Union cause. "A world that had produced Ahab and Hollingsworth [fictional characters of antebellum novelists Herman Melville and Nathaniel Hawthorne] was gone," explains Paludan. "The alleged brilliance of McClellan and even of Lee and Jackson faded before Grant's simple, deadly perseverance" (p. 315).

Paludan makes a persuasive case for the interconnectedness of politics, religion, social and economic development, military events, and the power of ideas in explaining Union victory. In the

The nation's capitol, May 1865.
Library of Congress

North political discussion and debate made government of, by, and for the people something very real. Northerners were reassured by the large number of immigrants who fought for the Union. "Their presence," Paludan argues, "suggested the truth of Lincoln's assertion that the United States exemplified ideas shared by right-thinking people everywhere" (p. 281). In advancing the cause of religion during the war, Northerners took on a sense of missionary zeal. Destroying slavery was God's work, they insisted, and they found comfort in believing that the thousands of dead and maimed young men had at least been sacrificed for a purpose. The booming economy, freed from the obfuscation of Southern congressmen, further vindicated the ideal of free labor and the righteousness of the Northern cause. The majority of Northerners embraced the goals of saving the Union and, eventually, of destroying slavery. Modernization and industrialization triumphed, as evidenced by the successful mobilization of Northern military might. Although challenged by the anarchy of the Confederacy's secession, the rule of law and the necessity of order remained bulwarks of Union ideals, Paludan contends.

Ironically, the foundations on which the North's victory was based imposed limits upon future development. The triumph of free labor unrestricted by government regulation allowed a few to amass tremendous fortunes while others sank deeper into poverty. The divide between haves and have-nots was especially apparent for former slaves, who depended heavily on federal protections. "The victorious Constitution and economic system provided the contexts that would limit the extent of the freedom blacks had gained," explains Paludan. "If it could be demonstrated that their status required increased national protection, if it could be argued that an enduring Union depended on the same thing, then for a time blacks might hope for special protection. But respect for a revitalized federal system and admiration for the validated free labor ideal might one day deprive them of that protection" (pp. 229–230). According to these dearly held values, it was assumed that after liberation former slaves were free laborers like any others, Paludan concludes.

Not since 1910, when Emerson Fite published *Social and Industrial Conditions in the North During the Civil War,* had an historian attempted to write a comprehensive, single-volume survey of the Northern wartime experience. Paludan's sophisticated and readable work fills this void. Combining intellectual vigor, a lively writing style, and broad themes, *"A People's Contest"* is essential to any Civil War bookshelf.

14.

Landscape Turned Red: The Battle of Antietam

by Stephen W. Sears

Washington, D.C., was on the verge of panic in late August 1862. Robert E. Lee's Army of Northern Virginia had just won another victory at the Second Battle of Bull Run, and rumors abounded that it was advancing on the capital. Against his cabinet's advice President Abraham Lincoln restored George McClellan to command of the Army of the Potomac, even though he had been Lee's victim in the Seven Days' Battles that June. As a Democrat McClellan favored a limited war that would not disrupt the old order, and he had consistently overestimated the size of the opposing forces. The president was well aware of McClellan's caution but believed he had no other options, because only Little Mac held the confidence of the soldiers.

Believing that his ragged veterans were unbeatable, Lee pushed across the Potomac River into Maryland. Fortune smiled on McClellan when a copy of Lee's campaign plans fell into Union hands. Outnumbering his enemy by nearly two to one, McClellan eventually attacked along Antietam Creek at Sharpsburg, Maryland on September 17, 1862. In this single day of combat more Americans were killed than in any other day in U.S. military history. Although the battle was a tactical draw, these heavy losses forced Lee to retreat into Virginia. Seizing the moment, on September 22 Lincoln made public his determination to issue an Emancipation Proclamation.

The Antietam battlefield, 1862.
PHOTOGRAPH BY MATHEW BRADY. LIBRARY OF CONGRESS

The president also recognized that McClellan had missed a golden opportunity to crush Lee's army at Antietam, however, a theme which dominates Stephen Sears's gripping account of this campaign, *Landscape Turned Red* (1983). McClellan's inadequacies are driven home in Sears's contrasting portrayals of the two army commanders. McClellan was "the captain who would not dare" (p. 181), a man of "imperious arrogance" (p. 23) who created, in a feat of mental gymnastics, an illusionary world in which he was chronically outnumbered and always the victim of the misguided policies of the Lincoln administration. By contrast, explains Sears, "behind the cool, calm, dignified face he presented to the world, Robert E. Lee had the calculating instincts of a riverboat gambler" (p. 73). Counting on McClellan's caution, Lee was marching north to give battle.

As Lee's hungry veterans moved into Maryland, the number of

stragglers increasing every step of the way, McClellan followed cautiously, careful to remain between the Confederate forces and Washington. On September 13, Sgt. John M. Bloss and Cpl. Barton W. Mitchell, both members of Company F, 27th Indiana Infantry, found a sheet of paper wrapped around three cigars. As they grabbed the cigars, they noticed that the paper was headed "Headquarters, Army of Northern Virginia, Special Orders, No. 191" and dated September 9th. The document, which eventually made its way to Union headquarters, turned out to be Lee's campaign plans. " 'Here is a paper,' " proclaimed a beaming McClellan, " 'with which if I cannot whip Bobbie Lee, I will be willing to go home' " (p. 127).

But even possession of Special Orders No. 191 could not cure McClellan's case of the slows, notes Sears. Because the commander failed to use his cavalry to gain information about the enemy, he continued to believe that Lee outnumbered him when the reverse was true. Precious time slipped away as McClellan carefully prepared the Army of the Potomac to strike the scattered Confederates. On September 14, neither he nor his subordinates pressed an attack at South Mountain, Maryland, that might have driven a wedge between Confederate forces. Then on the 15th, and again on the 16th, he refused to attack Lee because he was assembling his troops at Sharpsburg.

McClellan still enjoyed a large advantage in terms of manpower (75,000 Union soldiers versus 40,000 Confederates) when he finally struck on September 17th. His attacks were uncoordinated, however, and the battle devolved into what amounted to three separate engagements. In the morning the action focused upon Lee's left flank; in the early afternoon the Federals hit the Confederate center; and later that day the scene shifted to the enemy right. The fighting was savage throughout. In a cornfield that morning, minié balls mowed the fall corn crop to ankle level. In the center a sunken farm road became known as the Bloody Lane after it filled with the bodies of dead soldiers. That afternoon at Burnside's Bridge a few hundred Confederates delayed thousands of Union soldiers just long enough for reinforcements to arrive; they had marched seventeen miles that day to save their embattled army. By the end of the day Federal casualties numbered 2,108 dead, 9,540 wounded, and 753 missing; Confederate losses were estimated at 1,546 dead, 7,752 wounded, and 1,018 missing.

Sears documents that McClellan had missed opportunities at every stage of the battle. By failing to coordinate his efforts he allowed Lee to shift troops from one part of the line to another. Fully a third of McClellan's army had not fired a shot. Even after the fighting ended, Sears notes, McClellan had another opportunity the next day which he failed to take. The Confederate lines were more compact after the battering they had taken on the 17th, although about five thousand stragglers had made their way back to Lee's army during the night. With his back to the Potomac River, Lee waited defiantly that entire day for McClellan to attack before retreating that night. McClellan had more than 62,000 men still available for combat versus Lee's 33,000, yet he squandered his final chance to crush the most famous Confederate army while it was at its weakest, far from home and decimated by losses from hard marching and harder fighting.

Sears presents a convincing and compelling analysis of the entire Antietam Campaign, including the mysteries surrounding Lee's famous "Lost Order." The "carelessness" and "administrative neglect" (p. 382) of the Confederate staff, not treachery, allowed it to fall into enemy hands, Sears argues. Sears discounts claims that Lee knew as early as September 13 that McClellan had Special Orders No. 191 in his possession. The author acknowledges that a Confederate sympathizer had reported increased activity in McClellan's camp but concludes that it was "highly improbable" that any Union officer would have been careless enough to reveal this top secret information to a civilian. "The pattern of Lee's actions," Sears reasons, further supports this conclusion. "Robert E. Lee was a most daring general," he writes, "but not a foolhardy one. Had he actually known late on September 13 that his opponent possessed a copy of Order 191, it defies belief that he would not have met such an obvious crisis" by reacting differently than he did.

Landscape Turned Red is a splendid work of history that describes and analyzes one of the lost opportunities of the war. Well written and thorough without being tediously detailed, it is my favorite account of any single campaign, thus meriting its high rank in *The Civil War Bookshelf*.

15.

Mothers of Invention: Women of the Slaveholding South in the American Civil War

by Drew Gilpin Faust

Civil War enthusiasts are undoubtedly familiar with many of the effects wrought by the nation's bloodiest conflict upon the American South. Nearly 300,000 Confederates were killed or wounded during the four long years of fighting. Another 164,000 died of accident or disease. Areas occupied by Federal troops were often laid waste, setting back the Southern economy by half a century. Slavery, an institution upon which Southerners had based their society, was abolished. States' rights, the bedrock of mid-nineteenth-century Southern philosophy, fell to a more powerful federal government.

Amid the drama and agony of the battlefield, the emancipation of the slaves, and the defeat of the principle of secession, it is sometimes easy to forget about the war's dramatic effects on Confederate women. Two outstanding works—George Rable's *Civil Wars: Women and the Crisis of Southern Nationalism* (1989) and Drew Gilpin Faust's *Mothers of Invention: Women of the Slaveholding South in the American Civil War* (1996)—offer intriguing analyses of how Southern women influenced and were affected by the Civil War. The more recent of the pair, Faust's book boasts a slightly more sophisticated argument, so I have included it rather than Rable's able study.

Faust focuses on elite white Southern women, demonstrating

that the diaries, letters, and reminiscences of these privileged few make for fascinating social history. Antebellum Southern society, she argues, was organized according to hierarchies of race, class, and gender. Whites made blacks subordinate; the wealthy enjoyed privileges and status unknown to the poor; and men dominated public and professional life. Before the war genteel Southern white women had for the most part accepted an implicit bargain based upon the stratified society they knew, Faust claims. In return for the comforts of their station, the protection their husbands and fathers provided them, and the considerable influence they enjoyed over domestic relations, they acknowledged male dominance over their public lives.

The war gradually changed these relationships because the world Southern white women had known was lost. "With the departure of white men for battle and with the disintegration of slavery and the disappearance of prewar prosperity," argues Faust, "prerogatives of gender, class, and race eroded" (p. 7). The war forced new and unfamiliar roles upon elite Southern women. Newspaper editorials, songs, plays, poems, and official pronouncements implored them to contribute to the war effort by making clothes, becoming nurses and teachers, and suffering in silence the absences of their loved ones and companions. Patriotism, peer pressure, and conscription laws called upon their sons, husbands, and overseers to fight the Yankees, which left these aristocratic women in charge of perhaps the most important public duty of their civilization: managing and controlling the region's three and a half million slaves.

A true Southern lady, argued Confederate nationalists, would willingly and cheerfully assume these new burdens, and some did. But most women, concludes Faust, were more ambivalent about their new responsibilities. Wealthy Southern women often took up knitting and sewing but shortages of basic equipment (such as cotton cards), combined with their class-based reluctance to wear homespun clothing sharply limited domestic textile production. With some notable exceptions, elite women likewise refused to take up nursing, which would have exposed them to the very ele-

Jefferson Davis and his second wife, Varina.
LIBRARY OF CONGRESS

ments of society from which they had so assiduously distanced themselves. And few evidenced any desire to control their slaves. Because they had been long indoctrinated with a sense of their own weaknesses and sexual vulnerability to people of color, they faced intense emotional crises in managing their slave-based plantations. Their entire experience had suggested that this role, especially the terrible task of disciplining their bondsmen, was man's work. Disgusted with these ongoing emotional challenges, which cruelly tested their identities as women, many concluded that they, not slaves, were slavery's true victims.

Confederate society called upon women to sacrifice much in the defense of Southern civilization, and proper gender roles amid these changes and hardships came to be the subject of intense public debate, claims Faust. A few Southern women—probably about four hundred in the North and South combined—disguised themselves as men and joined the military. Female friendships and associations flourished. Many experimented with less feminine fashions, and virtually every diarist and letter writer Faust studied evidenced some desire to be a man. Hatred of the enemy led many Southern women to forget old notions of a woman's proper place and behavior. A notable example came when New Orleans was captured by Union forces in early 1862. Here Southern women demonstrated some of their most creative opposition, emptying chamber pots on the heads of occupying forces. This behavior led Gen. Benjamin Butler, military commander of the captured city, to decree that all women who "by word, gesture, or movement" demonstrated their contempt for Union soldiers "shall be regarded and held liable to be treated as a woman of the town plying her avocation" (p. 209). Faust brilliantly points out that Butler's infamous decree was a defacto recognition of women's public role.

Most elite Southern women, contends Faust, were not just angry at Union soldiers. As the war dragged on, they came to resent the seeming incompetence of Confederate males. Society and culture had not prepared these women for the new conditions brought on by the war. Material shortages had replaced antebellum prosperity and comfort. Slavery now seemed not a benefit but a terrible burden. By failing to protect their wives and daughters from the physical and emotional threats of the public sphere, Southern white men had broken their end of the prewar bargain.

Even if these changes weren't welcome, the war exposed these women to new challenges and responsibilities that made them question the gender identities of the past and gain valuable experience in public affairs. Why then did elite Southern females not mount a larger challenge to the social order after the war had ended? Once again, argues Faust, concerns about keeping race and class distinctions in place proved critical. Black emancipation was "a frightening reality" (p. 247) to Southern white women. Mob violence by disenchanted poor whites was a growing possibility amid the ashes of defeat. White women from slaveholding families did not embrace notions of equality for those of a different color or social class: they just wanted to preserve their own traditional privileges. Concludes Faust, "their disillusionment with the Confederacy arose chiefly from its failure to protect and preserve that privilege, to serve white female self-interest" (p. 247).

Acceptance of patriarchy seemed the least evil of the bargains offered by the postbellum Southern world.

But the new patriarchal system would differ from the paternalism of the Old South, Faust notes. Wartime experience and defeat had left Southern women doubtful of their own abilities and skeptical about the desirability of female emancipation. Yet it had also taught them that they could no longer blindly place their faith in men. The Altars of Sacrifice would be replaced by Steel Magnolias.

16.

Jefferson Davis: The Man and His Hour

by William C. Davis

During his lifetime Jefferson Davis was an extraordinarily controversial man whose reputation ultimately depended not on his long career in public service before the Civil War, but on his four years (1861–65) as president of the Confederate States of America. Supporters praised his intelligence, courage, integrity, and absolute devotion to the Confederate cause. They attributed the Confederate defeat not to President Davis, but to an overwhelming combination of internal rivalries and external might. Davis's critics, however, found him to be an inept administrator and a petty, vindictive bureaucrat wracked by poor health who allowed his personal likes and dislikes to dictate his personnel decisions. Poor presidential leadership, charged these detractors, played a major role in the Confederate collapse.

Considering the Confederate president a mysterious, enigmatic man, historians had for years bemoaned the lack of an adequate Davis biography. William C. Davis, author of several fine books about the Civil War, filled this void with his superb biography *Jefferson Davis: The Man and His Hour* (1991). Contrary to previous biographers, Davis believes that "there is nothing at all mysterious about" the Confederate president (p. xii). Rather, "it asks little more than a good grasp of human nature to come to grips with the man." The key, argues Davis, lies in his subject's basic insecurity. The son of a "remarkably undemonstrative and self-

Jefferson Davis.
NATIONAL ARCHIVES

contained" father (p. 692), Jefferson Davis idealized his friends and into his early adulthood sought out father figures to admire. He was by nature indecisive and his insecurities made him overly sensitive to criticism, unable to admit to his own errors, and ill-equipped to deal with men of rival stature. He found refuge in petty details and routine paperwork. "In his need to assuage his insecurity by accomplishing things," writes the author, "Davis often did not recognize the difference between doing business and just being busy" (p. 695).

Arguing that his subject's historical importance lies almost entirely in his work as president of the Confederacy, Davis devotes nearly half of this big (706 pages of text plus another hundred odd pages of introduction, notes, and bibliography) book to the Civil

War years. Another third describes the period before 1861, with special emphasis on events that most influenced Davis's character development. Especially important, theorizes the author, was the death of Davis's first wife, Sarah, after only three months of marriage. Ignoring her objections, Jefferson insisted that Sarah move to his family's estate in Mississippi during the summer, where she soon fell ill and died of either malaria or yellow fever. Although wracked by guilt he repressed outward displays of his emotions. The former fun-loving West Point cadet, whose undistinguished ranking (twenty-third of thirty-three graduates in the class of 1828) was in part attributable to demerits for misconduct, now cloaked his emotions behind a mask of self-control. Although he eventually overcame his grief and married Varina Howell in 1845, he would never regain his youthful gaiety. "Only after these reclusive days" explains the author, "would the adjective cold begin to occur to those who met Jefferson Davis" (p. 85).

William C. Davis acknowledges that his subject brought a wealth of experience—as army officer, planter, U. S. senator, and secretary of war—to the Confederate cause. Unfortunately "Jefferson Davis never possessed the temperamental, managerial, or interpersonal skills necessary to be a great chief executive," he claims. Through heroic self-discipline during the first year of the war, the Confederate president "rose above himself—above his health, above his wounded pride and fragile ego, even at times above his woeful inability to manage men" (p. 455). But as the conflict raged on it became increasingly difficult for Davis to act in a statesmanlike manner. His poor physical health left him tired and impatient with others. He was fiercely loyal to his friends and made disastrous appointments to important political and military positions. Then, unable to admit he was wrong, he immersed himself in mundane details better left to a minor bureaucrat.

Davis suggests that the president's biggest military mistake was in his decision not to replace one of his enemies, Joseph E. Johnston, with another of his enemies, P. G. T. Beauregard. President Davis's indecisiveness led him to be too patient with Johnston, a general the author blames for repeated Confederate defeats in the West. But the president demonstrated no such ambivalence when it came to Beauregard, who had dared to assume credit for the military successes in the West of one of the president's friends, Albert Sidney Johnston. Beauregard's fantastic plans for the Confederate army might very well have been impractical, but at least he *had* some plans, in contrast to the "uncommunicative, noncommittal, slow to follow instructions, and frequently insolent" Joe Johnston (p. 563).

Jefferson Davis: The Man and His Hour is a sensitive treatment of the Confederate president. The author's portrayals of President Davis's struggles to overcome his own frailties transform this difficult man into a sympathetic figure. William C. Davis also points out that this "onetime champion of localism" (p. 581) developed into one of the very few Southern leaders capable of embracing Confederate nationalism. Virtually nothing except a desire to save slavery, the existence of a common enemy, and the figure of Jefferson Davis held the Confederate states together in this impossible cause, the author argues. Union advantages in men and material were too great to overcome even if a great man, Abraham Lincoln, had exchanged places with a good man, Jefferson Davis. "For all his faults," William C. Davis concludes, "Jefferson Davis prolonged the life of his infant nation" (p. 704).

17.

The Civil War: A Narrative—Fredericksburg to Meridian

by Shelby Foote

The writing of history changes over time. For most of the eighteenth and nineteenth centuries historians sought to tell sweeping stories as thoroughly and comprehensively as they could. They viewed their craft as art rather than science, and their best works enjoyed broad popular appeal. In the late nineteenth and early twentieth centuries, however, this approach began to be questioned. Many scholars argued that historians needed to incorporate more scientific methods and focus more of their energies on analysis, rather than settling for mere narrative. Although the pendulum has since swung slightly away from this "social science" emphasis, modern historians are still by and large more interpretive and analytical in their writing than were their predecessors.

Shelby Foote is a throwback to the old narrative school of history. A successful novelist whose subjects were generally related to his native South, Foote began serious work on a history of the Civil War during the 1950s. What was planned as a one-volume account turned into a huge trilogy. *The Civil War: A Narrative—Fort Sumter to Perryville,* the first volume, was published in 1958. The second, *Fredericksburg to Meridian,* appeared five years later in 1963. The final volume, *Red River to Appomattox,* came out in 1974. In all, Foote's history of the war encompassed 2,934 pages and a million and a half words. It is recognized as one of the epic literary feats of the last half century.

The final product earned rave reviews in the popular press. Foote's magisterial style transports the reader back to the 1860s. Written for the classic Civil War aficionado, it focuses almost entirely on military events but with a comprehensiveness that verges on the astonishing. Moving from character to character and scene to scene with breathtaking vision and scope, Foote manages to describe every important person and subject relating to the war's battles and campaigns without becoming tedious or boring. Numerous quotations from contemporary witnesses and short bibliographical essays at the end of each volume attest to his command of published source materials.

Academics generally recognize the immensity of Foote's achievement but sometimes quibble with his novelist's methods. He did not footnote his work, depended too heavily on sources suspected by historians to be of questionable veracity, and paid insufficient attention to the diplomatic, political, social, and economic affairs so crucial to the war's outcome. Some have pointed out that his work lacks the interpretive, analytical framework now favored among professional historians. Others have suggested that his Southern roots made him too sympathetic to the Confederacy.

Foote anticipated much of the academic criticism his trilogy would encounter in a brief afterword to the first volume. True, he was a novelist, but "the novelist and the historian are seeking the same thing; the truth—not a different truth: the same truth—only they reach it, or try to reach it, by different routes. . . . [B]oth want to tell us how it was." Footnotes would have detracted from the work's narrative quality, Foote claimed, but he insisted that he made every effort to write an accurate account of the war. Born and bred a Southerner, Foote proclaimed: "If pride in the resistance my forebears made against the odds has leaned me to any degree in their direction, I hope it will be seen to amount to no more, in the end, than the average American's normal sympathy for the underdog in a fight" (pp. 815–16).

Shelby Foote's massive and magnificent trilogy clearly ranks as one of the great works about the war. But how do I choose one volume of *The Civil War: A Narrative*, given my self-imposed limitation of one book per entry? I've not included the first volume

Ulysses S. Grant.
LIBRARY OF CONGRESS

because I disagree (and I think most of my colleagues do as well) with Foote's emphasis on states rights rather than slavery, as the root cause of the war. In the third Foote's sympathies for the Southern cause occasionally come through too strongly as the Confederacy collapses.

But my reasoning in choosing the second volume is not entirely due to the minor flaws I see in the other volumes. *Fredericksburg to Meridian* is great narrative history, elegantly written and richly detailed. It begins with Jefferson Davis's arduous fact-finding journey across much of the area still under Confederate control in late 1862, and concludes with the promotion of Ulysses S. Grant to lieutenant general in early 1864. Herein one finds dramatic accounts of the major campaigns: Grant's multi-faceted attempts to take Vicksburg; the senseless slaughter at Stones River, Tennessee; Union general Joseph Hooker's advance across the Rappahannock River and the resultant ignominy at Chancellorsville; Robert E. Lee's ill-fated march into Pennsylvania culminating in the epic defeat at Gettysburg; the duel for Chattanooga, which included one of the Confederacy's greatest victories (at Chickamauga, Georgia) as well as its most shocking defeat (at Lookout Mountain). But Foote includes other campaigns, perhaps less recognized by modern readers but just as important to those engaged: the sparring for control of the Mississippi River between New Orleans, and Port Hudson, Louisiana; the fierce struggles in Missouri, Arkansas, and Kansas; the unsuccessful Federal attempts to batter through Confederate defenses at Charleston; and the terrifying exploits of Confederate raiders Nathan Bedford Forrest and John H. Morgan.

Foote rates Forrest highly, Grant somewhat less so than is currently the trend. The author's handling of the controversy between Braxton Bragg and his subordinates, which mixed genuine differences over wartime strategy with bitter personal quarrels more reminiscent of bickering children than professional soldiers, is superbly balanced. He gives equal weight to eastern and western fronts, thus serving as a nice counterbalance to Bruce Catton's great works on the Army of the Potomac, including *A Stillness at Appomattox* [2]. But any attempt to summarize such a massive narrative is probably fruitless. I've ranked it slightly lower than I initially projected, not because it lacks quality but because its huge size and comprehensive scope might put off some less devoted Civil War enthusiasts. By all means read Foote's trilogy—or at least *Fredericksburg to Meridian*—and relish it for its rich descriptions of two nations, and perhaps even two peoples, at war.

18.

The Life of Johnny Reb: The Common Soldier of the Confederacy

by Bell Irvin Wiley

Sometimes forgotten among discussions of the causes, course, and consequences of the American Civil War are the men who fought it. If one wants to get to know the Civil War soldier—the food he ate, the clothes he wore, the weapons he carried, the dangers he faced, and the feelings he had—the best, most readable studies are those written half a century ago by Bell Irvin Wiley, formerly professor emeritus at Emory University. Wiley wrote two classics on the subject: *The Life of Johnny Reb: The Common Soldier of the Confederacy* (1943) and the companion work, *The Life of Billy Yank: The Common Soldier of the Union* (1951). I've always considered *Johnny Reb* the superior of the two, perhaps because Wiley, who was a lifelong Southerner, had particularly good insights into what his forebears thought and felt.

"So impatient did I become for starting," wrote one soon-to-be Confederate from Arkansas, "that I felt like ten thousand pins were pricking me in every part of the body, and [I] started off a week in advance of my brothers" (p. 15). But the realities of camp life and battle, notes Wiley, soon dampened soldiers' initial enthusiasm. Desperate to escape the boredom of camp life, Confederates turned to music, reading, and sports. They arranged elaborate theatrical performances and gambled on everything that moved. Religious revivals swept through many Rebel camps in the spring of 1863 and once again in the winter of 1863 to 1864, but other soldiers drank, engaged in illicit sexual activities, and plundered the private property of those unfortunate enough to be in the army's wake.

Poor health, tattered uniforms, and inadequate rations made the Confederate soldier's life immensely difficult. Dysentery, diarrhea, malaria, measles, and the great killers typhoid and smallpox claimed far more casualties than battle, explains Wiley. In order to ease his burdens on the march, the average soldier took it upon himself to lighten his load. "'Reduced to the minimum,' recalled one observer, 'the private soldier consisted of one man, one hat, one jacket, one shirt, one pair of pants, one pair of drawers, one pair of shoes, and one pair of socks. His baggage was one blanket, one rubber blanket, and one haversack'" (p. 307). With resupply sporadic at best, he could expect to wear a ragged uniform and be in chronic need of blankets, socks, and shoes. But food was his biggest concern. Vegetables were scarce and the cornbread and beef which provided the bulk of his official ration were of dubious quality. He thus became an expert forager, scouring the surrounding countryside for edibles in order to remain alive. The shortage of food seemed particularly cruel given the South's agricultural prowess. Unfortunately for Johnny Reb, notes Wiley, the inefficiency of the Confederacy's subsistence department, the lack of preservatives or storage facilities, the poor transportation network, and the reductions in shipments from Texas, Arkansas, and Louisiana after the Federal capture of the Mississippi River precluded any effective attempts at distribution after mid-1863.

Johnny Reb took a casual attitude toward discipline. "To a much larger extent than in most military organizations," explains Wiley, "Rebel discipline was an individual matter between an officer and his men" (p. 234). Soldiers respected officers who demonstrated their bravery in battle but refused to cooperate with those who "put on airs" or tried to invoke overly harsh punishments. Discipline suffered accordingly and the laxness had a deleterious effect upon the war effort. Wiley suggests that tighter discipline might have reduced desertion, which became a major problem late in the war, and helped to reduce supply shortages, battlefield defeats, and resentment among active troops against those who

Pvt. William S. Askew, Company A, First Georgia Infantry, Confederate States of America.
LIBRARY OF CONGRESS

avoided military service. Indeed he pins much of the fault for the Confederate defeat on internal problems resulting from this general disorder and dissatisfaction.

Wiley also wrote a pioneering study about the role of blacks in the war, *Southern Negroes, 1861-1865* (1938) which demolished the myth that slaves were treated well by their masters. Some modern critics, however, note that *The Life of Johnny Reb* hardly reflects the cutting edge in Civil War scholarship. Wiley's chapter about the Confederate soldier's sentiments about women, for example, suffers in comparison to the more sophisticated analysis of Drew Gilpin Faust in *Mothers of Invention: Women of the Slaveholding South in the American Civil War* [15]. Likewise Wiley's suggestion that the average soldier cared little for ideology seems unconvincing given the conclusions of James McPherson's superb *For Cause and Comrades: Why Men Fought in the Civil War* [7], published in 1997.

Yet *The Life of Johnny Reb* remains a Civil War classic. Sympathetic to his subjects but aware of their flaws, Wiley mined a voluminous number of Confederate letters, diaries, and reminiscences to capture the true flavor of the times. Readers of this book come to know the Confederate soldier as a human being: alternately heroic and cowardly, bored and stimulated, dedicated and disgusted. Fiercely individualistic Johnny Reb began the war; fiercely individualistic he remained. Confederate officials often ordered the preparation of several days' rations when a battle loomed ahead. Unfortunately, Wiley explains, "this judicious measure generally fell short of its object because of Johnny Reb's own characteristics: he was always hungry, he had a definite prejudice against baggage, and he was the soul of improvidence" (p. 68).

This humanity makes the average Confederate soldier, for all of his faults and prejudices, even more admirable. As Wiley concludes: "He had a streak of individuality and of irresponsibility that made him a trial to officers during periods of inactivity. . . . He was far from perfect, but his achievement against great odds in scores of desperate battles through four years of war is an irrefutable evidence of his prowess and an eternal monument to his greatness as a fighting man" (p. 347).

19.

And the War Came: The North and the Secession Crisis, 1860–61

by Kenneth M. Stampp

Although written more than half a century ago, Kenneth Stampp's *And the War Came* (1950) remains the best one-volume analysis of why Northerners refused to take the steps which might have prevented the secession of eleven Southern states in 1860 to 1861. Like his later work *The Era of Reconstruction* [11], *And the War Came* is accessible to general readers and specialists alike. Stampp's readable and well-researched books fairly sparkle with insights and his clearly articulated arguments.

The 1950 publication date of *And the War Came* is worthy of notice. Disillusioned by what seemed to have been the failed crusade of World War I, many of Stampp's peers had been questioning the necessity of the Civil War. Often known as the revisionists, these historians blamed the onset of the American Civil War on a "blundering generation" of antebellum politicians whose repeated mistakes and personal ambitions threw the nation into a needless internal conflict. Their work has some appeal. Even the most ardent defenders of the presidents of the 1850s—Zachary Taylor, Millard Fillmore, Franklin Pierce, and James Buchanan—would rate them as marginal. And the period's political leaders—men such as Stephen Douglas, William Seward, Howell Cobb, and Nathaniel P. Banks—hardly compared with the great statesmen of the previous generation, Henry Clay, Daniel Webster, and John C. Calhoun.

And the War Came is a brilliant rejoinder to the revisionists' arguments. Perhaps as influenced by the hopefulness of the New Deal and the Second World War as his peers had been by the disappointments of the First World War, Stampp concludes that the Civil War was not unnecessary but "the product of deep and fundamental causes" (p. vii, 1964 edition). Slavery and the fundamental economic differences between North and South were very real, argues Stampp. Northerners and Southerners attended separate churches, read different books, and had their own interpretations of the Constitution—indeed of the Union itself.

Stampp acknowledges that these sectional distinctions did not necessarily mean the Civil War was inevitable. Northern Republicans, who stood to gain congressional majorities if Southern Democrats bolted from Congress in the wake of secession, had several alternatives. They could have accepted peaceful disunion, or compromised. A third option would have been to avoid any action which might further antagonize the situation, hoping that cooler Southern heads could rally their supporters and restore order over their mad cousins. Finally they could have resorted to military force to prevent secession or enforce law and order.

Peaceful disunion, once supported by militant abolitionists, found little favor in the North by 1860–61. Most Northerners hoped for a peaceful settlement and professed a willingness for conciliation if it would preserve the Union, but they denied the constitutional right of secession and insisted upon the enforcement of federal laws. Law and order had to be preserved or anarchy would have destroyed the stability needed to support continued economic growth. Stampp argues that even President Buchanan, long pilloried by historians as weak and vacillating, never deviated from his belief in a perpetual Union.

Others searched for compromises. Eastern merchants desperately hoped to avert a war, because war would disrupt traditional business patterns and threaten their ability to collect debts in the South. In the tradition of the great compromises of the past, a few legislators sought to cobble together an eleventh-hour agreement that would stave off the crisis. But these compromises, and those who proposed them, were at best "superficial"; at worst, they were

Republican campaign broadside, 1860.
LIBRARY OF CONGRESS

"fraudulent" (p. 158), claims Stampp. "The real purpose behind the conciliatory gestures of many of them," Stampp insists, "was not to save the Union by compromise but to gain some strategic advantage over the secessionists" (p. 172). Republican politicians had good cause not to agree to a real compromise: They knew that the old Whig Party had been destroyed by the perception that it had given in too often. The appearance of moderation, however, might split the South, earning their party the support of the border slave states, and consolidate Northern public opinion.

Practical considerations joined with ideological differences and political pragmatism to work against a deal between the North and South, Stampp explains. Northwesterners rabidly opposed secession because they stood to lose too much if the Union was dissolved. If the Mississippi River ran through a foreign country, the West's trade with the East would potentially be crippled. Even Northern businessmen, who had formerly opposed conflict, now feared that secession would endanger debt payments, reduce property values, and hurt the national economy. Having concluded "that southern society was essentially degenerate" (p. 253), Northerners believed they had every right to be belligerent toward their Southern cousins.

And what of President Lincoln's response to the Fort Sumter crisis? In Stampp's view, Lincoln "was guided by and not controlling public opinion" (p. 183). He understood that peaceful disunion was impossible, however. Pledging to oppose any compromise on fundamental issues, the president adopted a calculated defensive strategy designed to force the Confederates to fire the first shot, argues Stampp. By attempting to collect federal revenues, holding on to national property, and reinforcing isolated garrisons, Lincoln's policies forced the South into the role of aggressor. He kept a keen, instinctive eye on Northern opinion, and used the public resentment toward this defiance of federal authority. "In short," Stampp argues, Lincoln, "calculated the possible necessity of coercion to maintain the Union" (p. 187). The president didn't necessarily want to provoke a war, but believed, as did the majority of Northern voters, that it was in the country's best interests to prevent disunion.

Stampp's depiction of Lincoln's handling of the Fort Sumter crisis contrasts sharply with the conclusions of David Donald (*Lincoln* [6]), who believes the president allowed events to control him, rather than vice versa. Still, *And the War Came* offers a masterful explanation of why Northerners decided to fight to preserve the Union, and merits close reading by all Civil War enthusiasts.

20.

Stonewall Jackson: The Man, the Soldier, the Legend

by James I. Robertson, Jr.

Thomas J. "Stonewall" Jackson is one of the legendary figures of American history. He was a devout Presbyterian with ongoing concerns about his personal health, whose experimentation with odd cures and diets and other quirky behavior gave rise to a veritable industry of Stonewall Jackson tales. During the first two years of the war, his military reputation was on par with that of Robert E. Lee. Jackson's famous defensive stand at the First Battle of Bull Run, his brilliant Shenandoah Valley campaign, and the daring flank march which helped to win the Battle of Chancellorsville, took on almost mythical qualities. His premature death, owing to complications that stemmed from his having been accidentally shot by his own men, has led to endless debates about the difference his presence might have made later in the war.

Several biographers have told Jackson's story. For four decades Frank Vandiver's *Mighty Stonewall* (1957) held pride of place. But James I. Robertson, Jr., displaced Vandiver's venerable standard with his more recent biography, *Stonewall Jackson: The Man, the Soldier, the Legend* (1997). A lifetime of scholarship and teaching prepared Robertson for the task, and the massive narrative (760 pages), extensive bibliography, and thorough endnotes make this work a truly complete biography. Some may quibble with a few of

Robertson's interpretations, but this outstanding book joins the ranks of the Civil War classics.

Robertson takes to task those who have allowed Jackson's eccentricities to blind them to the true man, although he acknowledges that the Virginian said and did some odd things at odd times. Once while he and a comrade were watering their horses, Jackson wondered aloud: "'Did you ever think, sir, what an opportunity a battlefield affords to liars?'" (p. x). Some contemporaries claimed that he constantly sucked lemons. During the Civil War Jackson developed the unconscious habit of raising his left arm toward the sky, as if calling upon heavenly forces. The Virginian was also a hypochondriac. At one time or another he expressed genuine concern about his eyesight, hearing, throat, digestion, stomach, liver, kidneys, circulation, nervous system, joints, and muscles. To combat his real and imagined ailments, Jackson experimented with a bewildering variety of medicines, fads, ointments, and compresses—some helpful, others not. He was especially convinced about the virtues of hydropathy, the use of water to cure ailments.

But Robertson points out that often there was a method behind this seeming madness. Jackson loved fruits of all kinds (especially peaches), not just lemons. A strong believer in the importance of diet and physical fitness, he was careful about the types of food he ate, took long walks, and purchased exercise equipment—all habits we would encourage today. He tended to complain about his health only when he was bored or felt unproductive. During the Civil War he admitted that he was ill only once, and that was during the Seven Days' Battles, when the rigors of a season of hard campaigning would have debilitated a man less committed to his duty and his cause.

The key to Jackson, Robertson demonstrates, lies not in his unusual behavior, but in his personal experiences and religious convictions. Because he was orphaned as a young boy, Jackson developed a strong sense of honor, discipline, and responsibility. Those around him marveled at his self-control. Through hard work and absolute dedication, he overcame his scanty educational training to graduate in 1846 from the U.S. Military Academy. He kept a written set of maxims to guide his everyday actions. Jackson proved fearless in battle, and emerged from the war against Mexico as a genuine hero, but left the army in 1851 to accept a professorship at the Virginia Military Institute. There he developed into a somewhat pedestrian teacher, whose requirements of his students were as rigorous as they were rigidly enforced.

The professor also experienced a deepening of his religious faith. He was baptized in 1849 and joined the Lexington Presbyterian Church soon after his arrival at VMI. As Robertson explains, "Jackson did not accept this religion: he absorbed it—hungrily, constantly, totally" (p. 134). He prayed daily, read the Bible and other religious tracts faithfully, reserved the Sabbath for holy work, and gave up all amusements that he feared might divert him from drawing closer to his God. He owned six slaves but helped to organize and teach a Sunday School class for blacks. Through his reading of the Bible, Robertson argues, Jackson reasoned that God had sanctioned slavery and must have done so for divine purposes.

Religion affirmed Jackson's stance on secession and the Civil War. He was a lifelong Democrat who believed the conflict between North and South could have been avoided. But the federal government was trampling on the constitutional rights of Virginia, and honorable men had to smite the heathen invaders. Sure in his faith, he had nothing to fear in battle. Robertson explains it eloquently: "Jackson's stonewall-like determination lay in small part to his being a soldier; the dominant factor came from his complete belief in the guidance of the Almighty. Conquering for God, Jackson was confident in battle. His faith permitted nothing less" (p. 271).

In public Jackson was a courteous, shy, self-controlled, somewhat awkward man. He knew tragedy all too well: his father and a sister had died of typhoid fever when he was two; his mother had died five years later of dysentery and fever; his first wife, Ellie, had died shortly after delivering a stillborn son. Within the safe confines of his own home, he was open, tender, and even playful with his second wife, Anna. Oddly enough, Jackson also got along well with the flamboyant Rebel cavalryman J. E. B. Stuart. But few

Stonewall Jackson.
NATIONAL ARCHIVES

others got beyond Jackson's determination and steely reserve—at least until the First Battle of Bull Run. There his former VMI cadets "'saw the warrior and forgot the eccentric man'" (p. 263). Calm and grimly determined, safe in his faith in God, Jackson betrayed no sense of fear on the battlefield.

Obedience and audacity characterized Jackson's military thinking. Robertson argues that his frequent confrontations with subordinate officers—a much abbreviated list would include Richard Garnett, Turner Ashby, William Taliaferro, Richard Taylor, A. P. Hill, and Richard Ewell—stemmed from Jackson's expectation that they display the same unquestioning obedience that he did. Although many have accused Jackson of being too lethargic during the Seven Days' Battles, Robertson places most of the blame on the army's dysfunctional command system, and on Robert E. Lee's failure to issue specific orders. Jackson was merely doing what he was told. This same obedience made Jackson a veritable stone wall on the defense: when instructed to hold a position, he did so.

Boldness distinguished Jackson from most other Civil War generals. After the First Battle of Bull Run he wanted to march immediately upon Washington, D.C. With a comparatively small force in the Shenandoah Valley, he routed Federal armies, pinned down thousands of reinforcements bound for other fronts, and captured precious munitions. His daring provided a much-needed shot in the arm to sagging Confederate morale, and "changed the whole face of the Civil War in the state" of Virginia (p. 446), notes Robertson. Even at Antietam, where his lines were shattered during the enemy's morning assaults, he was by the end of the day investigating the possibility of a counterattack. Jackson's greatest day came at Chancellorsville, when he directed his corps over narrow wilderness roads to deliver a crushing blow to the Federal right flank.

Serious Civil War enthusiasts might challenge Robertson's defense of Jackson's leadership during the Seven Days' Battles and the Battle of Cedar Mountain in Virginia. But Robertson generally recognizes Jackson's faults and limitations. *Stonewall Jackson: The Man, the Soldier, the Legend* is a fair and sympathetic biography that transforms the eccentrically brilliant warrior of lore into a human being.

21.

The Destructive War: William Tecumseh Sherman, Stonewall Jackson, and the Americans

by Charles Royster

In the late morning hours of February 15, 1865, the lead elements of Union general William T. Sherman's army began entering Columbia, South Carolina, capital of the first state in the Union to secede and the veritable symbol of the Old South. Tired of the long war and ready to go home, gangs of Yankees rampaged through the city's business district and most fashionable residential areas. That night, fanned by high winds, uncontrolled fires raged through the city. Watching her house burn, a resentful Eliza Goodwyn, who had sent six sons into the Confederate army (two of whom had died), told an approaching Union soldier that her only regret was that she had not sent six more sons to fight. "Damn you women, you are the ones keeping up the war," replied the soldier (p. 22).

The following afternoon, Union troops departed and local residents began restoring order. Lottie Reynolds, whose house had been saved, was standing in her front yard as a vigilante approached with a captured Federal straggler in tow, her father recalled. "What shall I do with this man?" wondered the vigilante. Enraged and embittered by the destruction of her city, Lottie replied venomously: "Kill him." Her father remembered that she later expressed relief that the soldier was not killed, but he added: "In that moment all she had to suffer seemed to burn out every feeling of pity and she knew what war was" (p. 33).

For Charles Royster, these vignettes crystallize the effects of total war. From the outset of the Civil War, some citizens on both the Union and Confederate sides had called for the general devastation of their respective enemies. But as the conflict raged on, such rhetoric became the norm rather than the exception, observes Royster. In *The Destructive War* (1991), a multilayered series of essays, he examines and explains this progression, the results Americans believed would come from such total conflict, and the ways in which they attempted to justify their conduct during the war. "The destructive war grew from small beginnings," argues Royster, "yet it was also present or incipient at the start of the fighting. The people who made it surprised themselves, but the surprise consisted, in part, of getting what they had asked for" (p. xii).

Much of Royster's analysis revolves around two of the war's most notable characters, Stonewall Jackson and William T. Sherman. To many Southerners during and after the war, the pious Jackson came to symbolize the virtues of their cause. Jackson was relentless—whether it be in his pursuit of eccentric regimens which might improve his health, of his quest for closer association with God, or his desire to defeat the enemy. Southerners appreciated these qualities as the best means of guaranteeing their independence and of avenging the destruction of Confederate property by Federal invaders. In Royster's view, their tendency to overstate Jackson's achievements and to idolize his personality "conveyed their support for the kind of war Jackson wanted to wage" (p. 72).

Northerners, meanwhile, were justifying their own ruthless war. They believed Confederates deserved what they got for having started the conflict and having pursued it so persistently. The most obvious symbol of this vengeful mode of warfare and of the perceived need to restore order was Sherman, who Royster views as a counterpoint to Jackson. Sherman was a great admirer of the South before the war, and initially believed that destroying enemy property would only make the Confederates more determined to resist. His experiences in 1862 and 1863 trying to stamp out guerrilla activity around Memphis changed his mind. To win, argues

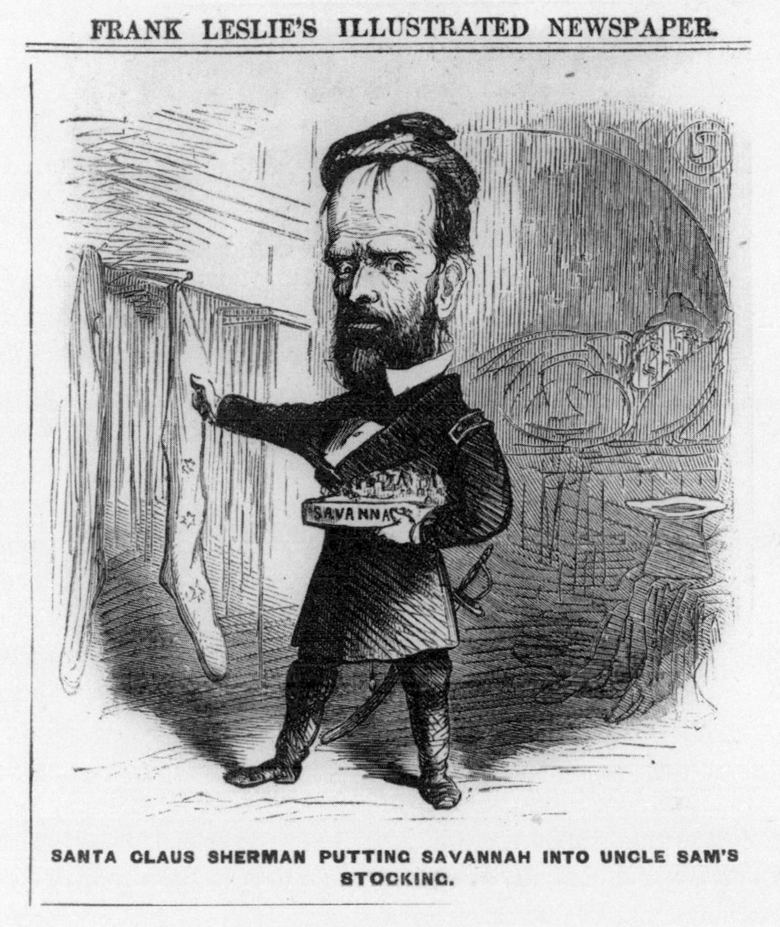

LIBRARY OF CONGRESS

Royster, Sherman concluded that the Union must make war upon the society he had once enjoyed.

How they viewed the country's history, culture, and future made it easier for Americans, Northern and Southern, to rationalize and justify their destructive wars. Neither side accepted responsibility for the conflict's outbreak or devastation, Royster observes. Jackson believed that fate rested in the hands of a Divine Providence. Sherman also absolved himself, reasoning that irresistible natural forces had been set in motion. Americans also came to see the war as a means of correcting the excesses and immorality of the antebellum period, notes Royster. By joining in the fighting or experiencing the war vicariously, all Americans could help in the cleansing process. They believed that winning this great moral victory would justify the means; thus Northerners and Southerners became willing to make the war their own. The killing and destruction was seen alternately as a progressive step or a necessary check against tyrannical impulses. In the process people on both sides created and shaped their images of what the nation was and should be. Either they would fight and win this conflict, or they would allow themselves to fall into a state of degradation. "The vicarious war was thus a civic necessity" (p. 295), concludes Royster.

Some of Royster's interpretations are not entirely convincing. Jackson's aggressive style of war might not necessarily have evolved into the destructive war waged by Sherman in Georgia and the Carolinas, or by Sheridan in the Shenandoah Valley. Robert E. Lee fought just as aggressively as Jackson, almost to the end, but generally resisted escalating the conflict. And Sherman's long marches were motivated as much by his penchant for raiding and avoiding pitched battles as by the guiding theory of destructive warfare. The Battle of Kennesaw Mountain, Georgia—the site of Sherman's unsuccessful frontal assault against the Confederate Army of Tennessee—was the exception rather than the rule in Sherman's Civil War campaigns.

The Destructive War is the most intellectually challenging volume recommended in *The Civil War Bookshelf.* The book is loosely organized around the general themes described above, but it is composed of a series of essays that venture far afield and occasionally seem repetitive. Five of its nine chapters are largely analytical; these have been the basis for most of my comments. The remaining four are brilliantly written descriptions of specific episodes—the burning of Columbia, the death of Stonewall Jackson, the battle of Kennesaw Mountain, and the grand procession of Sherman's triumphant army through Washington after the war. The sudden shifts in time and location, though somewhat disconcerting, remind the reader of the human consequences of the war.

And those seeking engrossing accounts of these events need look no further, for Royster has few peers as a stylist.

As the fires died out in the city of Columbia, Royster explains, the city's mayor and prominent civic leaders paid a visit to Sherman's headquarters. Their pleas for weapons, ammunition, and food to help restore order and feed the indigent were met by the Northern general's animated lecture on the South's role in starting the war. Sherman went on to comment on the large quantities of liquor on hand in the town, which, as anyone could have predicted, his men had confiscated and consumed. "It is true our men have burnt Columbia," reasoned he, "but it was your fault." (p. 31).

22.

The March to the Sea and Beyond: Sherman's Troops in the Savannah and Carolinas Campaigns

by Joseph T. Glatthaar

Having recently lost Atlanta, to Federal troops, in late September 1864, General John Bell Hood, Confederate commander of the Army of Tennessee, made a bold bid to regain the initiative in the western front. Rather than remain on the defensive against William T. Sherman's Union forces, Hood marched north to threaten a strategic railroad junction, the city of Chattanooga. After some initial indecision, Sherman opted not to follow Hood. Detaching one corps to reinforce Union troops already in Tennessee, Sherman cut loose from his own supplies and moved east toward Savannah. His self-appointed mission was simple. "I propose to demonstrate the vulnerability of the South," he explained, "and make its inhabitants feel that war and individual ruin are synonymous terms" (p. 7).

Sherman's 60,000 troops encountered little resistance: They cut a wide swath through the heart of Georgia, and confiscated nearly 7,000 mules and horses, over 13,000 head of cattle, over 10,000,000 pounds of grain, and nearly 11,000,000 pounds of fodder in the process. After briefly refitting in Savannah in January and February 1865 Sherman's legions pushed into South Carolina, on their way north, wreaking even more havoc along the way. "It seems hard for the women and children," explained one veteran to his sister back home, "but this rebellion must be put down and we are doing it" (p. 134).

Traditionally military historians have focused on generals, campaign strategy, and battlefield tactics. Although he provides basic outlines of these issues, Joseph Glatthaar is most interested in the soldiers of Sherman's army. What were their lives like, and what did they think about their comrades, their officers, blacks, Southern whites, and the war? By answering these questions, and by describing the hardship of the Union campaigns through Georgia and the Carolinas from the common soldier's perspective, *The March to the Sea and Beyond* (1985) explains why average Americans could conduct war so ruthlessly against one another.

Glatthaar reminds readers that Sherman's army was comprised largely of veterans. His random sample of twenty-five units reveals that all regiment and battalion commanders, as well as 98 percent of noncommissioned officers, had entered military service in 1861 or 1862. More than 90 percent of the lieutenants in these units had once been enlisted men, and nearly four out of every five privates had been in the army since 1862. A string of victories in the West had led these veterans to expect victory, unlike their counterparts in the East, who were accustomed to failure. Even the men of the Fourteenth Corps, who had been transferred from the Army of the Potomac to help break the siege of Chattanooga, had experienced victory at Lookout Mountain and in the recent Atlanta campaign. Already proud of their abilities to fight and suffer, the self-confidence of Sherman's soldiers rose even further following a rigorous medical examination on the campaign's eve. All those with even minor health problems were rejected, leaving an elite fighting force accustomed to success, hard marching, and self-reliance.

This army traveled light, notes Glatthaar. Every soldier carried a musket and bayonet, eighty rounds of ammunition, a small haversack for food, a canteen, a tin cup, a mess knife, a rubber blanket which doubled as a poncho, and a canvas-fly tent or woolen blanket. A few brought along an extra pair of socks or another shirt, and many brought a pen or pencil and some paper. Packed on a single mule was whatever cooking equipment an entire company thought worth the trouble of keeping. The army lived off the land, with teams of foragers, or "bummers," scouring the country-

The ruins of Charleston, South Carolina.
NATIONAL ARCHIVES

side for food and supplies. Although these hardened soldiers were disdainful of all discipline, they nonetheless performed well in the minor skirmishes along their march. They adored their commander, whom they referred to as "Uncle Billy" Sherman, for his reluctance to fight needless battles and his unassuming appearance.

Enemy resistance stiffened in the Carolinas, but the individual soldier's most consistent foe was mud. Heavy rains transformed roads into quagmires and turned quiet creeks into raging rivers that challenged even the expert engineers of Sherman's army. Shoes presented a special problem. "I am barefoot and my feet are extremely sore," recalled one Minnesota veteran. "When I step on them the blood oozes from the bottoms in such profusion that if I was on the snow I could be easily tracked. I have thought I could not go another step but some irresistible influence urges me along" (p. 116).

Sherman's troops fully shared President Lincoln's commitment to the cause of restoring the Union, argues Glatthaar. Few were ready to accept racial equality, but with the practicality characteristic of veterans, most had come to understand that ending slavery would hurt the Confederacy. As one veteran from Illinois put it, "I am no more in favor of negro equality now than I was three years ago. I am in favor of emancipation because Slavery stands in the way of putting down the rebellion" (p. 41). The soldiers' overwhelming support for the reelection of Abraham Lincoln in November 1864, whose victory they had ensured with their recent capture of Atlanta, also reflected their commitment to restoring the Union. A compelling picture emerges: Lincoln received strong majorities from Sherman's troops—ranging from a high of 99 percent in Missouri to a low of 75 percent in Michigan—in every state for which reliable voting data exists, Glatthaar notes.

Firm in their support for Lincoln and the goals of the Union, but tired of the war and saddened by the loss of so many former comrades, Sherman's men were ready to go home. As Glatthaar demonstrates, a hard war against the people of the South seemed the best means of accomplishing this task with the least amount of personal risk. The soldiers realized that devastating the countryside and pillaging private property would help crush the Confederate rebellion. Kind gestures toward individual Southerners were common, but most soldiers bore a good deal of animosity against the Confederate people as a whole. They especially hated South Carolinians, whom they held responsible for having started the conflict by seceding first. Officers turned a blind eye as Federal troops torched a string of towns throughout the Palmetto State. Upon reaching the North Carolina border, the army resorted to the methods they had used to demolish Georgia: barns, fences, and railroads were the objects of the main columns while private homes usually were victimized only by stragglers and foragers.

Glatthaar does not gloss over the soldiers' many indiscretions. Although relatively few civilians were killed, Southern homes were pillaged, women raped, and countless left destitute. But the author clearly respects Sherman's men for the conviction they had in their cause and for their military prowess. Elements of this army had participated in virtually every Northern victory of the war, notes Glatthaar; now they demonstrated that they could bring the realities of war home to the people of the Confederacy. As one soldier wrote, "there is nothing in this world like Sherman's army" (p. 15). This book, in helping us to understand the men of this remarkable army, does much to explain how Americans could make such terrible war upon themselves.

23.

The Civil War in the American West

by Alvin M. Josephy, Jr.

In 1860 less than 15 percent of the population of the United States lived west of the Mississippi River. Yet the Trans-Mississippi had long exerted a profound influence upon the nation's political development. Missouri's application to enter the Union as a slave state had led to a terrible sectional crisis from 1819 through 1821. Fearing that the addition of another slave state would disrupt the fragile political balance, Congress delayed Texas's effort to join the Union for a decade, until 1846. The same year, Representative David Wilmot's demand that all territories acquired during the war with Mexico be free sparked another firestorm. Controversies concerning the status of California, Utah, and New Mexico were temporarily quieted by the Compromise of 1850, but by the middle of the decade, questions over Kansas and Nebraska once again brought the nation to the brink of civil war.

Too often Civil War historians focus on small pieces of the vast Trans-Mississippi region rather than tackling it as a collective whole. Alvin M. Josephy, Jr., filled this yawning gap in Civil War literature with his far-reaching *The Civil War in the American West* (1991), the first one-volume work to deal with the region in a comprehensive fashion. Confederates and Yankees engaged in bitter struggles in New Mexico, Texas, Louisiana, Arkansas, and Missouri, and western volunteer armies also launched a series of vicious campaigns against the Indians, notes Josephy. "During the four years of the Civil War," the author explains, "more Indian tribes were destroyed by whites and more land was seized from them than in almost any comparable period of time in American history" (p. xiii).

Josephy approaches the war in the far West thematically, opening with the effort by Henry Hopkins Sibley and Texas volunteers to wrest New Mexico from federal control in 1861 and 1862. Like most observers Josephy challenges Sibley's overly optimistic assumption that his men could live off the land as they moved across the Trans-Pecos and into the upper Rio Grande Valley. He then shifts his attention to the north, where a massive uprising among the Dakota Indians of Minnesota resulted in the slaughter of several hundred whites in August 1862. Crucial here was the decision of the well-known shaman and hereditary chief Little Crow (Taoyateduta), long an advocate of peaceful relations with the whites, to support those among his people who wanted a full-scale war against them. Little Crow, argues Josephy, saw the uprising as "an opportunity to regain his prestige" (p. 112) among his tribe. The government's response was swift and decisive, and thirty-eight Indians and mixed bloods were eventually hanged in a mass execution in Mankato, Minnesota. But the conflict between Indians and whites spread west and south, eventually inflaming most of the Great Plains.

The Civil War in the American West then returns south, to cover Federal campaigns along the Texas coast and in the Red River country of Louisiana. The action is portrayed largely as a result of the need for cotton in northern factories, fear of the growing French presence in Mexico, and President Lincoln's desire to speed the free-state organization of occupied Louisiana. Josephy sharply criticizes the Union's campaigns along the Texas coast and especially the Red River campaign of 1864. "Ill-conceived, poorly planned, and indecisively conducted," he concludes that the latter "became remembered principally as a waste of men and time. Motivated by political considerations of the Lincoln administration, in the full context of the war it was militarily irrelevant" (p. 223).

The book continues with a description of the escalating ten-

Contemporary sketch of the execution of thirty-eight indians involved in the rebellion led by Little Crow.
Library of Congress

sions between whites and Indians which eventually led to a massacre at Bear River, Idaho (January 29, 1863), the destruction of an entire people in New Mexico (1863–66), and another massacre at Sand Creek, Colorado (November 29, 1864). Josephy labels the Bear River attack, carried out by General Patrick E. Connor's Union column on a northwestern Shoshoni camp, as "one of the largest, most brutal, and, because of its eclipse by other Civil War news, least-known massacres of Indians in American history" (p. 259). The Federal soldiers killed some 250 Indian men, women, and children. In New Mexico Union General James H. Carleton systematically annihilated several groups of Mescalero and Mimbreños Apaches and forced the Navajos onto the desolate Bosque Redondo Reservation. More widely known is John Chivington's massacre of Black Kettle's followers near Sand

Creek, where "in an orgy of brutality and hate" (p. 311), more than 150 Cheyenne and Arapahos (two-thirds of whom were women and children) were killed and mutilated by Colorado volunteers.

Josephy concludes with an extended description of the contest for control of Arkansas, Missouri, Kansas, and Indian Territory. Here invading armies, guerrilla forces who sometimes amounted to little more than murderers (such as the pro-Confederate leader William Quantrill and his followers, who sacked the town of Lawrence, Kansas, slaughtering 150 defenseless citizens in the process), and Indian tribes waged a bitter war for domination or survival. Josephy's designation of this part of the war as "The Wasteland" is only slightly hyperbolic, for the struggle was often conducted without quarter.

Throughout the book Josephy interweaves the twin themes of westward expansion and Indian removal. He points out that whites continued to move West even in the face of the Civil War. Determined that this migration should continue, officials on the scene waged a more aggressive war against the tribes. "It was a natural continuum of the prewar westward movement and the dispossession of Indian tribes," Josephy explains. "The differences were that now the western volunteer armies that moved against both secessionists and Indians were tougher and harder on the tribes than the prewar Regulars had been, and the Federal government, preoccupied with the task of restoring the Union and impatient with any diversion that seemed to help the Confederacy, did little to control the volunteers' anti-Indian zeal" (p. xiii).

When I first read *The Civil War in the American West,* I was not terribly impressed. Most significantly, Josephy omits coverage of the wars against the Indians in Texas. Conflicts in the Lone Star State are highlighted by the victory of migrating Kickapoo Indians over a force of several hundred Texans at the Battle of Dove Creek. I also disliked the book's organization. Rather than approach the war in the West chronologically, Josephy does so by region. I found it disconcerting to find the description of the massacre at Sand Creek, Colorado (November 29, 1864), precede the Battle of Pea Ridge, Arkansas (March 7 to 8, 1862).

Although I'm still concerned about the omission of the Texas-Indian wars, I believe my first impression that the organization is flawed was wrong. I can't think of a better or more logical way to deal with the complex events west of the Mississippi River than the regional presented used in *The Civil War in the American West*. Further, Josephy is a master stylist with a firm command of the subject matter, especially of the campaigns against the Indians. Readers will find this book to be an informative and enlightened discussion about the Civil War west of the Mississippi River.

24.

Jefferson Davis and His Generals: The Failure of Confederate Command in the West

by Steven E. Woodworth

When the subject of the Civil War is raised, I must admit that I, like many others, invariably think of military events in the East. Perhaps this reaction stems from the often larger-than-life, historical characters who were involved there: Robert E. Lee, Ulysses S. Grant, Stonewall Jackson, George McClellan, J. E. B. Stuart. Or this fascination with the eastern front might be attributable to the exceptional work on the subject by writers such as Bruce Catton (*A Stillness at Appomattox* [2]) and Douglas Southall Freeman (*Lee's Lieutenants* [4]), whose books have influenced generations of academic historians and lay enthusiasts. Ken Burns's more recent documentary series (books based on it are *The Civil War: An Illustrated History* [42] and *Ken Burns's The Civil War: Historians Respond* [43]) stressed the war in Virginia, Maryland, and Pennsylvania, and has undoubtedly had a similar effect on modern audiences.

When I pause to analyze the conflict more carefully, however, I inevitably ask myself: Where did the Confederacy really lose the war? Conversely, where did the North win it? Of course, Robert E. Lee surrendered at Appomattox, Virginia. But he would not have been forced to do so if events in the West had not gone so badly for the Confederacy for so long. What if his men had not deserted in droves at the same time that William T. Sherman's Union legions cut their way through Georgia and the Carolinas? What would have happened if Vicksburg had not fallen in July 1863? What if Union forces had not captured Nashville, with its key industrial plants, in early 1862? Or what if the Confederates had made a better showing in Kentucky, a slave state, at the outset of the war?

Intrigued by these questions of where the Confederacy's losses were most serious, modern historians have given more attention to western affairs than was once the case. Among the most important of these were Thomas Connelly and Archer Jones, whose controversial *The Politics of Command: Factions and Ideas in Confederate Strategy* [25] stimulated tremendous interest. Among the best recent works are Richard M. McMurry's *Two Great Rebel Armies: An Essay in Confederate Military History* [41], published in 1989, and Steven Woodworth's *Jefferson Davis and His Generals* (1990), a more comprehensive introduction to President Jefferson Davis's handling of western affairs.

Woodworth points out that the Confederate president—a graduate of West Point, hero of the war against Mexico (where he had commanded a regiment in battle, something neither Lee nor Grant had done before 1861), secretary of war, and United States senator—seemed exceptionally well-trained for the job. Abraham Lincoln, by contrast, had no military training and hardly any military or administrative experience. With this seeming imbalance between Union and Confederate supreme commanders, why then did the Confederacy fail in the West?

Woodworth gives Davis moderately good marks for his military strategies. His offensive-defensive strategy, whereby Confederate armies looked to exploit enemy weaknesses while holding as much territory as possible, was "well suited to the military, defensive, and industrial realities facing the South" (p. 19), he concedes. At Shiloh; in the fall 1862 Kentucky offensives; at Stones River, Tennessee; and at least three times during the Chickamauga campaign; the strategy nearly paid off. Davis also made a good decision when he placed all western affairs under a single commander, his trusted fellow West Pointer Albert Sidney Johnston. Following Johnston's death at Shiloh, however, the Confederate president committed what Woodworth calls his

Joseph E. Johnston, who sparred frequently with Jefferson Davis.
NATIONAL ARCHIVES

"principal conceptual error of the war in the west" (p. 123): He broke off the Trans-Mississippi region and placed it under a separate military command. Rather than cooperating with one another against a common enemy, troops on one side of the river often operated independently of those on the other side, with disastrous results.

Woodworth is even more critical of Davis's personnel decisions. The president, he argues, was far too loyal to his friends and expected too much from them. Generally speaking, "the closer his [Davis's] personal association with the officer in question, the less reliable was his judgment" (p. 33). Woodworth blasts Davis's failure to relieve Leonidas K. Polk, his old West Point chum, from command. The latter's blunders helped the Confederacy lose Kentucky in 1861; more importantly, his behind-the-scenes machinations poisoned relations within the high command of the Army of Tennessee. Similarly, Davis erred in appointing his bumbling friend Theophilus H. Holmes (who had ranked forty-fourth of his forty-six-member West Point class of 1829) to lead the Trans-Mississippi Department, which orchestrated all Confederate activities west of the Mississippi, in 1862. The president then compounded his mistake by not insisting that Holmes send aid to the strategic citadel at Vicksburg.

Woodworth identifies several weaknesses in Davis's character that exacerbated his errors. The Confederate president was determined that others acknowledge that he was right, which led to needless bickering. His "tendency to overwork and overworry" (p. 315) compounded his health problems. Most serious was Davis's indecisiveness, which revealed itself in his hesitation to issue direct orders, "compel cooperation" (p. 316) among his bickering western generals, concentrate scattered forces, or take risks.

Not all readers will agree with Woodworth's analysis. Although the author is successful in portraying Davis as a complex man "of great ability and great dedication" (pp. xii–xiii) who nearly achieved his goals, Woodworth's depictions of other Confederate leaders tend to be one-dimensional. He rates Sidney Johnston and Braxton Bragg very highly, while Polk, Holmes, and Joseph E. Johnston almost never do anything right in his view. Despite the lack of balance in some instances, however, experienced Civil War readers will find *Jefferson Davis and His Generals* a challenging, thought-provoking work and a good read.

25.

THE POLITICS OF COMMAND: FACTIONS AND IDEAS IN CONFEDERATE STRATEGY

by Thomas L. Connelly and Archer Jones

Some readers may find *The Politics of Command* (1973) a bit frustrating. Its subject—the factions and ideas which shaped Confederate military strategy—is complex. The frequently changing alliances and personal relationships which influenced Confederate policy confounded the authors' efforts to weave a cogent narrative, as detail needs to be built upon detail and connection upon connection. The reader experience naturally suffers as a result. Nonetheless, this influential work has had a major impact upon our understanding of Civil War strategy.

Connelly and Jones argue that the ideas of Baron Antoine Henri Jomini, a Napoleonic war veteran and military theorist, greatly influenced Civil War thinking. Jomini stressed the importance of concentrating one's forces, maintaining interior lines, and striking against enemy communications. By massing against the adversary's weak points and marshaling the advantages gained by shifting resources more quickly than one's foe, even a numerically inferior force could emerge victorious. Jomini's works about the campaigns of Napoleon and Frederick the Great were widely read in the United States in the 19th century, often served as the basis for instruction at West Point (an educational experience shared by most high-ranking officers on both sides), and were a key ingredient in Henry Halleck's *Elements of Military Art and Science* (1846), one of the first American texts on military strategy. Civil War strategists, maintain Connelly and Jones, often followed Jomini's dictums.

Unfortunately, an ill-designed administrative structure worked against Confederate efforts to implement Jominian designs, claim Connelly and Jones. In order to conduct the war over a huge geographic area plagued by an inadequate transportation network, the Confederate War Department divided the South into several administrative departments. However, inter-departmental cooperation proved extremely difficult, inhibiting a Jominian concentration of forces. Duplication and fragmentation of scarce resources were all too common. Quite naturally, departmental commanders had a tendency to look after the needs of their own areas rather than sacrificing for the general good. Even worse, argue the authors of *The Politics of Command,* "the means often seemed to take precedence over the end" (p. 183). Rather than using the department structure to help achieve Confederate war aims, Richmond officials shaped policies to fit the system.

Connelly and Jones challenge the widely held belief in the effectiveness of that Confederate icon, Robert E. Lee. Despite the prestige he enjoyed as a result of his tactical victories and his close relationship with President Jefferson Davis, Lee offered little strategic advice relevant to affairs outside Virginia. The few suggestions he did make, according to the authors, reflected his ignorance of military geography outside Virginia and his miscalculations about logistics on the western front. They argue that Lee never recognized Federal strength or Confederate weakness in the West, and paid insufficient attention to the need to protect strategic munitions supply areas in Georgia, Alabama, and Tennessee.

A loose group of Southern generals and politicians struggled to counter Lee's Virginia-based advice. Unlike Lee, members of this informal alliance emphasized the strategic value of the Nashville, Chattanooga, and Atlanta corridor into the lower South. This group also called upon the government to abandon its attempt to defend the West in its entirety, instead trading territory in some areas in return for the chance to concentrate scarce resources

P. G. T. Beuregard, one of the most fractious Confederate generals.
NATIONAL ARCHIVES

against a single enemy force. Such a policy, argue Connelly and Jones, would have been consistent with true Napoleonic principles.

Often labeled the "western concentration bloc," this group of dissenters was led by P. G. T. Beauregard. It was Beauregard who, in Connelly and Jones' opinion, saved the Confederate cause in the West early in the war by taking effective command from a "dazed" Albert Sidney Johnston, who "seemed close to a mental collapse" (p. 98). Beauregard, they insist, had been the "guiding light" (p. 103) behind the concentration of scattered Confederate forces around Corinth, Mississippi, which made possible the counterstrike against Ulysses S. Grant's advancing Federals at Shiloh. Relegated to less important commands in the Carolinas after that loss, Beauregard bombarded relatives, friends, and friends of friends with lengthy letters and memoranda, even publishing a pamphlet, *Principles and Maxims of the Art of War* (1863), for the edification of his correspondents and colleagues.

Although President Davis was torn between competing factions, in the end he came to favor a concentration of western forces, despite his personal distaste for Beauregard. Davis emerges in this study "as a harried leader, beset by personnel problems and responding to pressures and ideas generated within his organization" (p. 200). He peaked about 1863, but then, beset by a lack of talented general officers, he became increasingly slow to react to changing conditions. In the end, Davis "seemed to have a less complete grasp of the whole" (p. 197), conclude the authors.

The Politics of Command has stimulated much debate among historians, with its criticisms of Lee proving especially controversial. Connelly further elaborated his attacks on Lee in a 1979 biography, *The Marble Man: Robert E. Lee and His Image in American Society*. It portrays Lee as a frustrated man tormented by feelings of inadequacy and self-doubt, and again takes issue with his subject's generalship, pointing out that Lee's troops suffered heavy casualties and that the leader focused too narrowly on Virginia. Further, Connelly contends that Lee's image as a great general emerged largely after the war had ended.

This view has not gone unchallenged. Admittedly, Lee had imperfections. Even his victories were bloody, and he did, as Connelly and Jones argue, tend to view the war through the lens of Virginia rather than that of the Confederacy. Still, their conclusions miss two critical points. As the Confederacy's wealthiest, most populous, and strongest state, Virginia merited the close scrutiny of its best general. And, despite Lee's faults, the Confederacy's cause was far better served with him than without him.

These criticisms having been noted, *The Politics of Command* still has much to offer students of the Civil War. Especially significant is the authors' reassessment of Beauregard's contributions. Though aware of his flaws, they see the flamboyant Louisianan as a central figure in Confederate strategic planning. In addition to their reconsideration of Southern strategy, Connelly and Jones unravel the "family ties, personal friendships, common strategic views, and political rivalries" (p. 55) within the western concentration bloc. They also deserve credit for forcing subsequent historians to recognize the conflicts in the West as an essential part of the war, not simply a subtext to the battles in Virginia. These contributions merit this ranking of *The Politics of Command* in *The Civil War Bookshelf.*

26.

Been in the Storm So Long: The Aftermath of Slavery

by Leon F. Litwack

Despite claims to the contrary by apologists for the Old South, it now seems clear that slavery would not have died of its own accord. For at least in the short run, slavery remained profitable in the 1850s. It also served as the lynchpin for maintaining social order in the South. A good many white Southerners who might otherwise have been expected to oppose it instead viewed slavery as something akin to holding the proverbial wolf by the ears: they were terrified to hold on to the wolf, but even more terrified of letting it go. It took a bloody Civil War to force the South to let go of its "peculiar institution."

Leon F. Litwack's *Been in the Storm So Long: The Aftermath of Slavery,* awarded a Pulitzer Prize in 1980, is a magnificent account of the impact of the end of slavery on the American South. Basing his work upon contemporary government records and newspapers, manuscript collections, and interviews with ex-slaves conducted during the 1930s by the Federal Writers' Project, Litwack describes the complex sets of events, relationships, tensions, and perceptions that characterized racial relations as slavery dissolved and a new society emerged. Throughout, he emphasizes the mutual dependency of all Southerners—white as well as black—as they lost and then looked to recover from the Civil War. "The extent to which blacks and whites shaped each other's lives and destinies and were forced to respond to each other's presence," explains Litwack, "had never been more starkly apparent" (p. xi) than in the immediate aftermath of slavery.

Descriptive rather than analytical, this narrative focuses on the expectations, fears, accomplishments, and uncertainties of the four million newly freed men and women. Litwack recognizes that the experiences of slavery could not suddenly be erased, and frequently reminds us that "the old ways of living, working, and thinking did not die easily" (p. xiv). Thus the rules for survival and accommodation that slaves had learned during lifetimes of bondage remained a vital influence even after slavery had ended. Similarly, many whites had convinced themselves that their slaves were loyal and happy in their bondage; when their expectations were shattered after the slaves were freed, they often reacted bitterly and angrily.

Through the eyes of contemporary observers and participants, Litwack takes the reader through the entire experience of emancipation and its aftermath. Especially memorable are his depictions of black soldiers marching into towns and rural communities, delivering the freedom they had hoped for themselves for so long (of the 186,000 blacks who joined the Union Army, 134,111 were from the slave states). For many slaves in areas not occupied by Union troops, however, liberation was neither swift nor decisive. Whites knew that the Confederacy had lost the war, and that with that loss came the end of slavery, but many still clung to the institution that had been the basis of their society. "Only gradually, often belatedly, did many of them concede freedom to their slaves," writes Litwack, "but not without considerable self-torment, bitterness, and anxiety about the future" (p. 179). Often it took the presence of a federal agent to actually bring about the end of slavery.

There were few guidelines for freedom, and both whites and blacks were filled with uncertainties about their new roles, notes Litwack. Vanquished Confederates often clung tenaciously to old habits, and were sensitive about any challenges to their presumed racial superiority. Blacks, by contrast, needed to demonstrate their newfound independence, and did so in an extraordinary variety of ways. Many former slaves adopted surnames (many slave-owners

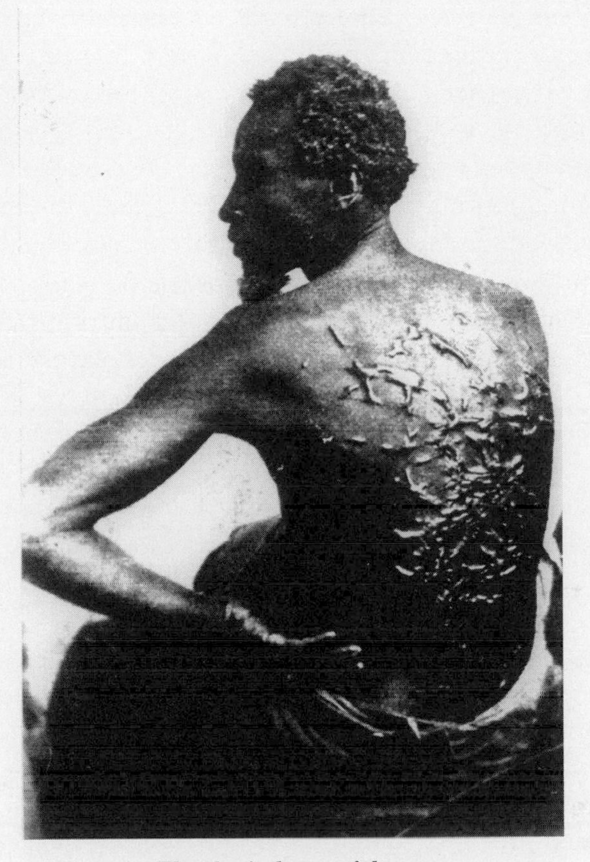

The physical scars of slavery.
NATIONAL ARCHIVES

had only given their slaves a first name); a good number left the plantation, at least temporarily; some families, adopting middle-class notions of gender divisions, withdrew wives and mothers from the work force. Most made extraordinary efforts to locate lost family members. "Whatever action a freedman deemed appropriate, no matter how restrained or insignificant it may have appeared to others," writes Litwack, "the objective remained essentially the same—to achieve some recognition, even if only grudgingly given, of that new sense of dignity and self-respect which emancipation encouraged in them" (p. 228).

Not surprisingly, clashes between whites and blacks frequently turned violent. However, cooler heads on both sides realized their continued interdependency—freedmen were in need of employment, and whites needed labor. Blacks soon discovered that freedom did not necessarily denote equality, notes Litwack; every Southern state passed a series of laws, known as Black Codes, designed to limit opportunities for blacks. Especially important were the contract labor laws, under which laborers could be required to speak respectfully to their employers, forego rights to have visitors during working hours, or obtain their employer's permission to leave the workplace. Almost invariably, local agents of the Freedmen's Bureau (established in 1865, the Freedman's Bureau was designed to provide limited federal assistance to former slaves), anxious to stabilize labor relations, supported the inviolability of contracts, no matter how one-sided they were.

But blacks were not simply passive observers. They established separate black churches, which became "the central and unifying institution in the postwar black community" (p. 471). They also placed great importance upon education. Because they were more interested in getting their children educated than in fighting over the issue of racial segregation in the schools, black parents usually acceded to white demands for separate schools, notes Litwack. Blacks also organized their own political conventions, where they demonstrated much more interest in political and civil rights than in challenging the economic system, in which pitifully few freedmen secured any land. "In their overriding concern for realizing the same rights to life, liberty, and property as whites enjoyed, black spokesmen did not wish to undermine their own position by appearing to advocate confiscation," explains Litwack (p. 521). Suffrage, theorized many freedmen, was the key in these still-heady days immediately following emancipation.

Been in the Storm So Long successfully describes the actions of former slaves and slaveowners in the aftermath of slavery. By taking on this important and controversial subject, it has filled a much-needed void in the Civil War enthusiast's bookshelf.

27.

The Class of 1846, From West Point to Appomattox: Stonewall Jackson, George McClellan and Their Brothers

by John G. Waugh

As James McPherson notes in the forward to *The Class of 1846* (1994), it is more than a cliché to describe the Civil War as a brothers' war. Thomas Crittenden, son of U.S. Senator John Crittenden, became a major general in the Union army, while his brother, George, rose to the same rank in Confederate service. Seven brothers and brothers-in-law of first lady Mary Todd Lincoln fought against her husband's armies. But the fraternal connection was more than just biological; many who fought the Civil War had long known one another in the classrooms of West Point, on the battlefields of Mexico, and in the garrisons of their nation's far-flung western forts. Studying, fighting, and suffering together created strong bonds among men, transforming comrades-in-arms into brothers. John G. Waugh explores this theme in his *Class of 1846*, a narrative describing the lives and shared experiences of a unique West Point class.

In the early summer of 1842, 122 prospective cadets assembled on some cliffs overlooking the Hudson River in hopes of gaining admission into the U.S. Military Academy. Physical and academic entrance exams weeded out 30 of their number. Over the next four years, death, homesickness, misconduct, and academic deficiencies reduced them to 59 men. The survivors became an illustrious group, including men like George Derby, an acclaimed humorist; Archibald Botts, Thomas Easley, and Alexander Perry

George McClellan.
NATIONAL ARCHIVES

Rodgers, all of whom died during the Mexican War; and James Stuart and Oliver Hazard Perry Taylor, both killed fighting Indians during the 1850s. Their ranks also included 22 future Civil War generals—10 Confederate and 12 Union. Several others who tried to start with the class—most notably Ambrose Powell Hill—(who became a corps commander under Lee in the Army of Northern Virginia at Antietam) and John Gibbon (one of the North's best cavalrymen) were delayed but would graduate a year later.

The two real stars were an ungainly Virginian, Thomas J. Jackson, and an aristocratic Pennsylvanian, George McClellan. Waugh's characterizations of Jackson are stunningly effective. He offers, for example, this vivid description of the underprepared young man's struggles to pass his qualifying exams in math.

"Jackson was so singlemindedly bent on passing that it was painful to watch," writes Waugh. "Sweat streamed down his face. . . . Tension gripped the room as he strove to come to terms with fractions. His anguish, and the examining board's, ended only when he was told that he could sit down" (p. 13). In the end, Jackson qualified—his name was at the very bottom of the list. Slowly, agonizingly, surely, the young Virginian edged his way up in his class rankings: first year—fifty-first; second year—thirtieth; third year—twentieth; final class rank—an amazing seventeenth.

Through faith, ambition, honor, and perseverance, Jackson transformed himself into a great general. The same could not be said about his precocious classmate George McClellan, observes Waugh. Although he was just fifteen years, seven months old when he entered West Point (the academic board had waved the normal minimum age requirement in his case), McClellan graduated second in his class. The handsome, dapper Pennsylvanian seemed destined for greatness. He went on to organize and revere the mighty Army of the Potomac, and his soldiers returned his devotion. But, while he inspired his army, Waugh explains that he could never seem to find a way "to translate that hypnotic sway he held over it into victory in the hour of battle. Nobody could concoct a sounder strategy. Nobody could organize a great army better or faster than he could. Nobody could then do less with it" (pp. 517–18).

Waugh interweaves the development of Jackson and McClellan with the experiences of the other members of the class of 1846, discovering fascinating connections through their years at West Point, during the wars against Mexico and the Indians, and in the Civil War. With his characteristic eye for the interesting or telling anecdote, he describes the friendly rivalry between former West Point roommates A. P. Hill (who graduated fifteenth in the class of 1847) and McClellan for the hand of the beautiful Mary Ellen Marcy. After a five-year-long campaign for the popular Miss Nelly (who had, by her count, entertained nine marriage proposals), McClellan finally won, demonstrating a dogged determination he would never replicate in the Civil War.

The paths of the class of 1846 crossed frequently during the

Civil War, and Waugh chronicles these fascinating connections. Truman Seymour (ranked nineteenth) and John G. Foster (fourth) both belonged to the Union garrison at Fort Sumter, while David R. Jones (forty-first) was a peace emissary for the Confederate besiegers. Jackson and George H. Gordon (forty-third) both fought in the Shenandoah Valley. Jesse Reno (eighth) died while leading Federal attacks at South Mountain, Maryland, against Jackson's brother-in-law, D. H. Hill. A. P. Hill's finest hour came at Antietam, when his division arrived just in time to save the Confederate army from the piecemeal attacks of his former roommate and rival suitor McClellan. At the Battle of Gettysburg, George Pickett (who had graduated dead last in the class) led the climactic Confederate charge on the third day of fighting. Among his subordinates were Birkett Davenport Fry (whose failure to master mathematics had led to his dismissal from West Point) and Cadmus Marcellus Wilcox (fifty-fourth), who had served as best man in Ulysses S. Grant's wedding in 1848. In the thick of the Union defenders at Gettysburg was John Gibbon (who had been put back a year), who had three brothers who fought for the Confederacy.

This is a book whose subject I wish I had thought of and whose stylistic grace I wish I could match. A former journalist who has also served as a staff member for a Republican vice-president and as a Democratic Senator, Waugh laces his story with interesting and often poignant details. *The Class of 1846* is not, nor does it pretend to be, a balanced history of the Civil War, or even of the role played by its protagonists—as evidenced by the single paragraph devoted to Jackson's role at the First Battle of Bull Run. But though an incomplete history of the Civil War, it is a delightful account of the lives of many of the war's most famous officers.

28.

The Fate of Liberty: Abraham Lincoln and Civil Liberties

by Mark E. Neely, Jr.

Historians have traditionally formed two distinct camps when describing the Lincoln administration's policies toward civil liberties and dissent. One group tends to take the same view of the situation as the contemporary Republican Party. Because the Union was faced with a substantial, fairly well organized body of dissenters, they maintain that Abraham Lincoln's wartime suspensions of the writ of habeas corpus (which traditionally protected an individual from illegal detention or arbitrary arrest) were justified. Others, however, insist that Lincoln established a virtual dictatorship, using the guise of a wartime emergency to purge his political enemies.

Mark E. Neely, Jr., author of several well-regarded books on the Civil War era, has written the definitive analysis of these issues in his *Fate of Liberty: Abraham Lincoln and Civil Liberties* (1991). Lincoln's policies, argues Neely, were the product of an administration more concerned with winning the war than with respecting constitutional niceties. This did not mean, however, that Lincoln persecuted dissenters as a means of eliminating his political opposition. Instead, government attacks against civil liberties usually stemmed from efforts to enforce conscription laws, prosecute fraudulent government contractors, and deal with blockade-runners, arms dealers, foreign nationals, deserters, and Confederate citizens caught behind Northern lines, claims Neely.

Less than two weeks after South Carolinians had fired on Fort Sumter, Lincoln authorized Gen. Winfield Scott to suspend the writ of habeas corpus if such action was needed to protect communications between Washington, D.C., and the rest of the Union. In early May the president announced a similar policy in Florida. These moves were taken in response to particular local situations, claims Neely; they were not a means of crushing political opposition or portents of a more general policy. In the former case pro-Confederate sentiment in Maryland threatened to block reinforcements into the nation's capital. In Florida, which had already seceded, Lincoln was trying to protect Federal positions at Key West and the Tortugas. Little public protest accompanied either decision. "From this point on," argues Neely, "theory usually followed fact with President Lincoln in matters having to do with civil liberties. Once he suspended the writ of habeas corpus without suffering dire political consequences, similar actions grew easier and easier" (p. 10).

Neely praises Lincoln's methods in Maryland and Kentucky, two slave states which could very easily have left the Union were it not for the president's "shrewd mixture of tough policies and sympathetic treatment" (p. 49). Missouri, unfortunately, was another matter. With insufficient direction from Washington, early in the war, military officers often took matters into their own hands, arresting civilians, confiscating newspaper presses, declaring martial law, and organizing trials by military commissions. As Lincoln finally awoke to the crisis in Missouri, the ensuing guerrilla war along the Kansas-Missouri border led many to conclude that civil liberties were an unaffordable luxury. The state "became a nightmare for American civil liberties," Neely concludes, "a sorry blemish on the administration's record" (p. 50).

Most of the administration's policies on civil liberties were related to the need for soldiers, the author observes. The Militia Act of July 17, 1862, allowed Secretary of War Edwin Stanton to conscript militiamen from states that had failed to satisfy their manpower quotas. With opposition to this act on the rise, three weeks later Stanton suspended the writ of habeas corpus for all persons arrested for having dodged the Militia Act. To more fully ensure

Abraham Lincoln.
NATIONAL ARCHIVES

compliance, on September 24 Lincoln suspended the writ of habeas corpus throughout the nation. Thousands were arrested; indeed, Neely labels the months which followed "the lowest point for civil liberties in the North during the Civil War . . . and one of the lowest for civil liberties in all of American history" (p. 53). As dangerous as they were, however, these efforts did not represent an effort to stifle dissent. Rather, they were the administration's crude effort to enforce what amounted to conscription.

Neely goes on to explode several other myths regarding the track record of Lincoln's administration on civil liberties. Secretary of State William Seward, whose department handled internal security until the spring of 1862, was not an arbitrary zealot, as he is so often portrayed. Though an outspoken nationalist, Seward did not crush dissent—the vast majority of the eight hundred civilians arrested under his watch involved cases that had nothing to do with political opposition. Further, Neely explores the *Ex parte Milligan* case, often cited by twentieth-century scholars as a victory for civil liberties during wartime, in which the Supreme Court deemed unconstitutional the arrest of anti-war Democratic politician Lambdin P. Milligan. Neely minimizes the case's importance, pointing out that several hundred trials by military commission were held *after* the Milligan decision, which was largely ignored until rediscovered by latter-day jurists.

Equally important are Neely's conclusions about the number of civilians subjected to arbitrary arrest—and the reasons they were held. He demonstrates that the traditional count of such arrests—13,525, a number provided in 1897 by the chief of the Record and Pension Office of the War Department—is far too low. But the vast majority of those charged, explains Neely, were profiteers, traffickers in contraband, Confederate civilians, and draft dodgers. Arrests in the border states were especially high. "There were more arrests," he concludes, "but they had less significance for traditional civil liberty than anyone has realized" (p. 138).

The Fate of Liberty is not an easy book to read, owing largely to the complex legal issues with which it deals. But it is an important one, well deserving of the Pulitzer Prize it received in 1992. Through its pages Neely has fundamentally changed the way we think about Lincoln's policies on civil liberties during the Civil War. The president emerges not as a tyrant determined to crush his political enemies, but as a pragmatic leader who believed that only by winning the war could civil liberties be permanently preserved. A sick man might temporarily be fed emetics, reasoned Lincoln in his typically folksy response to a query on the subject, but would surely not insist on "feeding upon them the remainder of his healthful life" (p. 221).

29.

Why the South Lost the Civil War

by Richard E. Beringer, Herman Hattaway, Archer Jones, and William N. Still, Jr.

This is an unusual book. Unlike their academic colleagues in many other disciplines, historians generally work alone. Thus a collaborative effort by four professors at four different universities goes against the grain. Further, most academics tend to write in careful, tentative prose, couching their narrow conclusions within innumerable qualifications. To their credit, Richard E. Beringer (University of North Dakota), Herman Hattaway (University of Missouri, Kansas City), Archer Jones (North Dakota State University; also coauthor of *The Politics of Command* [25]), and William N. Still, Jr. (East Carolina University) set out their arguments boldly and without equivocation. Their goal is "not to settle the controversy over Confederate defeat." Rather, by synthesizing "the best and most appropriate conclusions of our predecessors in this field and by presenting the best and most provocative of that earlier work . . . we hope to stimulate fresh thought and to move future discussion onto more complex ground" (pp. x–xi). Their book has done just that: *Why the South Lost the Civil War* has been alternately praised and damned since its publication in 1986.

The authors set forth two basic premises. First, they challenge traditional assumptions by asserting that the North and the South were on relatively equal military terms. Officers in both armies, though sometimes lacking strategic genius, had a fairly good understanding of basic tactics. The new nation's huge geographic size, the rapid troop transfers made possible by the South's interior lines, and the recent development of rifled weapons all favored the Confederacy. Further, the dramatic wartime expansion of Southern industry combined with the relatively ineffective Northern naval blockade to provide Confederate armed forces the means by which they could have won.

Their second premise holds that adherence to the principle of states rights did little to impair Confederate efficiency. To a remarkable extent, they note, the Confederates centralized the war effort. The central government levied taxes, impressed slaves, and created national armies. Although state governors like Zebulon Vance (North Carolina) and Joseph Brown (Georgia) tried to obstruct the Confederacy's efforts, on almost every major issue Richmond eventually triumphed. And local defense organizations, often assumed to have been counterproductive to the general war effort, actually helped the cause far more than they hurt it, the authors find.

Beringer, Hattaway, Jones, and Still instead attribute Confederate defeat to psychological and spiritual factors. Although many individuals were fanatical nationalists, the great mass of Southerners never wholly committed themselves to the Confederate cause. A significant minority had opposed secession. Others, whose loyalties to their section had temporarily eclipsed their loyalty to the Union, found it too easy to accept the possibility of defeat. "We have little hesitation in expressing our serious doubts that the average Georgia plowman sensed a distinct nationality from the average Ohio plowman, even after the war began" (p. 81), argue the authors of *Why the South Lost the Civil War*.

Religious beliefs contributed to this failure of will. Convinced that an all-powerful God was on their side, many Southern preachers sought to inspire a veritable jihad against the enemy. Since God controlled events, victories on the battlefield would be an irrefutable sign of His favor. Some Confederates came to realize that the same logic also held in the reverse: defeat must mean that God was not with them. "If the South began to lose battles," write the authors, "it could only mean that God did not side with the Confederacy, and if God sided with right, it would mean that the South did not have right on its side and God favored the ad-

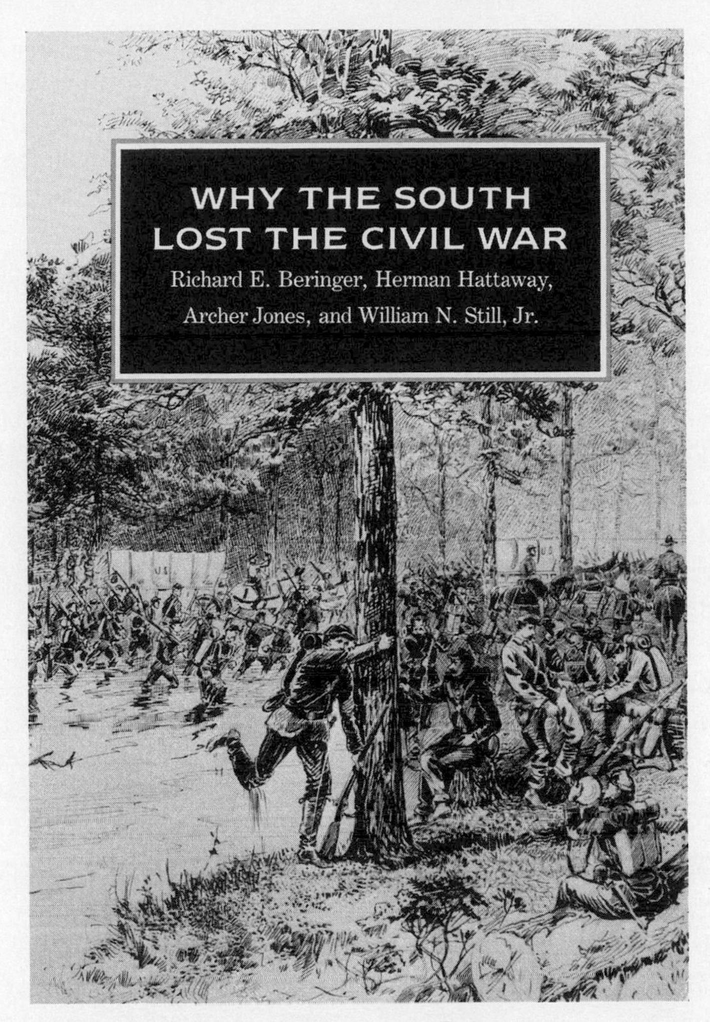

COURTESY OF THE UNIVERSITY OF GEORGIA PRESS

versary. God, then, had not chosen the Confederates, and it would be wrong for the South to continue to fight" (p. 98). By late 1864 the fall of Atlanta, Philip Sheridan's victories in the Shenandoah Valley, and the reelection of Abraham Lincoln suggested just that. Because of these military disasters, which seemed to demonstrate that they were not favored by God's graces, Confederates had adopted a more fatalistic view of the world. Repentance of their sins would be essential.

Guilt about slavery, explain the authors, was a major factor in the loss of Confederate morale. Many Southerners concluded that the institution of slavery had ignited God's wrath. Guilty Southerners unconsciously saw Union victory as a relief from a war that few had really wanted and which might free them from an institution whose burdens now seemed insurmountable. Defeat might have its own rewards, reasoned many. Thus instead of rallying to the Confederate cause at this time of darkness, they simply resigned themselves to defeat.

Beringer, Hattaway, Jones, and Still acknowledge that Confederate soldiers and civilians fought harder than any other Americans in history, but they claim that Southerners could have given even more to the war effort. As an example of a nation that sacrificed much more than the Confederacy, the authors cite Paraguay, which fought a losing war against Brazil, Uruguay, and Argentina from 1865 to 1870. Paraguay had a population of half a million people and kept 15 to 20 percent of its population in the military (compared with 3 to 4 percent under the Confederacy). At the conclusion of the country's disastrous conflict, only 221,000 Paraguayans were still alive—106,250 women, 86,000 children, and 28,750 men. "Paraguayan tenacity," conclude the authors, "based on a fundamental commitment to their country and hatred of the invaders, does exhibit how a people can fight when possessed of total conviction" (pp. 441–42). Confederates, they claim, never expressed this level of national determination.

As readers of this volume know, *Why the South Lost the Civil War* has not gone unchallenged. Gary Gallagher's *The Confederate War* [5], for example, points out some of the logical fallacies in the loss of will thesis. Gallagher makes a compelling case: the Confederates lost heart *after* a series of demoralizing defeats on the battlefield. Military events led to the loss of will, not the reverse. States rights and Northern industrial, financial, and demographic superiority, point out others, were far more important than Beringer, Hattaway, Jones, and Still acknowledge. Even so, in reinvigorating the debate about the South's defeat, *Why the South Lost the Civil War* has served an important purpose, and is essential reading for the Civil War enthusiast.

30.

Union in Peril: The Crisis Over British Intervention in the Civil War

by Howard Jones

How close did Britain, the world's greatest naval and industrial power in the mid-nineteenth century, come to intervening in the American Civil War? Very close, argues noted diplomatic historian Howard Jones in *Union in Peril* (1992; rpt. 1997), a provocative survey of wartime Anglo-American relations. According to Jones neither Britain nor the United States really understood each other's national interests. Even though neither side sought out a direct confrontation, the suspicions caused by these misunderstandings very nearly brought one about.

Jones portrays British Prime Minister Lord Palmerston and Foreign Secretary Lord John Russell as pragmatic men seeking to protect their nation's interests who found themselves in a no-win situation. Britain wanted peace in North America because the war threatened the lucrative Anglo-American trade. But whatever Britain did seemed doomed to alienate either the Union or the Confederacy. United States diplomats had threatened war if the British recognized Confederate independence, and neither Palmerston nor Russell wanted to endanger their important economic relationships with Northern farmers and industry. By the same token the British economy—along with thousands of mill workers—depended heavily upon shipments of Southern cotton, which the Union blockade had cut off.

Jones also gives high marks to the chief Union policymakers,

President Abraham Lincoln and Secretary of State William Seward, who had to chart similarly treacherous diplomatic seas. Lincoln wisely blocked Seward's April 1861 effort to provoke a foreign war in order to avert secession, while at the same time allowing Seward's aggressive policies and statements to be seen as implied threats to other nations. Seward soon matured as a statesman; his "combative diplomacy and rock-hard allegiance to the Union" (p. 7) became vital factors in preventing British intervention.

The problems between the two nations were largely attributable to their mutual inability to understand the forces driving the other's actions, argues Jones. British efforts to remain neutral were often misinterpreted in Washington. Union diplomats accused the British of being pro-South, when that country's ministers were trying to follow international law as they charted a course of neutrality. Further, Americans did not grasp the subtleties of British diplomacy. The British sought to distinguish between outright recognition of the Confederacy and mediation, which they believed would "resolve differences between belligerents and not between nations" (pp. 128–29). The Union, however, regarded British involvement of any type as unwelcome meddling in American domestic affairs. For their part the British failed to recognize either the intensity of the ongoing conflict in America or the depth of Northern commitment to the Union. Many in Britain saw the war not as a crusade, but as a needless bloodbath which, for humanitarian reasons, needed to be ended. Too often the British based their policies on the incorrect assumption that the United States could never be restored, observes Jones. Those favoring some form of intervention (and a European-inspired mediation seemed the best solution) never recognized that compromise was impossible.

Within this context of mutual misunderstanding a series of complex questions and events threatened the Anglo-American relationship. Was Lincoln's blockade of the Confederacy real, or merely a paper one? What rules of international law applied to a blockade that, at the beginning of the conflict, extended over an area too large for the U.S. Navy to patrol? What were the rights of

Secretary of State William Seward
LIBRARY OF CONGRESS

neutral ships and shippers? Was the Confederacy a nation, or simply a belligerent?

As casualties mounted in the summer of 1862, Russell and Palmerston moved closer to insisting upon mediation. The excess supply of raw cotton on hand in England before the war was rapidly dwindling, and Robert E. Lee's victory at the Second Battle of Bull Run seemed to confirm the belief that the North could not restore the Union by force of arms. "European mediation—and perhaps recognition [of the Confederacy]—seemed imminent" (p. 159), concludes Jones. Ironically, Lee's subsequent invasion of the North delayed British action, because a decisive battle was clearly pending. The Confederate victory that most expected would result from this great contest would force a mediated settlement.

Of course, Lee did not win the Battle of Antietam. Most historians believe that this strategic defeat, combined with Lincoln's subsequent Emancipation Proclamation, ended any real threat of British intervention. Not so, Jones contends. Many British policy makers, still believing Northern military victory to be improbable, reasoned that the Union victory at Antietam simply demonstrated the need for outside intervention to stop the futile bloodbath. Skeptical British observers also questioned the motives behind Lincoln's decision to call for emancipation following the battle; rather than a moral act to end an immoral institution, many saw it as an act of desperation by a Union incapable of winning a military victory. Russell in particular feared the measure would spark a horrible race war and redoubled his efforts to push for mediation, emerging "as the chief advocate for stopping the war in the name of peace" (p. 180).

Jones identifies early November 1862 as "the Union's time of greatest crisis in foreign affairs" (p. 210). Britain, France, and Russia were now seriously considering a joint proposal to intervene. The chief opponent to this intervention was Britain's secretary of war, George Cornewall Lewis, who circulated a 15,000-word memorandum that argued that the Confederacy had not earned the right of recognition. The South, he contended, had not met the criteria for independence according to international law. Further, the act of recognition would encourage a war between Britain and the Union. Finally, Lewis wondered, what would the terms of the mediated peace be? Until this latter question was resolved, he argued, no action should be taken. In the end, Lewis won, and Britain refused to demand that the United States and the Confederacy reach a mediated settlement.

Union in Peril offers a fresh interpretation of relations between the Union and Britain during the Civil War. By raising British intervention (or at least mediation) as a very real possibility, Jones has forced Civil War historians to reconsider their assumptions about the men who determined British policy and the factors that most influenced these leaders. More significantly, he has demonstrated that the greatest threat of European intervention came *after* the Battle of Antietam, when most historians considered intervention a moot point.

31.

Free Soil, Free Labor, Free Men: The Ideology of the Republican Party Before the Civil War

by Eric Foner

Why did the North refuse to allow secession? In *And the War Came: The North and the Secession Crisis* [19], Kenneth Stampp explains how, in the months following Abraham Lincoln's election as president, Northern public opinion reached a consensus. Few favored war, but most eventually concluded that national order and the Union must be preserved against Southern lawlessness. Stampp helps us understand the North's reaction to the immediate crisis of 1860 to 1861. We can then move to a related question: What had led a majority of Northern voters to cast their ballots for the fledgling Republican Party, which had not even existed before 1854 and against which Southerners had repeatedly threatened secession? Eric Foner's *Free Soil, Free Labor, Free Men* makes a compelling case for the power of ideas in explaining this political behavior. Based upon the notion of free labor, Republican party chiefs espoused a pragmatic national program with the crusading fervor of the abolitionists, constructing a brilliant and persuasive ideology. In so doing, the platform appealed to the practical interests as well as the moral sensibilities of most Northerners. Their rhetoric inspired commitment by championing the superiority of the Northern system while simultaneously demonizing Southerners and their rival society.

Antebellum definitions of labor were far more expansive than modern readers might suspect. In general, the term was used to encompass all those directly involved in the production of goods. This definition was consistent with the dynamic, expansive Northern economy of the 1840s and 1850s, which still centered upon independent farms and small shops. But the free-labor system could succeed only if average workers had reasonable opportunities to improve their lot. Specifically, argued Republicans, this meant that if wage earners worked hard and lived frugally, they had to be able to obtain their economic independence, either by going to the West to take up farming or by opening up their own businesses. The federal government could help this process by sponsoring internal improvements and making public lands available to western settlers.

The South, Foner argues, loomed as a major obstacle. Northerners saw the Southern social and economic systems as backward and stagnant. The root of the problem, claimed Republicans, was slavery, which unfairly rewarded owners and discouraged individualism and hard work among laborers. The system was bad enough if it simply remained where it already existed. But what if slavery expanded west, into Kansas or Nebraska, or south, into Cuba or the Caribbean? Free laborers migrating into the slave territories could hardly compete fairly against slaves. Northerners thus feared the "peculiar institution" not just because of the injury it did to blacks, but because of the harm it threatened to do to *them*.

Key to the popularity of the Republican Party's free-labor ideology was antislavery's gradual transformation from moral crusade to political movement. The leading figure in this process, argues Foner, was Salmon P. Chase of Ohio. A prominent lawyer and congressman, Chase fused antislavery elements with more mainstream political parties. He was at the forefront in convincing many Northerners that the founding fathers had deplored slavery and wished for its abolition. A conspiratorial "Slave Power" (p. 92), theorized Chase, had contrived to make the federal government an active sponsor of the expansion of slavery.

Foner reminds us that the Republicans were a coalition of several diverse groups. Radicals, who drew most of their support from rural New England or areas settled by descendents of New

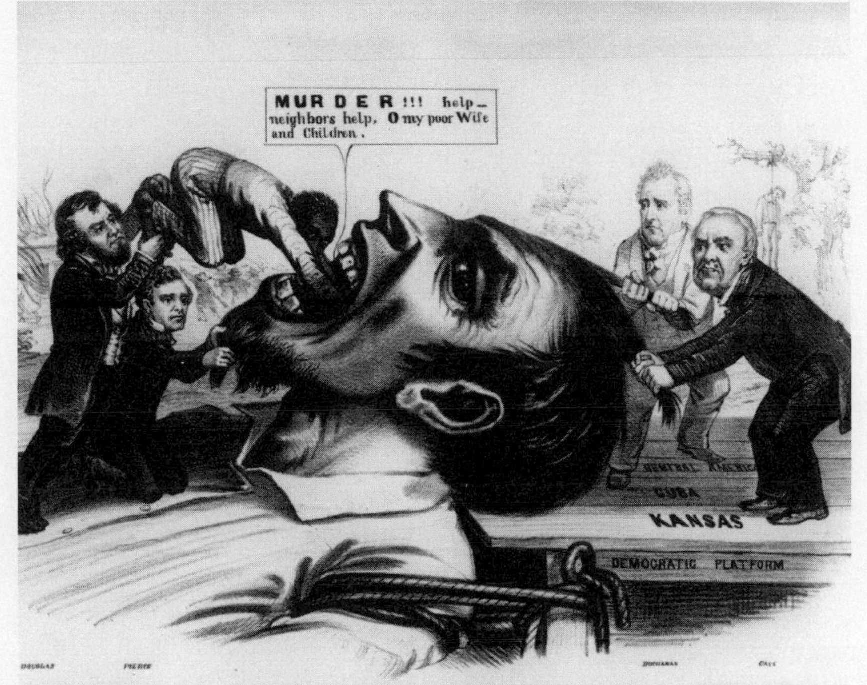

A contemporary cartoon lampooning those who had allowed slavery to expand.
LIBRARY OF CONGRESS

Englanders, insisted that the party oppose slavery. Their past record of affiliation with the Liberty and Free-Soil Movements made it clear that they would bolt any organization which abandoned this standard. But the group also included former Whigs, who disliked the notion of slavery but believed the federal government had better things to do—like promoting economic development—than abolishing slavery. The Republicans also attracted a significant number of former Democrats, who were disaffected with what they perceived to be their old party's capitulation to Southern interests. As heirs to the legacy of Andrew Jackson, they most cherished the notion of the Union.

Support from each of these factions would be necessary if the Republican Party hoped to win the presidency in 1860. Many assumed that slavery, if limited to the states where it already existed, would eventually wither away. But the repeal of the Missouri Compromise (in 1854, with passage of the Kansas-Nebraska Act) and the Supreme Court's Dred Scott decision (1857), which made it much more difficult for the federal government to restrict the expansion of slavery, legitimized fears of a Southern "Slave Power" conspiracy. Even so, intraparty compromises were still necessary to garner enough support for Lincoln, and only careful wording of controversial issues in the platform managed to avoid offending too many people too badly. Moderates such as Abraham Lincoln held the balance, and when secession came, they "refused to abandon either of their twin goals—free soil and the Union" (p. 219).

Central to this book's success is Foner's identification of the complex set of values and beliefs which lay at the heart of the Republican notion of free labor. As he points out, it was the "multifaceted nature" (p. 10) of the ideology which made it acceptable to a broad range of Northern voters. Part appeal to economic self-interest, part moral crusade, part popular vision for national greatness, and part denunciation of the South, the concept of free labor seemed to offer something for everyone. This notion now seems deceptively simple, but therein lies the contribution of *Free Soil, Free Labor, Free Men.*

32.

LINCOLN AND THE TOOLS OF WAR

by Robert V. Bruce

This delightful book is one of the great old classics of Civil War literature. After studying to be a mechanical engineer and serving as a combat engineer in the Pacific during the Second World War, Robert V. Bruce went on to specialize in the history of science. In 1988 he received the Pulitzer Prize for his *Launching of Modern American Science*. But Bruce's earlier work, *Lincoln and the Tools of War* (1956), is more relevant to the Civil War reader. It remains the most readable and entertaining account of the development, procurement, and production of new weapons in the North.

President Abraham Lincoln, argues Bruce, was an active champion of new military technology. Long delighted by machines, gadgets, and novelties, the president took a keen personal interest in ordnance matters. Lincoln's personal secretaries were aware of their boss's proclivities, and amused by the quirks and enthusiasm of the inventors who flooded the executive office with letters, samples, and prototypes, called many such appeals to his attention. The president carved out time to meet with these inventors or to watch their demonstrations in and around Washington. Largely through his personal intervention or sponsorship, many new weapons—some successful and others best left forgotten—were introduced into the Northern war effort. These included aerial balloons, ironclad ships, machine guns, mortar gunboats, Greek fire, incendiary shells and exploding bullets, and breech-loading

Adm. John A. Dahlgren.
NATIONAL ARCHIVES

artillery. The exploding bullets Lincoln once favored, were later outlawed as barbaric, and his "coffee mill" guns (Lincoln's term for an unwieldly, cumbersome early prototype of a wheeled repeating gun) spent most of the war in storage. On the other hand, Lincoln sponsored several important innovations, such as breech-loading rifles and carbines.

In his enthusiasm for new military gadgets, Lincoln offset the conservatism of the army's chief of ordnance, James W. Ripley, notes Bruce. A tradition-bound bureaucrat who would be forced into retirement in 1863 after forty-five years in the service, Ripley took pride in protecting the army from unsolicited new inventions or gimmickry. His unswerving commitment to producing all small arms with interchangeable parts proved a major military advantage and served as "a powerful impetus to the American system of mass production" (p. 34). But he refused to make time to see inventors or to conduct tests of new inventions unless specifically ordered to do so by Lincoln. Without Lincoln's intervention, Ripley would have excluded from the army's attention several worthwhile projects, such as the mortar gunboats used so effectively on the Mississippi River and the breech-loaders so popular among Union soldiers, alongside the works of quacks and charlatans.

Bruce finds John A. Dahlgren, chief ordnance officer at the Washington navy yard when the war broke out, to be a welcome contrast to the disinterested Ripley. Dahlgren was an inventor and tinkerer in his own right, who pioneered an effective new type of naval gun during the 1840s. He soon came to the attention of the president, who helped to engineer Dahlgren's promotion to chief of the U.S. Navy Ordnance Bureau in 1862. Lincoln enjoyed Dahlgren's company, and frequently visited his office. Some believed that the officer was too eager to exploit his personal connections for self-promotion. Still, Dahlgren provided useful technical advice to a president unable to find it elsewhere.

Bruce is at his best when describing the inventors, an eccentric hodgepodge of outright frauds, impractical dreamers, original thinkers, and technical geniuses from all backgrounds and walks of life. "Whatever else might be said about the inventors," writes a bemused Bruce, "they were not dull . . . Lincoln had always enjoyed meeting odd specimens of the human race, and the inventors were usually [in the words of his secretary, John Hay] 'men of some originality of character, and not infrequently carried to eccentricity.' Furthermore, the devices they lugged in with them appealed to Lincoln's zest for things mechanical" (p. 81).

Although Bruce is sympathetic to Lincoln, he identifies two major War Department mistakes regarding the introduction of new technology. The first, attributable to Secretary of War Simon

Cameron, concerned the federal government's failure to use its enormous economic power to purchase modern rifles from Europe at the outset of the war. In addition to providing Union soldiers with good weapons while Northern manufacturers geared up for wartime production, such a move would have kept a good many English and French guns out of Confederate hands. A second and more systemic flaw was administrative. Responsibility for research, development, and procurement of all weapons lay with the army and navy ordnance bureaus. However, these goals were often antithetical to one another. As Bruce puts it, "the proving ground's peach was the assembly line's poison" (p. 223). The War Department should have established an independent agency to handle research projects. Although the U.S. Navy established a permanent commission and Congress set up the National Academy of Sciences during the war, neither organization had the funds or the authority to effectively research and develop new weapons, explains Bruce.

Civil War enthusiasts should find this book enlightening as well as entertaining. It fills a large gap in the literature about the conflict, and paints an engaging portrait of President Lincoln and the technicians, inventors, and charlatans who hoped to change the way the war was fought.

33.

The Fremantle Diary: Three Months in the Southern States

by James Arthur Lyon Fremantle, edited by Gary Gallagher

On April 2, 1863, Captain James Arthur Lyon Fremantle, a twenty-eight-year-old graduate of the Royal Military Academy in Sandhurst, England, on a six months' leave of absence from the British army, landed at the desolate little border port of Bagdad, Mexico, at the mouth of the Rio Grande. Eager to see some fighting, he made his way overland, via horseback, stagecoach, and railroad to Galveston, Texas, before heading north to Shreveport, Louisiana. Fremantle crossed the Mississippi River at Natchez in mid-May, then visited Joseph E. Johnston's Confederate army. From Meridian, Mississippi, he took the railroad to Mobile, Alabama, then rode north through Chattanooga, Tennessee, stopping at Shelbyville to observe Braxton Bragg's Army of Tennessee. Fremantle then went east to Charleston, South Carolina, to visit with P. G. T. Beauregard. On June 17, he entered Richmond, Virginia, securing meetings with Confederate Secretary of State Judah P. Benjamin and President Jefferson Davis. Fremantle finally caught up to Robert E. Lee's Army of Northern Virginia as it moved north, and observed the Battle of Gettysburg from behind Confederate lines. Bidding adieu to his Southern hosts, the indomitable Englishman then crossed into Union lines on July 7 and made his way to New York City, just in time to watch the draft riots there a week later.

Fremantle kept a diary of his three-month journey across

America and published a short excerpt from it about Lee's most recent campaign in the September 1863 issue of *Blackwood's* magazine. Later that year the entire diary was published in England; it was reprinted for American audiences in New York City and Mobile in 1864. Hailed as a classic contemporary account of life in the Confederacy, *The Fremantle Diary: Three Months in the Southern States* has been reprinted several times since then. I particularly like the 1991 edition, published by the University of Nebraska Press, which boasts an introduction by Gary Gallagher (*The Confederate War* [5]) as well as a new index.

Fremantle, who was the son of a major general in the British army, quickly became enamored with the rough frontier lifestyle of Texas, and claimed to have gotten along well with whites of all classes and backgrounds. "I no longer shrink at every random shower of tobacco-juice; nor do I shudder when good-naturedly offered a quid," he joked (p. 87). His obvious good humor and peculiar appearance (editor Gallagher describes Fremantle as "a diminutive Ichabod Crane. . . . Long sidewhiskers accentuated his already elongated face; drooping eyes peered from beneath a high-crowned hat set at a jaunty angle" [p. xiii]) undoubtedly endeared him to his Southern hosts.

Civil War readers will find Fremantle's vivid descriptions of army life and biographical vignettes unmatched in quantity or quality. Also a professional soldier, he quickly grasped the importance of personal courage to effective Civil War leadership. Soldiers on both sides expected their officers to physically lead them into battle. Without such demonstrations of personal courage, an officer's influence over his men was extremely limited. As Fremantle learned from Col. George St. Leger Grenfel, a British soldier of fortune in the western Confederate armies, "'every atom of your authority has to be purchased by a drop of your blood'" (p. 159).

Fremantle's descriptions of high-ranking Confederate officers and of Lee's army have become a staple for Civil War historians. Jefferson Davis "struck me as looking older than I expected" (p. 211); Bragg was "very thin; he stoops, and has a sickly, cadaverous, haggard appearance, rather plain features, bushy black eyebrows which unite in a tuft on the top of his nose, and a stubby

Braxton Bragg: "His eyes are bright and piercing."
—James Arthur Lynn Fremantle.
LIBRARY OF CONGRESS

iron-gray beard; but his eyes are bright and piercing" (p. 145). Fremantle also offers a classic description of the hardened veterans of John Bell Hood's division: "They certainly are a queer lot to look at. They carry less than any other troops; many of them have only got an old piece of carpet or rug as baggage; many have discarded their shoes in the mud; all are ragged and dirty, but full of good-humor and confidence" (p. 239).

Fremantle's record of the third day of fighting at Gettysburg is particularly rich. After the failure of Gen. George Pickett's charge against the Union center, Confederate forces fell back in disarray. Fremantle marveled at Lee's calm as he rallied his men against a Yankee counterattack that never came. According to Fremantle, Lee told one of his generals: " 'All this has been my fault—it is I that have lost this fight' " (p. 269). But Lee's controversial subordinate, James Longstreet, became Fremantle's real hero. "No person could have been more calm or self-possessed than General Longstreet," admired the Englishman. "I could now thoroughly appreciate the term bulldog, which I had heard applied to him by the soldiers" (p. 266).

Of course, *The Fremantle Diary* must be read with some skepticism. His depiction of Bragg as "a rigid disciplinarian . . . rather unpopular on this account, and also by reason of his occasional acerbity of manner" (p. 143) seems right on target, as does his impatience with the deliberative Joseph E. Johnston, who could always think up good reasons *not* to move against the enemy. But few would agree with the Englishman's high regard for Leonidas K. Polk, characterized by most as a disputatious schemer. And Fremantle's descriptions of blacks and slavery were clearly influenced by the views of his white hosts. Slaves, he claimed, were more afraid of Northern invaders than their Southern owners. He admitted that some aspects of the institution were distasteful, but if the slave states were only "left alone, the system would be much modified and amended" (p. 191). His bold prediction that the Confederacy would win its war for independence was, of course, utterly wrong.

Though Fremantle is at times a victim of his own prejudices, as well as many adopted from those with whom he traveled and spoke, his diary remains the best record left by any contemporary observer during the Civil War. His vivid descriptions of the South, from the rough backcountry of Texas to the more refined districts of Richmond, provide an unparalleled glimpse of life in the Confederacy. Quoted or referred to by every serious historian of the Confederacy, *The Fremantle Diary* belongs in every Civil War enthusiast's library.

34.

The Civil War and Reconstruction

by David Herbert Donald, Jean H. Baker, and Michael F. Holt

This book has a long history. In 1937, James G. Randall, then professor of history at the University of Illinois, published the first edition of *The Civil War and Reconstruction*. Randall went on to write scores of articles and thirteen books, including a multivolume history of Abraham Lincoln's presidency, *Lincoln, the President* (4 vols. 1945–55). But his *Civil War and Reconstruction* had the greatest impact. A readable, comprehensive survey of the years between 1850 and 1877, it was quickly acknowledged as the best single-volume history of the period. Widely used in college classrooms, it influenced an entire generation of future historians.

Although Randall's book reigned supreme for two decades, it inevitably seemed more dated as new scholarship changed our understanding of the period. Randall's sympathetic treatment of antebellum Southern political interests, belief that the war could have been avoided had extremists (particularly abolitionists) not deliberately flamed the fires of sectional controversy, and sharp criticisms of Radical reconstruction seemed out of step with newer trends in the field. Following his mentor's death in 1953, David Donald, one of Professor Randall's former students, took on the massive task of updating the original edition.

Editor of *Why the North Won the Civil War* [3] and author of *Lincoln* [6], Donald accomplished his goal magnificently, updating Randall's original text when appropriate but retaining the book's basic structure. Donald did add additional chapters on black reconstruction and the wartime Confederacy. Sections on the antebellum years placed less emphasis on possible alternatives to war, presented slavery in a darker light, and were less critical of abolitionists. Union general George McClellan and Confederate president Jefferson Davis both came out less favorably. But Donald saved his most sweeping changes for reconstruction. Blacks, scalawags, carpetbaggers, and Republicans received much more sympathetic treatment from Donald that they had in Randall's original survey.

The Randall-Donald 1961 edition again became the standard by which all competition was measured. Thousands of college students—a few of whom have gone on to become Civil War historians—were first exposed to the conflict through the lens of the new edition. But time once again took its toll, for our understanding of the past changes as scholars gather new information and adopt fresh modes of analysis. James M. McPherson's newer surveys, *Battle Cry of Freedom* [1] and *Ordeal by Fire: The Civil War and Reconstruction,* came to supplant the Randall-Donald edition in classrooms and among scholars during the 1980s and 1990s.

In 2001, the newest version of *The Civil War and Reconstruction* appeared. Now coauthored by Donald and two of his former graduate students, Jean Harvey Baker and Michael F. Holt, this fine new volume presents a major challenge to McPherson's works. Wholesale changes are evident, with Baker taking the lead in rewriting the antebellum and wartime material, and Holt reponsible for the reconstruction era. The first sentence of this newest work, "The American Civil War was not inevitable," (p. 1) suggests something of a return to the original Randall thesis. But one soon discovers that this is a nuanced and sophisticated analysis of the 1850s, one that clearly reveals the horrors of slavery and the growing differences between North and South. Rather than establishing guilt or innocence as the nation broke apart, Holt depicts men and women throughout the nation as struggling to maintain their respective ways of life. The twenty-one chapters on the war itself in the 1961 edition have been streamlined to fifteen in the present book, with the authors still largely favorable to

McLean House, Appomattox—site of Robert E. Lee's surrender to Ulysses S. Grant.
NATIONAL ARCHIVES

Lincoln and critical of Davis. In an evaluation reflecting contemporary scholarship, Robert E. Lee emerges as a leader of initiative and talent whose early victories did much to sustain Confederate morale but whose "predilection for the offensive" (p. 212) cost his side dearly. Acknowledging the superiority of Northern resources, the authors nonetheless attribute the Confederacy's defeat to "reverses in the field, tension between state governments and Richmond, [and] the failure of the central government to maintain the morale of the people" (p. 475), all of which combined to destroy the morale of a people who built their nationalism on battlefield victories and a dedication to slavery.

Most notable to those familiar with earlier editions of this title, however, is Michael F. Holt's fresh depiction of reconstruction. A noted student of antebellum politics in his own right, Holt sucessfully links economic and political trends in North as well as South to explain the period. Moderates, not Radicals, eventually took control of reconstuction, he argues, but any consensus and commitment about what to do in the former Confederate states eventually became embroiled in politics. Endemic corruption and the threat posed by "Liberal Republicanism" (p. 617) to the regular Republican Party, the "preoccupation with the northern ramifications of . . . southern policy" (p. 615), and the economic Panic of 1873 combined to retreat from reconstruction. Still, the increased participation by black men and women in all aspects of Southern life left many with "a sense of independence and self-esteem" and "a rich institutional life" (p. 644) that would never be erased.

In sum, the authors have succeeded admirably in updating and revising these earlier classics. Comparisons of *The Civil War and Reconstruction* with McPherson's *Battle Cry of Freedom* are thus inevitable. Donald, Baker, and Holt are particularly strong on political and social complexities, and their survey effectively incorporates more recent scholarship. Further, *The Civil War and Reconstruction* covers the years through 1877, whereas *Battle Cry of Freedom* stops at 1865. Even so, I continue to favor McPherson's older work. Whereas he has written an eloquent history with a flair for the dramatic, *The Civil War and Reconstruction* is primarily a textbook—a well-written one, but a textbook nonetheless. Too, McPherson's thematic emphasis on slavery, argument that secession represented a counter-revolution, and "contingency" thesis regarding the war's outcome still speak to its superiority for a broad audience.

35.

Ulysses S. Grant: Triumph over Adversity, 1822–1865

by Brooks D. Simpson

Ulysses S. Grant is the most elusive of all major Civil War personalities. A reticent, modest man born to a talkative, egotistic father, Grant disliked slavery but married into a slaveholding family. He graduated from West Point in 1843 an unspectacular twenty-first out of his graduating class of thirty-nine cadets. As a junior officer in the Mexican War, he compiled an outstanding record. But the monotony of peacetime army life, poor health, long absences from his beloved wife, and disputes with a post commander led him to resign from the army in 1854. Grant then endured a series of failures as a farmer, realtor, and small businessman, ending up a humble clerk in his father's store. Many believed he was an alcoholic. Returning to the army upon the outbreak of the Civil War, Grant worked hard, learned from his mistakes, overcame continued rumors of his alcoholism, and eventually forced Robert E. Lee to surrender the vaunted Army of Northern Virginia. Through it all, Grant remained an enigma.

What holds the key to understanding this unprepossessing man, who most would have categorized as a failure before 1861 and who did not own a single book of military history? His wife Julia Dent Grant, whose confidence in her husband had never flagged, was never able to communicate to others what she herself knew so well. William T. Sherman, who liked and respected Grant and who was usually ready to offer judgment about anything, found his friend too mysterious to understand, once declaring: "I knew him as a cadet at West Point, as a lieutenant of the Fourth Infantry, as a citizen of St. Louis, and as a growing general all through the bloody Civil War. Yet to me his is a mystery, and I believe he is a mystery to himself" (p. xvii).

Historians have agreed with Sherman. No complete multi-volume biography of Grant comes close to matching Douglas Southall Freeman's magestic account of his rival *R. E. Lee* (1934–35). William S. McFeely's *Grant: A Biography* (1981) won a Pulitzer Prize and provides an excellent account of Grant's presidency, but most Civil War scholars have not been satisfied with McFeely's assessment of his subject's generalship.

In 2000, Brooks D. Simpson, author and editor of several well-regarded books on Grant and reconstruction, completed the first entry of what is projected to be a two-volume biography of Grant. His *Ulysses S. Grant: Triumph over Adversity, 1822–1865* offers the best and most comprehensive account of Grant's life through the Civil War now in print. Grant once described his way of making war as follows: "Find out where your enemy is. Get at him as soon as you can. Strike at him as hard as you can and as often as you can, and keep moving on" (p. 458). Simpson's straightforward biography thus seems especially well suited to its subject.

This direct approach should not be mistaken for a simplistic one. According to Simpson, bad luck and the misfortune to have attempted to strike out on his own during a time of economic depression, rather than some deeper personality flaw, hold the key to explaining Grant's prewar adversities. This foundation helps us better understand Grant's subsequent success. Rather than a hapless failure, Simpson's Grant rejoined the army in 1861 a serious if unlucky businessman who had endured a great many setbacks. A devoted family man, he kept up with politics and impressed shrewd observers with his determination and common sense.

Simpson points out that the very adversity Grant had known served him well during the Civil War. Possessing an underappreciated natural intelligence tempered by a self-confidence (which in some cases became *over*confidence) forged in his many trials,

Ulysses S. Grant, who was dying of throat cancer, completing his memoirs, 1885.
LIBRARY OF CONGRESS

Grant was in Simpson's view better versed in military affairs than usually acknowledged. He was a flexible improviser with a keen eye for details and perceptive listener who stood resolute in the face of unforseen challenges. "A survivor" (p. 146), Grant was also a shrewd political infighter who managed—just barely, especially considering the repeated frustrations of the Vicksburg campaign and in the face of trumped-up charges of drinking to excess—to protect his own interests against critics both in and out of the army.

After his victory at Chattanooga in late 1863, Grant was called east and eventually appointed general-in-chief. Once there, Simpson argues, Grant understood that he not only had to draw up a coordinated strategic plan which would capitalize upon the Union's advantages of manpower and resources, but that also had to cultivate a close relationship with President Abraham Lincoln. Simpson mounts a spirited defense of Grant against charges that he needlessly squandered the lives of his men. "Disharmony and incompetence" (p. 346) among Union generals in the Army of the Potomac plagued Grant's efforts to strike against Lee; bungling on the part of the president's political appointees (Franz Sigel, commander of an ill-fated force in the Shenandoah Valley, and Ben Butler, slow-moving head of the Army of the James) prevented Grant's grand strategy from crushing the Confederacy much earlier.

Simpson makes a compelling case, although it is too early to determine the full impact of his interpretations on our broader understanding of the Civil War. Though not hagiography (Simpson sharply criticizes Grant's anti-Semitism and occasional outbursts of anger and frustration, for example), *Ulysses S. Grant: Triumph over Adversity* depicts Grant in highly favorable terms. Union general Phil Sheridan once pointed out that Grant "was so self-contained, and made you feel that there was a heap more in him than you had found out" (p. 461). Perhaps, as Simpson suggests, we all have underestimated Grant and his abilities.

36.

REHEARSAL FOR RECONSTRUCTION: THE PORT ROYAL EXPERIMENT

by Willie Lee Rose

On November 7, 1861, Commodore Samuel Du Pont's Union squadron sailed into Port Royal Sound, key to Port Royal Island, the largest of South Carolina's Sea Islands. The islands, whose fertile soils grew some of the world's finest cotton, were home to about 2,000 whites (a number which swelled to 4,000 during the summer) and 11,000 black slaves. The hastily constructed Confederate defenses proved no match for the big guns of Du Pont's fleet, and the entire white population, along with a thousand or so slaves, evacuated to the mainland. Federal troops landed the following day.

Little did either the white soldiers or the remaining black inhabitants know that many would be involved in one of the Civil War's most notable social experiments. As Willie Lee Rose describes in *Rehearsal for Reconstruction* (1964), the Sea Islands provided a unique situation. White South Carolinians had abandoned the islands and their property. But thousands of black slaves had been left behind; others would arrive later in the conflict, freed by the campaigns of Union general William T. Sherman's veterans as they rampaged through the South Carolina mainland. "On these islands, within gunshot and shouting distance of the Confederate pickets," explains Rose, "American anti-slavery men and women . . . met the American slave on his home ground and were asking

A school for former slaves.
NATIONAL ARCHIVES

him to work out his own salvation by working cotton—voluntarily" (p. 79).

Shortly after Union occupation the slaves were declared "contraband of war," and as such not liable to be returned to their owners. The Treasury Department, headed by the antislavery secretary Salmon P. Chase, was authorized to deal with the abandoned lands. He and other abolitionists saw a golden opportunity at Port Royal, notes Rose. By demonstrating that the former slaves could succeed on their own with minimal outside assistance, abolitionists would aid the war effort and force the Federal government to move more decisively to end slavery. Chase summoned Edward L. Pierce, a young Boston attorney, personal friend, and political supporter, to supervise efforts on behalf of the freedmen. Pierce gathered together several dozen teachers and missionaries, and by March 1862 the group, known as Gideon's Band, was at work in Port Royal.

At first few Gideonites recognized the immensity of their task, claims Rose. Old habits and practices developed over generations of slavery were difficult to break, despite the enthusiasm of the teachers and missionaries. Only gradually did Pierce and the others recognize that if they were to succeed, they would need to move beyond their instinctive emphasis on moral instruction to more practical matters facing the freedmen. As fellow New Englander John Adams had long ago realized, the cornerstones of a civil society included not only religion and education, but also self-defense and self-government. To truly gain the respect of most Northerners, blacks would have to fight for their freedom and prove that they could govern themselves. "Now," explains Rose, "the Port Royal Islands would indeed become a testing ground for the full panoply of an ever broadening radical program for the Negro. The black man would be given his chance as a free soldier of the Union as well as a free laborer upon the land where he had toiled as a bondsman" (p. 191).

The reformers as well as the freedmen soon found that theory often clashed with practical realities. While the Gideonites focused upon improving the lives of the former slaves, other federal agents seemed more concerned that they produce the cotton desperately needed by idle Northern factories, Rose explains. Though well meaning, few of the philanthropists had experience either in managing the production of raw cotton or in organizing labor. The freedmen refused to work in the old "gang" system the teachers and missionaries initially encouraged, and many of the males joined the Union army, thus depriving the Sea Islands of a vital segment of the labor pool.

Rose offers a sensitive and balanced analysis of the intricate relations between Pierce's Yankee reformers and the blacks of Port Royal. Despite innumerable problems, the freedmen built a functioning society on the Sea Islands during the Civil War. They repeatedly showed their willingness to fight for the cause of freedom, and they established schools and churches. Blacks also demonstrated their political independence and came to dominate the local government, often to the annoyance of those Gideonites accustomed to deciding what was best for their charges. In developing a rich variety of interests—from learning to read to driving hard bargains with whites in labor contracts or political arrangements—blacks at Port Royal acted like freed persons, notes the author.

In one crucial area, however, the Port Royal experiment failed to live up to the expectations of the freedmen and served as a precursor of the major failure of the reconstruction policies to come, argues Rose. In the controlled experiment on the Sea Islands, confiscation laws had made it possible for the government to seize property in lieu of unpaid federal taxes. At Port Royal some of these abandoned lands were reserved for individual freedmen who could afford to purchase small lots. Still other ex-slaves pooled their resources to make collective purchases. But the federal government failed to recognize squatter's rights. Instead they discouraged efforts to allow large numbers of freedmen to preempt the plots that they were farming, and made it possible for many whites who returned to the islands after the war to reclaim their land. The government's desire not to interfere with the sanctity of laws regulating property—even that owned by Southern secessionists—outweighed their desire to create policies that would truly help the former slaves.

Rehearsal for Reconstruction is a brilliant account of the Port Royal experiment, which served as a classic case study of the problems the nation would face as it entered the period of restoration and reconstruction. Based largely on the letters and diaries of the antislavery men and women who went to Port Royal, it explains the transition from slavery to freedom on the Sea Islands of South Carolina. By understanding their successes and failures, Civil War enthusiasts will gain a much greater appreciation for the dramatic social changes that accompanied emancipation throughout the nation.

37.

Lincoln, the War President: The Gettysburg Lectures

edited by Gabor S. Boritt

For nearly four decades Gettysburg College has sponsored a Civil War–related lecture to celebrate the anniversary of Abraham Lincoln's Gettysburg address. The annual affair has featured many of America's most accomplished historians, and this remarkable anthology includes contributions (revised for publication) from five Pulitzer Prize winners who have spoken there: Robert V. Bruce, David Brion Davis, Carl N. Degler, James M. McPherson, and Arthur M. Schlesinger, Jr. In addition, *Lincoln, the War President* (1992) includes the addresses given by noted Civil War scholar Kenneth M. Stampp, and an introductory essay by the book's editor Gabor S. Boritt. Here readers will discover many fascinating insights into Abraham Lincoln's wartime leadership.

Lincoln inherited a national crisis. The first official document he read after taking office—which was handed to him about one o'clock in the morning following his inaugural ball—was a message from Maj. Robert Anderson, commander of Federal forces at Fort Sumter, South Carolina. Unless his garrison was resupplied, warned Anderson, he could hold out only a few more weeks. In his essay for this collection, Robert Bruce (*Lincoln and the Tools of War* [32]) reminds us that Lincoln had steadfastly refused to face the extent of the tensions between North and South in the years

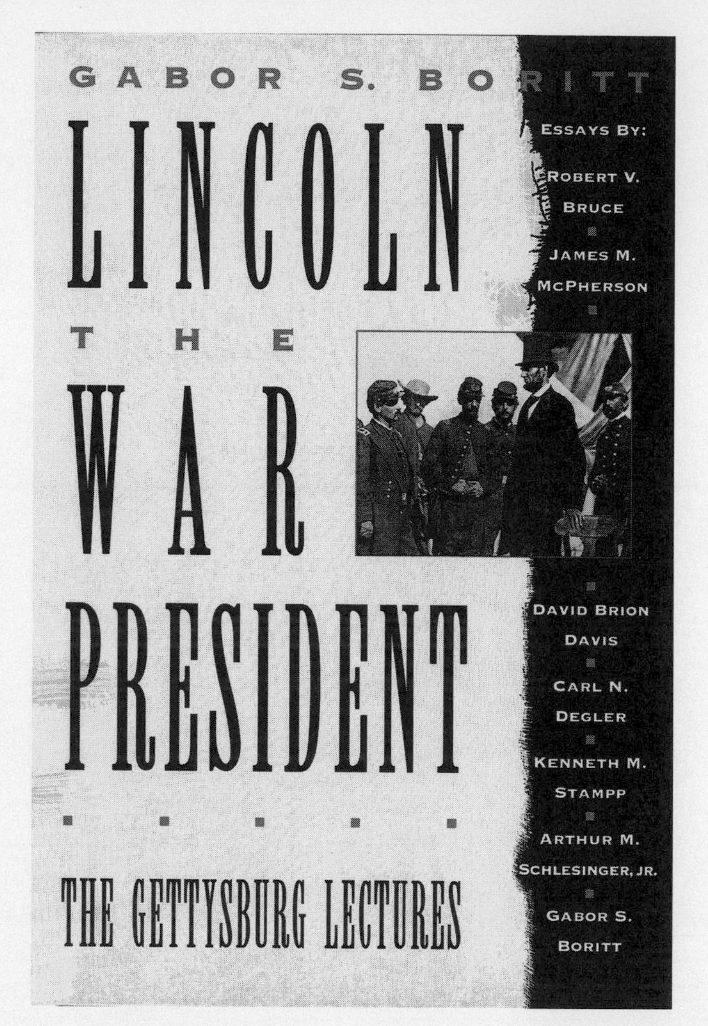

leading up to the Civil War. Even in the face of repeated sectional disputes—the Whiskey Rebellion (1794), the Virginia and Kentucky Resolutions (1798–99), the Hartford Convention (1814), the Nullification Crisis (1831–33), the Compromise of 1850, and the Kansas-Nebraska controversy (1853–57)—Lincoln did not accept the seriousness of the nation's internal jealousies. During his round of debates with Northern Democratic candidate Stephen Douglas in 1858, for example, he insisted that "there will be no war, no violence" (p. 26).

Lincoln's unwillingness to prepare himself for the possibility of armed conflict helps us to understand the depths of his wartime anguish. The war had been "forced upon the Government" (p. 28), Lincoln believed. His struggles to find a way to defeat the South are the subjects of James McPherson's contribution to *Lincoln, the War President*. In his essay McPherson (*Battle Cry of Freedom* [1] and *For Cause and Comrades* [7]) emphasizes Lincoln's skills as a national leader. In forming the coalition needed to win the war, the president admittedly appointed generals to appease various political factions rather than on the basis of their military abilities. While not excusing such calculations, McPherson points out that this patronage sometimes paid huge dividends, as in the cases of William T. Sherman and Ulysses S. Grant, both of whom owed their initial wartime commissions to political connections.

When war actually came in April 1861, Lincoln, like most Americans, believed it would be short. As hopes for a quick victory evaporated, the president adopted a national strategy of total warfare. In this context we can understand Lincoln's changing position on emancipation, the subject of David Brion Davis's contribution. Davis, a Pulitzer Prize winner for *The Problem of Slavery in Western Culture* (1966), in this essay emphasizes the gradual approach taken by most world leaders (including Lincoln) who hoped to end slavery. They wanted not only to protect property holders, but also to provide for a lengthy period during which society, and slaves, would be prepared for emancipation. As late as December 1, 1862, notes Davis, Lincoln proposed a plan by which slaveowners would be partially compensated for the loss of their slaves, who would be emancipated over the next thirty-seven years!

McPherson and Davis both see Lincoln's changing views on the prosecution of the war as key to explaining his Emancipation Proclamation. Fellow contributor Kenneth Stampp (*The Era of Reconstruction* [11] and *And the War Came: The North and the Secession Crisis* [19]) takes this argument a step further, arguing that the war's horrors transformed the president from a "narrowly focused, almost obsessive defender of the Union" (p. 140) to the

Great Emancipator. By the time of his second inaugural address, concludes Stampp, Lincoln had come "full circle, for the cause of the Union now seemed ancillary to the approaching liberation of four million slaves" (p. 142).

Carl Degler examines the American Civil War in a broader international context. Degler, who received a Pulitzer Prize for *Neither Black Nor White* (1971), compares the incomplete state of American nationalism at the time of the Civil War to national unification movements then going on in Italy, Germany, Switzerland, and Canada. In the process he insists that Lincoln emerged as the true creator of American nationalism. In his first inaugural address, notes Degler, Lincoln used the word "Union" twenty times, never once using "nation." By the second inaugural, however, the president was describing the war as one to save the "nation," not simply the "Union." Degler also points to the importance of military power in affirming nationalism during this period, and suggests intriguing parallels between the way Lincoln and his German counterpart, Otto von Bismarck, used "iron, as well as shed blood, in order to build a nation" (p. 108).

Arthur M. Schlesinger, Jr., whose books on Andrew Jackson (1945) and Franklin Roosevelt (1957) both won Pulitzer Prizes, takes a comparative approach in examining our greatest wartime presidents, Lincoln and Roosevelt. He admits that each man expanded the power of the presidency and occasionally flouted the Constitution. However, Schlesinger insists that neither leader based his actions on any claims of expanded presidential prerogatives, instead justifying their deeds on the basis of a national emergency. They were acting out of necessity, not setting dangerous precedents which lesser men might abuse. "These two Presidents," concludes Schlesinger, "remained faithful to the spirit, if not the letter, of the Constitution: acting on the spirit to save the letter" (p. 178).

In reading *Lincoln, the War President,* I am struck by just how much this man grew in office. From one whose vision seemed limited to that of preserving an imperfect Union, Abraham Lincoln emerges as a leader who built a nation, freed four million slaves, and implemented a successful strategy for winning his nation's largest war. Perhaps his genius lay in his ability to manage all these things without losing his endearing sense of humanity. An anecdote from David Donald's *Lincoln* [6] sums it up best. The evening of Lincoln's 1864 reelection was a rainy one in Washington. Wet and muddy after having fallen, one of his aides came in to the War Department, where Lincoln and several supporters were awaiting results. The president remembered how it had also been raining in Springfield, Illinois, on the evening of his 1858 senatorial race against Douglas. That night, he had only barely managed to avoid a fall of his own as he made his way back home. " 'For such an awkward fellow,' he explained to his aides, 'I am pretty sure-footed' " (Donald, p. 545). Indeed our sixteenth president was.

38.

Sherman: A Soldier's Passion for Order

by John F. Marszalek

William Tecumseh Sherman was one of the most complex and controversial figures in American history. Sherman loved the South and once supported slavery, yet came to be reviled by Southerners for having pillaged Georgia and the Carolinas. He was named after a Shawnee leader who formed a powerful Indian confederacy, but later helped to crush Indian armed resistance to the Federal government. Although bitterly critical of the press, he was a remarkably quotable public figure. Sherman was disdainful of politics and politicians, but he was frequently seen as a potential presidential candidate, even after he repeatedly rejected calls that he run for public office.

In *Sherman: A Soldier's Passion for Order* (1993) John Marszalek comes closer than any other biographer to explaining this enigmatic man. This is a balanced account, with six chapters devoted to the pre-Civil War period, eight chapters to the war itself, and eight chapters to Sherman's postbellum career. In Marszalek's view, the search for order, stemming in large measure from childhood traumas, dominated Sherman's long life. His father died when young Tecumseh ("Cump") was just nine years old, leaving the family penniless. Thomas Ewing, a prominent lawyer, politician, and next-door neighbor, took over the care of Tecumseh to help out. Baptized a Catholic at his foster mother's insistence, his first name was deemed unsuitable, so he was christened William.

These upheavals intensified Sherman's insecurities and anxieties, argues the author, and explain some of his erratic behavior later in life.

The antebellum years were not easy. Sherman graduated from West Point in 1840, sixth in his class of forty-two, and later married his foster sister, Ellen. They loved one another but argued frequently over what his profession should be and where they should live. Sherman loved the army for its order, but after much consternation and frequent transfers resigned his commission. He managed a bank in San Francisco, and endured a short stint as a businessman and a lawyer (apparently, he lost both of his cases) in Kansas before accepting a position as superintendent of the Louisiana Military Seminary in 1859. Sherman enjoyed life in the South and supported slavery as part of the "natural order" (p. 45), claims Marszalek. Still, he equated secession with anarchy, and left Louisiana upon that state's departure from the Union.

Sherman then joined the Union Army and fought in the First Battle of Bull Run. Most historians have maintained that the Battle of Shiloh, where he performed well as a brigadier general in the thick of the fighting, gave him the self-confidence needed to be a successful general. Marszalek, however, argues that the defining point in Sherman's career came while he was serving as military governor of Memphis, a post he held from July to November 1862. As head of Federal occupation forces, Sherman "imposed order on the chaos of Memphis through his own methods" (p. 201). He emerged from the experience confident in his own abilities and, in Marszalek's view, with "a new philosophy of war" (p. 189). Battling enemy guerrillas who did not respect traditional lines of operation or property rights had transformed his thinking. During his Memphis experience Sherman "came face to face with the fact that war was more than soldiers, more than set conflict," writes the author. "The idea that war included the entire populace—its determination to fight and its material goods—became evident to him."

By the Vicksburg campaign, according to Marszalak, Sherman had become "an early psychological warrior" (p. 230). He perfected his destructive war against the enemy's psyche, as well as

William T. Sherman.
LIBRARY OF CONGRESS

his resources and property, during his raids on Meridian, Mississippi (February 1864), throughout his more famous March to the Sea following the capture of Atlanta (November to December 1864), and in his ensuing march through the Carolinas (February to May 1865). In Marszalek's view, Sherman made war against the Southern people he so admired in order "to reimpose Union and stability" (p. 332). As Sherman had explained to a fellow Union officer at the outset of his move against Savannah: "I propose to demonstrate the vulnerability of the South, and make its inhabitants feel that war and individual ruin are synonymous terms" (p. 296).

Sherman remained a public figure after the war ended. He had always promised the South a hard war and a soft peace, and opposed the strict reconstruction imposed by a Republican Congress. Appointed commanding general of the U.S. Army in 1869, Sherman often quarreled with politicians who were eager to cut military spending and willing to feed from the public trough of corruption. In 1874, disgusted by Secretary of War William Belknap's corrupt behavior and intervention in what Sherman believed to be army affairs, the general transferred his command headquarters from Washington, D.C., to St. Louis, Missouri, for nineteen months. From St. Louis and Washington, Sherman observed the final defeat of the Indians. Not surprisingly, Marszalek views these campaigns against the Indians as consistent with his subject's desire to impose order on a disorderly West.

Although generally favorable toward his subject, Marszalek acknowledges Sherman's imperfections. Sherman and his wife argued frequently, and after the Civil War he was at best a flirt and at worst an adulterer. In addition to acknowledging Sherman's wildly pessimistic estimates of enemy capabilities while holding down a semi-independent command in Kentucky in 1861, Marszalek attributes his failed assault against Kennesaw Mountain, Georgia, to "impatience" (p. 274). He also reminds readers that Sherman erred in not crushing John Bell Hood's Confederate army situated around Atlanta; his primary objective had been the enemy's army, not the city itself. Most significantly, Sherman was "blind to the time bomb" represented by the aftermath of emancipation (p. 315), claims Marszalek. His views about race remained those of a former slaveowner; in his desire to restore order in the South, he ignored the real needs of black Americans during reconstruction.

I'm not entirely convinced that all of Sherman's actions should be viewed through the lens of a search for order. The Catholic Church, for example, would seem to have offered a rock-solid haven for a man seeking order and stability, but Sherman rejected the repeated entreaties of his stepmother and wife that he become a practicing Catholic. Further, he surely understood that his decision to transfer his headquarters out of Washington during the 1870s left the army—which he loved for its order—in turmoil. But these are interpretative quibbles. Well-researched and clearly written, *Sherman: A Soldier's Passion for Order* is superior in all respects to other biographies of William Tecumseh Sherman, one of the greatest and most controversial of all Civil War generals.

39.

Under Two Flags: The American Navy in the Civil War

by William M. Fowler, Jr.

Civil War naval operations have yet to undergo the intense, sustained scrutiny accorded to the conflict's land warfare. This is not intended to slight the contributions made by naval historians; rather, it is simply to point out that the naval section of the typical Civil War enthusiast's bookshelf is likely to be thinner than that accorded the armies. Of the one-volume histories of naval affairs, *Under Two Flags: The American Navy in the Civil War* (1990), holds pride of place, replacing Bern Anderson's earlier *By Sea and By River: The Naval History of the Civil War* (1962).

William M. Fowler, Jr. is the author of several well-respected books about naval affairs during the American Revolution, and his *Under Two Flags* serves as an excellent introductory survey of naval operations during the nation's sectional conflict. Judicious and balanced, Fowler's book avoids the exaggerated claims made for the Union navy in Anderson's earlier work. Rather than a rival for preeminence with the army, as is often implied by Anderson, Fowler rightly describes the Federal navy's role as that of a partner in a great enterprise.

Ironically the basis for Union naval strategy came from an army man, Winfield Scott. As commanding general of the army, Scott proposed what would be dubbed his Anaconda Plan, which called for a gradually tightening stranglehold upon the Confederacy. A tight naval blockade of the Confederate coast would be accompa-

Battered turret of the Union Ironclad Passaic.
NATIONAL ARCHIVES

nied by the North's capture of the Mississippi River. Secretary of the Navy Gideon Welles was enough of a political realist to defend the navy's interests and promote its victories whenever he could, and he recognized the basic virtues of Scott's strategy. Unfortunately, Welles had precious little with which to enforce the blockade when he took office, thanks largely to the mistakes of his predecessor, Connecticut Democrat Isaac Toucey. Secretary Toucey "was simply a fool" (p. 34), Fowler insists, for not having brought the scattered U.S. Navy home from its far-flung overseas duties as the war clouds began to darken. Further, the peacetime navy had built no ironclads. Fowler concludes that the navy "was light of head and weak in the body" (p. 33) on the eve of war.

Welles moved quickly to overcome the initial confusion. He and his assistant secretary, Gustavus Fox, "formed a harmonious team that brought energy, integrity, and skill to the administration of the navy" (p. 50). Fortunately for Welles and Fox, the Union possessed the economic, industrial, and technical strength to mobilize a large fleet. Stephen Mallory, secretary of the navy of the Confederate States of America was not as fortunate. "A convivial, high-living raconteur" (p. 39), Mallory enjoyed the services of 125 officers who had resigned their U.S. commissions (representing about 25 percent of the existing naval officer corps in 1861). But the South lacked adequate shipbuilding facilities and money to provide these men with ships. Especially early in the war, Mallory was further hampered by the refusal of several states to cede any rights or privileges to the central government. Yet he was not without options. He planned a crash construction program of ironclad rams that would render the wooden vessels of the Union navy obsolete. Mallory also believed that the Confederacy could build or purchase from abroad enough commerce raiders to inflict serious damage upon the North's merchant marine, thus drawing off Union warships from the blockade.

Mallory was partially right on both counts, claims Fowler. Though chronically underpowered and prone to mechanical breakdowns, Confederate ironclad rams struck fear in the hearts of many a Yankee captain. The North was busy producing armored craft of its own, however. The first Rebel ironclad, the *Virginia,* wreaked havoc among the wooden Union fleet at Hampton Roads, Virginia, for one March day in 1862. But almost as if by divine providence, the first Union ironclad, the tough little *Monitor,* arrived in time to battle the larger *Virginia* to a draw the next day. After that, it was only a matter of time until the superior Northern shipyards were constructing new armored vessels at a pace the Confederacy could not match.

Mallory's other stratagem—commerce raiders—proved devastating to Yankee shipping but failed to break the Northern blockade. High-seas Confederate raiders such as the *Alabama, Shenandoah,* and *Florida* took about three hundred prizes and drove insurance rates for American-flagged ships to intolerably high levels. But trans-Atlantic commerce continued because hundreds of American shipowners simply placed their ships under foreign flags. Equally significant was Secretary Welles' refusal to weaken the

Union blockade by diverting ships to hunt the speedy Confederate raiders. "Whatever his faults," writes Fowler admiringly, "Welles never once lost sight of the fact that maintaining the blockade was paramount" (p. 299).

To tighten the blockade, the North mounted several operations against key Confederate ports. In 1861 Union warships forced the surrender of Forts Hatteras and Clark in North Carolina and captured Port Royal, South Carolina. The following spring, David Farragut's fleet ran past Confederate forts at the mouth of the Mississippi River and forced the surrender of the South's largest city, New Orleans. Farragut followed this up with a daring attack against enemy defenses guarding Mobile Bay, Alabama, two years later. According to Fowler, steam power and the increased range and destructive power of naval guns had rendered obsolete the old sailor's maxim, "'A ship's a fool to fight a fort'" (p. 65).

But naval firepower alone was not always enough to ensure victory. In the spring of 1863 Farragut's attempt to seize the Mississippi River citadel at Vicksburg without ground support failed, as did the attacks by Samuel F. Du Pont and John Dahlgren against Charleston, the following summer. Much more effective, Fowler points out, were joint army-navy strikes against Forts Henry and Donelson, Island Number 10, and Fort Pillow, on the Tennessee and Mississippi Rivers.

Fowler brings naval engagements come to life in *Under Two Flags*. The reader can see and hear the dangerous but unreliable Confederate ironclad ram *Arkansas* come wheezing out of the Yazoo River against the Union river squadron above Vicksburg, and feel the exaltation of Union sailors as they passed the deadly Confederate underwater torpedoes at Mobile Bay. Excellent maps and illustrations and a useful naval chronology supplement the text. My only criticism of the book is Fowler's short and inconclusive analysis of the Federal blockade's economic impact on the Confederacy. Readers should consult Robert M. Browning, Jr.'s *From Cape Charles to Cape Fear: The North Atlantic Blockading Squadron During the Civil War* (1990), and Raimondo Luraghi, *A History of the Confederate Navy* [46] for a more thorough account of this aspect of the war.

40.

The Secessionist Impulse: Alabama and Mississippi in 1860

by William L. Barney

On November 6, 1860, Abraham Lincoln was elected the sixteenth president of the United States. South Carolina seceded from the Union the following month. In early 1861 the remaining states of the lower South—Mississippi, Alabama, Florida, Georgia, Louisiana, and Texas—followed suit. Four states—Virginia, Arkansas, North Carolina, and Tennessee—would join the others later that spring. Why did the Southern states secede, and why did they do it then?

The secession movement was a product of regional as well as local conditions. Complaints about the federal government's failure to provide adequate protection to frontier settlers against Indian attacks in Texas, for example, hardly resonated with the voters of Georgia. William L. Barney's *The Secessionist Impulse: Alabama and Mississippi in 1860* (1974) remains the best study of how these sectional and local influences shaped the secession movement. Barney's work was originally a dissertation, and can sometimes be difficult reading, given its careful documentation, use of statistics, and close arguments. But it offers great rewards; nowhere else is the secession movement in the lower South more cogently explained.

Cotton was king in the South. The 1850s, argues Barney, were difficult years for many Southern cotton farmers. Although the economy was growing, the largest slaveholders and landowners

CHARLESTON MERCURY

EXTRA:

Passed unanimously at 1.15 o'clock, P. M. December 20th, 1860.

AN ORDINANCE

To dissolve the Union between the State of South Carolina and other States united with her under the compact entitled "The Constitution of the United States of America."

We, the People of the State of South Carolina, in Convention assembled, do declare and ordain, and it is hereby declared and ordained,

That the Ordinance adopted by us in Convention, on the twenty-third day of May, in the year of our Lord one thousand seven hundred and eighty-eight, whereby the Constitution of the United States of America was ratified, and also, all Acts and parts of Acts of the General Assembly of this State, ratifying amendments of the said Constitution, are hereby repealed; and that the union now subsisting between South Carolina and other States, under the name of "The United States of America," is hereby dissolved.

THE

UNION

IS

DISSOLVED!

Defiant announcement proclaiming secession, 1860.
LIBRARY OF CONGRESS

seemed to be gathering a disproportionate share of the wealth. For smaller farmers the costs of land, slaves, and supplies were rising faster than prices for cotton. Cheaper slaves and more land seemed the only alternatives to social and economic ruin. At about a thousand dollars for a good field hand, slave ownership seemed beyond the reach of most yeoman farmers. Reopening the slave trade with Africa might flood the market with imported labor and depress prices for slaves. Since they recognized that this option stood little chance of winning congressional approval, many Southerners placed greater emphasis upon securing new land. They were well aware of the terrors of soil erosion in this age of relatively unscientific farming. If they wanted new agricultural opportunities—or at least the possibility of moving to the West with their slaves when the land they were farming gave out—they had to have congressional protection for slavery in the western territories, explains Barney.

These opportunities of expansion were especially important for ambitious young Southerners trying to make their fortunes during the 1850s. If they could not find new areas suitable for cotton and plantation agriculture, there seemed little realistic hope of maintaining their lot in the world. And now, faced by a growing antislavery movement in the North, their demands that the federal government guarantee their right to take their property (slaves) into western territories seemed to be in danger as well. "Increasingly," Barney explains, "the South felt hemmed in and betrayed" (p. 23).

Amidst this economic discontent Southerners feared for their safety. Theorists had long argued that the diffusion of slaves over a wide area was essential to preventing slave rebellion. By avoiding the heavy concentration of slaves in any area, social control could be maintained. But fueled by the fires of John Brown's raid against the federal arsenal at Harpers Ferry, Virginia, Southern fears of slave rebellions "reached pathological proportions during 1860," writes Barney (p. 163).

The politics of fear were easy to exploit during the summer drought of 1860, which hit that year's corn crop in Mississippi and Alabama particularly hard. For slaveholders anxious to acquire more slaves and more land, leaving the Union seemed the only answer, argues Barney. To secede they needed the support of nonslaveholders, however, since most white Southerners did not own slaves. In Mississippi and Alabama secessionists convinced many poor whites that the preservation of slavery was in their best interests. If the "peculiar institution" were destroyed, argued those in favor of a break from the Union, the resultant social chaos "would fall heaviest on the poor" (p. 124). Southern whites understood that slavery elevated all of them—even the poorest—above blacks. Leaving the Union, they concluded, seemed the only way to preserve their society.

What about those who opposed a break with the North? In Mississippi and Alabama age, social composition, and location, rather than wealth or likelihood of slave ownership, tended to separate the conservatives from their secessionist rivals. "In broad terms," Barney explains, those favoring cooperation rather than secession "represented the South's old wealth and more specifically the yeomanry of northern Alabama, the very wealthy planters of the Mississippi-Yazoo Delta, slaveholders in the previously developed plantation areas, and the Northern and Virginia-born business groups in the towns" (p. 295). In other words, those who had "something to save" (p. 100) under the current system tended to oppose secession.

It was under these conditions, that Abraham Lincoln, a Republican, pledged to oppose the expansion of slavery into the territories, was elected president in November 1860. Conservatives, who had voted for Stephen Douglas or John Bell in the 1860 presidential contest, now seemed powerless to respond to the secessionists' appeals. Calls for patience had little attraction when measured against promises of a better life outside the Union, notes Barney. Faced with higher costs for slaves and land, squeezed by failing crops and tight money, even nonslaveholders "had little to lose by backing secession" (p. 296). And so they did.

41.

Two Great Rebel Armies: An Essay in Confederate Military History

by Richard M. McMurry

Two great armies dominated the Confederate military effort. The Army of Northern Virginia, operating in Virginia, Maryland, and Pennsylvania, won some of the most spectacular battles of the Civil War. It mounted two major invasions of the North and surrendered only after having been battered into submission by a more numerous and better-supplied enemy. By contrast, the Army of Tennessee was largely unsuccessful in its campaigns from Missouri to Georgia. Its only major victory (at Chickamauga) was in large part attributable to the two divisions that had been loaned to it from the Army of Northern Virginia. Why was one Confederate army so successful, and the other not?

Two Great Rebel Armies (1989) offers convincing and compelling answers to this basic question. Several preexisting factors worked against the Army of Tennessee. Whereas a relatively narrow area east of the Allegheny Mountains defined the Virginia front, the western front extended two and a half times that distance, from the Cumberland Gap to the Mississippi River. Terrain features compounded the problem. The major rivers of Virginia ran west to east, providing the Army of Northern Virginia with convenient defensive lines that blocked Union advances. Further west, however, the Mississippi, Cumberland, and Tennessee Rivers ran like daggers into the heartland of the Confederacy. Dominated by Union gunboats, these rivers became invasion

Generals Joseph E. Johnston and Robert E. Lee after the war.
LIBRARY OF CONGRESS

routes for advancing Federal armies. Finally, the eastern Rebel states, especially Virginia, boasted a superior infrastructure of railroads and industry as compared to the western states of the Confederacy. The Army of Northern Virginia defended a smaller area with superior natural defenses and a stronger economic base, concludes McMurry.

The Federals contributed to this imbalance. Northern political leaders generally placed more emphasis on western affairs than did their Southern counterparts, devoting more men and additional resources to fight an already inferior enemy. The most successful of the Union generals—Ulysses S. Grant, William T. Sherman, Philip Sheridan, and George Thomas—operated outside of Virginia for most of the war. They easily outmatched their counterparts in the East—Irvin McDowell, George McClellan, John Pope, Ambrose Burnside, and Joseph Hooker. "Until some historian puts the question to a computer," quips McMurry, "we shall not know what would have happened if a Rebel army commanded by Lee, Longstreet, Jackson, and Stuart had faced a Union force under Grant, Sherman, Thomas, and Sheridan" (p. 43).

The Army of Northern Virginia was also superior to that of Tennessee in terms of preparation and leadership. The Dominion's antebellum militia, much better than any in the western states, became the nucleus of the Army of Northern Virginia. And the west had no educational institution comparable to the Virginia Military Institute, which provided the eastern army with a large pool of potential officers. Forces in Virginia were also mobilized more effectively, thanks to the efforts of Gov. John Letcher and the commander of Virginia state troops, Robert E. Lee.

Generals in the Army of Tennessee were more quarrelsome and less cooperative than their counterparts in Virginia, argues McMurry. Such behavior stemmed at least in part from the examples set by their commanding generals. In the east subordinates looked to the stable and stately Robert E. Lee. But five men of indifferent abilities commanded the Army of Tennessee. Albert Sidney Johnston had difficulty controlling his generals. P. G. T. Beauregard openly and persistently voiced his criticism of President Jefferson Davis. If anyone hated Davis more than Beauregard, it had to be another commander of the Army of Tennessee, Joseph E. Johnston. Braxton Bragg spent as much time quarreling with his subordinates as he did fighting the Yankees. Finally, there was John Bell Hood, gallant in battle but hapless as an army commander. "Some historian who really wants to melt the microchips might try asking one of the infernal machines what would have happened if a Union army led by McClellan, Pope, Burnside, and Hooker had tangled with a band of Rebels under Joseph E. Johnston, Bragg, [and] Hood" (p. 132), suggests McMurry.

In a final flourish McMurry lambastes Robert E. Lee's greatest critic, historian Thomas Connelly. In a series of articles and books, including *The Politics of Command* [25], Connelly has accused Lee of focusing too much attention on Virginia and not understanding western conditions. McMurry counters by arguing that Lee cannot be fairly held responsible for "the almost criminal incompetence of the Confederate generals who served in the West" (p. 152). "If Bragg had had, say, fifteen thousand more men at Chickamauga, would it have made a difference?" wonders McMurry. "Or would it only have meant that there were a few thousand more troops whose lives Bragg could waste and a few more generals in the Army of Tennessee with whom he could quarrel?" (p. 153).

The western theater was important, concludes McMurry, and the problem, he insists, was not a lack of attention. Rather, the Confederates did not have sufficient manpower or leadership to hold everything together. The best thing they could have done was what they did: concentrate their best army under their best general in defense of their most important state near the North's most vulnerable point—Washington, D.C.

Two Great Rebel Armies is a provocative little book (155 pages plus appendices) that readers should find enjoyable to read and challenging to think about.

42.

The Civil War: An Illustrated History

by Geoffrey C. Ward, with Ric Burns and Ken Burns

In September 1990 the Corporation for Public Broadcasting launched *The Civil War,* a nine-part, eleven-hour documentary, directed by Ken Burns. The project captured the public imagination. One of PBS's top-rated shows of all time, approximately forty million people watched at least part of the series, which stimulated increased interest in the Civil War. *The Civil War: An Illustrated History* (1990) was published as a companion volume to the film project.

As the series was panned by some scholars, my inclusion of this book in *The Civil War Bookshelf* will undoubtedly raise the hackles of some of my academic colleagues. *The Civil War: An Illustrated History* is divided into five chapters each covering one year, beginning with 1861. (This organization probably resulted from the original plans for the film project, which called for a five-hour, five-part series.) Respected Civil War historians Don E. Fehrenbacher, Barbara J. Fields, James McPherson, and C. Vann Woodward have contributed brief yet enlightening essays which conclude four of the five chapters. The remaining chapter closes with partial transcripts from Ken Burns's two days of interviews with Shelby Foote (*The Civil War: A Narrative—Fredericksburg to Meridian* [17]) in preparation for the series. The main text of the book closely mirrors the narrative of the documentary, so those who liked the broadcast series will probably enjoy reading this book.

Lincoln and his generals and admirals.
NATIONAL ARCHIVES

Military and political events receive the closest scrutiny, and slavery is portrayed as the fundamental cause of the war. Robert E. Lee emerges as a brilliant champion of the Confederacy, and affairs in the East receive more attention than those on the western front. Joshua Chamberlain assumes a central role in the Union victory at Gettysburg.

Academic historians admired Burns's ability to garner general interest in the period, but pointed out many factual errors in his work and challenged many of his conclusions. Given the impact of Burns's documentary on the public's impression of the Civil War, I also have included the most systematic critique of his series, *Ken Burns's* The Civil War: *Historians Respond* [43] in *The Civil War Bookshelf*.

Why, then, with so many extraordinary books written about our nation's most terrible war, would *The Civil War: An Illustrated History* rank number forty-two on my list? First, the book is truly a visual feast. The Burns brothers, Ric and Ken, along with lead writer Geoffrey C. Ward, selected for this lavishly illustrated work 475 of the 16,000 images used in the original documentary. Famous paintings, such as Richard Norris Brooke's depiction of the weeping veterans of the Army of Northern Virginia furling their Confederate battle flag for the last time and James Walker's magnificent portrayal of George Pickett's charge at Gettysburg, are reprinted in magnificent color. Hundreds of photographs collected by Mathew Brady's teams of cameramen are also included, from the portraits of Abraham Lincoln, simple and moving in their understated elegance, to the images of the battlefield, which horrified Americans then and now in their grisly detail. And in addition to the extraordinary pictorial offerings, the campaign maps, so important to understanding the war, are presented clean and uncluttered. These collective images helped make the conflict *real* for many average viewers and readers in a way that words could not.

I've also included *The Civil War: An Illustrated History*, because Geoffrey C. Ward, the lead author, has a good eye for the telling anecdote and moving tribute. His eloquent description of Lee's postwar career serves as an excellent example. After the war ended, Lee never returned to his prewar mansion at Arlington, instead accepting a position as president of tiny Washington College in Lexington, Virginia. "There, for the rest of his life," writes Ward, "he showed Americans that one can lose as well as win with grace" (p. 410). Ward then relates the famous example of Lee dressing down one of his professors who had made disparaging remarks about his old rival Ulysses S. Grant. " 'Sir, if you ever again presume to speak disrespectfully of General Grant in my presence, either you or I will sever his connection with the university.' " An educational reformer as a college president, Lee concluded that his greatest mistake had been attending military school. Thus, "whenever his students and those of neighboring Virginia Military Institute marched together, Lee made a point of staying out of step."

Reprinted also are excerpts from the saddest of letters, that written by Maj. Sullivan Ballou of Rhode Island to his wife Sarah a week before the First Battle of Bull Run. Viewers of the documentary will recall the segment, Honorable Manhood, in which narrator David McCullough reads this unforgettable expression of Ballou's love for his wife and country. " 'Sarah my love for you is deathless, it seems to bind me with mighty cables that nothing but Omnipotence could break; and yet my love of Country comes over me like a strong wind and bears me unresistably on with all these chains to the battlefield. . . . Never forget how much I love you,' continues Ballou, 'and when my last breath escapes me on the battlefield, it will whisper your name' " (pp. 82–83). Ward's conclusion is elegant in its simplicity, for nothing could possibly match the emotions expressed by Ballou to his wife. "Sullivan Ballou was killed at the first battle of Bull Run."

For more nuanced interpretations and a fuller understanding of the Civil War, readers can find better books. But I've often used this book to find a fitting quotation or an insightful passage about a particular incident. And no single volume can match the collection of contemporary broadsides, paintings, and photographs found in *The Civil War: An Illustrated History*. It deserves a place in any Civil War enthusiast's library.

43.

Ken Burns's The Civil War: Historians Respond

edited by Robert Brent Toplin

During the 1960s the centennial of the American Civil War led to an upsurge in popular interest in the subject. Ken Burns's PBS miniseries had a similar effect in the early 1990s. Shelby Foote, one of the documentary's featured analysts, quipped that the documentary had made him a millionaire. His highly respected trilogy *The Civil War: A Narrative (Fredericksburg to Meridian* [17]), had sold about 30,000 copies in the fifteen years before the Burns series was aired. Audiences loved Foote's soft Southern drawl and homespun insights so much that in the six months following the broadcast, they snapped up more than 100,000 copies of his three-volume work.

Though popular reviews of Burns's *Civil War* were overwhelmingly favorable, academics proved to be more critical. Burns went to great lengths to seek out the advice and counsel of historians throughout the five years of production, but factual errors still slipped through. Other Civil War experts challenged the filmmaker's interpretations. *Ken Burns's* The Civil War: *Historians Respond* (1996) is a superb compendium of the debate about the project, offering seven reviews (two favorable, three mixed, and two distinctly unfavorable) by academics as well as responses by Burns and Geoffrey C. Ward, the series' principal writer.

In general, those who praise Burns's effort emphasize the project's artistic excellence and popular appeal. Through the medium of television, Burns captured the imaginations of millions of Americans and engaged them in the Civil War as no one else has ever done since the war itself. His biggest champion is C. Vann Woodward, a respected specialist in Southern history recently retired from Yale University, who served as a series advisor. Woodward praises Burns's efforts to get the historical record straight and champions the filmmaker's right, as an artist, to tell the narrative in a manner which would make the tragedies and glories of the Civil War come alive. Historians, insists Woodward, should support artists without the expectation that they champion any particular social, economic, or political cause.

Editor Robert Brent Toplin, professor of history at the University of North Carolina, Wilmington, and a filmmaker himself, describes the contemporary themes which most impacted Burns's work. Because it was made in the maudlin era following the Vietnam War, the project reveals the darker side of armed conflict, claims Toplin. Likewise the influence of the civil rights movement is strong. Burns believes the war was about slavery; thus the title for program number one: "1861: The Cause." Toplin also points out how Burns managed to be critical of slavery without portraying Southerners in a negative light. This, argues Toplin, reflected the decreasing sectional divisions in the late twentieth-century United States. "With considerable intelligence," Toplin concludes, "Burns demonstrated the relevance of the present for shaping an understanding of the past" (p. 36).

Gabor Boritt, editor of *Lincoln, the War President* [37], Gary Gallagher, author of *The Confederate War* [5], and Catherine Clinton, who formerly taught at Harvard University, are not persuaded. Boritt compliments the documentary's treatment of Lincoln and praises the Gettysburg segment as "miraculously good art" (p. 93). But numerous factual errors leave him uneasy. As Boritt quips, "What [Burns] and his co-workers badly needed was a team of graduate-student fact-checkers" (pp. 89–90). A specialist in the war's military events, Gallagher chides those who have criticized *The Civil War*'s emphasis on campaigns and battles. After all, he notes, "the subject of Burns's documentary was a mam-

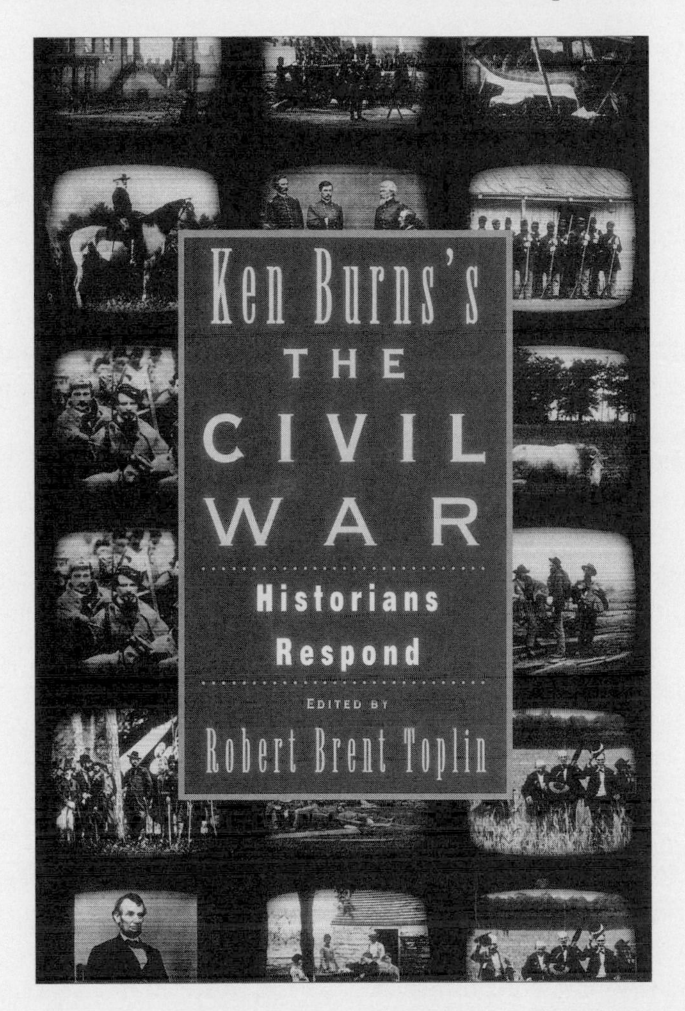

moth *war*" (p. 41). But he believes that Burns could have more effectively incorporated recent scholarship, offered a more geographically balanced coverage of military events, and better explained connections between the battlefields and the home fronts. The result, concludes Gallagher, is "a skewed sense of the war's military dimension" (p. 43). Catherine Clinton praises Burns for having rekindled interest in the Civil War, but charges that "women were all but invisible" (p. 67) in the eleven-hour film.

Positively scathing are the reviews by Eric Foner and Leon F. Litwack. Foner, author of *Free Soil, Free Labor, Free Men: The Ideology of the Republican Party Before the Civil War* [31] and two books on reconstruction, charges that Burns devoted too much time to the theme of reunification and not enough to the failures of reconstruction. "To this turbulent period [reconstruction] and the issues it raises Burns devotes exactly two minutes," Foner writes (p. 109). The focus on the reunification of white veterans is "an exercise in selective remembering" (p. 117) which omits discussions of racial justice and injustice, he charges. Litwack, author of *Been in the Storm So Long: The Aftermath of Slavery* [26], attacks the documentary for "virtually ignoring" (p. 129) the domestic changes that accompanied the war. "None of the great battles," he asserts, "compare in sheer drama with the way in which the Civil War came to be transformed into a social revolution." Further, although the series did show many visual images of ordinary black men and women, "they are seldom given any voice" (p. 134). Good history and good film, he contends, should challenge traditional assumptions and "take risks—even disturb the peace" (p. 140).

Ward and Burns acknowledge that they should have caught some of the factual errors, but respond vigorously to their critics. Ward claims to have anticipated the protests of those who believed states' rights, rather than slavery, caused the war, but declares that he was "personally astonished" that some academic critics "evidently saw our whole enterprise as little more than an exercise in racism" (p. 145). Pointing out that films are inherently limited by time constraints, and that television seems better suited to narrative than analysis, he reminds his critics "that by including one historian's opinion among several on matters over which scholars continue to differ does not imply that his or her view is to be taken as gospel" (p. 148). Burns too seems genuinely hurt by the tenor of the attacks, especially since he believes that the perspectives of many of the academics who were harshest in their criticism were "so close to our own sensibilities" (p. 173). A popular medium like television, he insists, has certain advantages—but also some disadvantages—over more traditional literary scholarship. Wasn't there value, he wonders, in the series having opened up a new national debate about the causes, course, and consequences of the Civil War?

Toplin's well-crafted anthology reveals the tensions between academic and popular historians. It also provides a fascinating glimpse into the production of Ken Burns's extremely influential documentary *The Civil War*. In so doing, it has earned a place in *The Civil War Bookshelf*.

44.

MARY CHESTNUT'S CIVIL WAR

edited by C. Vann Woodward

Mary Boykin Miller was born to wealth in 1823, and at age seventeen married James Chestnut, Jr., one of the largest slaveowners in South Carolina. A former United States senator, her husband initially served as an aide to Confederate general P. G. T. Beauregard before returning to Richmond to join President Jefferson Davis's staff in late 1862. He and his family returned to South Carolina in 1864, but had to flee their home in early 1865 to escape William T. Sherman's fast-approaching invasion. They never recovered their shattered fortune.

While staying at a younger brother's Alabama plantation in February 1861 Mary Chestnut began keeping a journal, and she continued to write regular entries in it for much of the war. Seven volumes of the original journal remain, covering most of 1861 and parts of 1862 and 1865. She burned several other volumes in May 1863 in anticipation of a Federal cavalry threat against Richmond. Others were probably lost, either during her family's frequent wartime moves or during the confusion which often characterized her life after the Civil War. Some historians suspect that she did not regularly keep a journal of any type for much of 1863 and 1864.

Chestnut had a keen awareness of the importance of recording history, and hopeful that her writing would restore her family's antebellum prominence, she made a serious effort to prepare her journals for publication in 1875 to 1876. Comparisons of the original and this revision (some four hundred pages of this effort survive) suggest that she did a good deal of editing and rewriting. But then she set aside this project in favor of other literary efforts (she eventually drafted three full novels, a biography of her husband, translations of French fiction, and family memoirs). During the 1880s she turned to her journals of the war years once again. Chestnut "took many liberties" (p. xxv) in selecting, revising, cutting, and expanding upon her original journal for the latter version, but died before completing this task. Parts of two drafts of this revision—some forty-two hundred pages in all—remain.

In 1902 *The Saturday Evening Post* and D. Appleman and Company published heavily edited versions of Chestnut's journals, entitled *A Diary from Dixie*. Another edition, edited by novelist Ben Ames Williams, appeared in 1949. This version strove for readability above all else, shifting passages, altering sentences, and adding completely new opening and concluding passages. Irritated by the "excessive liberties taken by previous editors" (p. liv), historian C. Vann Woodward took up the task of publishing a more complete, authentic version of Chestnut's wartime writings, producing *Mary Chestnut's Civil War* in 1981. In contrast to the earlier editions Woodward has attempted whenever possible or reasonable to remain faithful to the 1880s drafts, even though Chestnut had clearly intended to do more polishing and revising.

Woodward's edition received the Pulitzer Prize in 1982, and readers will find unparalleled insights into the inner workings of the Confederate government in Chestnut's untainted work. Countless luminaries grace the pages of her journals, which are laced with her own personal observations and comments about contemporary events. She became a good friend of Varina Davis, wife of the Confederate president, and faithfully supported him against his many critics. "Seceding can go on indefinitely with the dissatisfied seceders" (p. 121), she wrote icily of those who resisted President Jefferson Davis's attempts to centralize Confederate policies. "Sometimes I think I am the only friend he has in the world" (p. 746), she added later. She offered biting criticisms of Confederate general Joseph E. Johnston, who hated Davis and

Northern view of Mulberry, the Chestnut plantation in South Carolina.
LIBRARY OF CONGRESS

whose generalship has since sparked intense controversy. "He is a born retreater" (p. 730), she concluded venomously.

Mary Chestnut's Civil War mixes wartime gossip, insights, and characterizations about life in high Confederate society. Surprisingly, Mary Chestnut hated slavery more than perhaps any other thing in the world—save Yankees. "God forgive us, but ours is a *monstrous* system," she wrote. "Like the patriarchs of old our men live all in one house with their wives and their concubines, and the mulattoes one sees in every family exactly resemble the white children—and every lady tells you who is the father of all the mulatto children in everybody's household, but those in her own she seems to think drop from the clouds, or pretends so to think" (p. 29). "Slavery has to go, of course," (p. 88) added Chestnut in July 1861. A strong feminist, she also bitterly decried the relegation of women to purely domestic duties. "There is no slave, after all, like a wife" (p. 59), she complained. "All married women, all children, and girls who live on in their father's houses are slaves" (p. 729).

Mary Chestnut was nonetheless devoted to the Confederate cause, and frequently speculated about the reasons for the South's defeat. "Did we lose by imbecility or because one man cannot fight ten for more than four years?" she wondered. "We waited and hoped. They [the Yankees] organized and worked like moles, with the riches of all the world at their backs. They have made their private fortunes by their country's war. We talked of negro recruits. The Yankees used them—18 million against six. The odds [were] too great" (p. 794). But she also chastised those who had, in her view, shirked their duty. "Such a hue and cry—whose fault? Everybody blamed by somebody else. Only the dead heroes left stiff and stark on the battlefield escape. Blame every man who stayed at home and did not fight. I will not stop to hear excuses," she continued, blasting her own cousin and the brother of one of her friends who in 1865 "said they would be found ready enough to take up arms when the time came! Rip Van Winkle was a light sleeper to these two—their nap has lasted four years" (p. 814).

Mary Chestnut's Civil War might be difficult going for some readers. Diaries and memoirs written without the assistance of editors and copy editors usually are. But in addition to providing an insider's view of life in the Confederacy, it is a poignant reminder of the suffering endured by women who waited in dread for news of the men they had loved and tended. "When I remember all the true-hearted, the lighthearted, the gay and gallant boys who have come laughing, singing, dancing in my way in the three years past, I have looked into their brave young eyes and helped them as I could every way and then seen them no more forever. They lie stark and cold, dead upon the battlefield or moldering away in hospitals or prisons," Chestnut writes. "I think, if I consider the long array of those bright youths and loyal men who have gone to their deaths almost before my very eyes, my heart might break, too."

"Is anything worth it? This fearful sacrifice—this awful penalty we pay for war?" (p. 625). One wonders.

45.

The Red Badge of Courage

by Stephen Crane

First published in 1895, Stephen Crane's *The Red Badge of Courage* has often been hailed as the first great American war novel. It retains its emotional power more than a century later. This impressionistic work describes the psychological and physical struggles of a young Union soldier, Henry Fleming (usually referred to merely as "the youth"), as he overcomes his fears to prove his manhood on the field of battle. Through the experiences of this fictional character, Crane brilliantly portrays the sudden mood swings and contradictory images of the Civil War battlefield.

Born in 1871 in Newark, New Jersey, Crane was educated at Lafayette College and Syracuse University before becoming a freelance reporter in New York City. His first novel, *Maggie, a Girl of the Streets* (1893), was the story of a suicidal young prostitute. Unable to find a publisher, Crane paid for the manuscript's printing himself. It won some critical acclaim, but sold poorly. His second book, *The Red Badge of Courage,* first appeared in condensed, serialized form in the *Philadelphia Press,* from December 3 to 8, 1894. D. Appleton and Company, a New York–based publisher, published the full text the following autumn.

Remarkably, Crane had never seen military service when he wrote *The Red Badge of Courage*. Apparently he came to imagine combat by looking at the celebrated Civil War images taken by Mathew Brady's photographers, in conversations with veterans, and by reading accounts of the war. Following the spectacular success of *The Red Badge of Courage,* Crane finally experienced combat first hand as a war correspondent during the Greco-Turkish War (1897) and the Spanish-American War (1898). He emerged from these experiences triumphant; legend has it that upon his return from the former conflict, he exclaimed to fellow writer Joseph Conrad, " 'My picture of war was all right! I have found it as I imagined it' " (p. 201).

Although never acknowledged in the text, the narrative is loosely based upon the Battle of Chancellorsville. Readers will recognize that some of the routed soldiers Fleming encounters behind the Union right flank were those fleeing from Stonewall Jackson's last great attack, which shattered that section of the Federal line. Those familiar with the long string of poor commanders who plagued the Union Army of the Potomac will also identify with the realism of Fleming's complaint: " 'B'jiminey, we're generaled by a lot 'a lunkheads' " (p. 76). In reality, the men of the Army of the Potomac had been outgeneraled; the Union commander, Joseph Hooker, had somehow managed to lose to an army half the size of his own.

But *The Red Badge of Courage* is by no means a history of the Battle of Chancellorsville; instead, it is a gripping story of the quest for manhood on the Civil War battlefield. The book's opening lines have often been mimicked but rarely duplicated: "The cold passed reluctantly from the earth, and the retiring fogs revealed an army stretched out on the hills, resting. As the landscape changed from brown to green, the army awakened, and began to tremble with eagerness at the noise of rumors" (p. 5). Almost immediately, the reader is thrust into the psyches of Fleming and his green regiment of fellow recruits as they come to grips with the subject of the rumors—impending combat. Would they stand and fight as men, or would they fail the test of manhood and run?

The pressure intensifies as the fighting approaches. The regiment holds against the initial Confederate assault, but then, to the stunned disbelief of Fleming and his comrades, the enemy attack begins anew. Amidst the carnage and confusion, Henry throws

Union soldiers (probably 2nd Rhode Island Inf.).
NATIONAL ARCHIVES

down his rifle and bolts for the rear. "He ran like a rabbit. . . . He ran like a blind man," writes Crane as the youth leads the rout, with other comrades following in his wake. "In his flight the sound of those following footsteps gave him his one meager relief. He felt vaguely that death must make a first choice of the men who were nearest; the initial morsels for the dragons would be then those who were following him. So he displayed the zeal of an insane sprinter in his purpose to keep them in the rear" (pp. 36–37).

Exhausted and bewildered, Fleming eventually falls in with a group of wounded men making their way back from the fighting. By now, certain that his regiment has disintegrated, he rationalizes his flight as having been necessary to save one small cog in the army's machinery—Henry Fleming. But the youth's mood, like the battle, swings dramatically from smug rationalization to abject failure when he abandons a badly wounded soldier, "the tattered man," to die a painful death alone. He repeats this foul deed when he encounters a wounded friend from his regiment, Jim Conklin ("the tall soldier"). Wandering aimlessly toward the Union right flank late that afternoon, young Henry is then engulfed by panic-stricken soldiers fleeing another terrifying Confederate attack. The experience is a grim reminder of his own craven flight.

Seeking information, Fleming tries to stop one of the fleeing Yankees. Desperate to get away from the advancing Rebels, the man savagely strikes the youth's head with his rifle. Dazed and bloodied by the blow, Fleming manages to stagger back to his regiment, convinced that his comrades had witnessed his cowardice. But to his amazement, they knew nothing of his having fled, and assumed that the enemy had inflicted his bloody head wound. "His self-pride was now entirely restored," writes Crane. "He had performed his mistakes in the dark, so he was still a man" (p. 73).

On the second day of the battle, Fleming is transformed into a raging Achilles as he seeks to wash away the shame of the previous day. Critical comments about his regiment's performance by superior officers are taken as an affront to his manhood. Hatred of the enemy blinds him to anything—even temporary halts in the furious action. "Some of the men muttered and looked at the youth in awe-struck ways," writes Crane. "It was plain that as he had gone on loading and firing and cursing without the proper intermission, they had found time to regard him. And they now looked upon him as a war devil" (p. 81). As the fighting climaxes, the youth and his comrade, Wilson ("the friend") spearhead a successful counterattack which blunts a Confederate advance, capturing a Rebel battle flag in the process.

Fleming knows, of course, that he will never forget his sins of the first day, when he had run from the enemy and deserted two wounded comrades. "Yet gradually he mustered force to put the sin at a distance," writes Crane. "He felt a quiet manhood, non-assertive but of sturdy and strong blood. He knew that he would no more quail before his guides wherever they should point. He had been to touch the great death, and found that, after all, it was but the great death. He was a man" (p. 109).

Were this a study of the literature, rather than the history, of the Civil War, I would rank this book much higher than number forty-five. Since it is not, my bias toward history rather than fiction has led me to make this judgment. However, I should add that *The Red Badge of Courage* provides a better feel of the emotional and psychological highs and lows experienced by Civil War soldiers in combat than any other source.

46.

A History of the Confederate Navy

by Raimondo Luraghi, translated by Paolo E. Coletta

This work lends an international flavor to *The Civil War Bookshelf.* Italian historian Raimondo Luraghi spent twenty-seven years researching the Confederate navy, during which time he made over forty research trips to the United States. His original manuscript appeared as *Marinai del Sud: Storia della Marina confederata nella Guerra Civile Americana, 1861–1865* (1993); three years later, the Naval Institute Press published the English translation, *A History of the Confederate Navy.* Based upon archival research in four countries and boasting 150 pages of notes and bibliography in addition to its 349 pages of text, Luraghi's work is now the foundation for studies of the Confederate navy.

A History of the Confederate Navy focuses on two basic problems. "First," writes Luraghi, "how did an agricultural country with a limited industrial plant and almost no merchant marine succeed in building a navy that successfully confronted the formidable navy of the Northern states through four years of merciless fighting? Second, why despite a staggering number of books on the American Civil War, has almost no historian tried to answer that question?" (p. xi). In part, he explains, this resulted from the destruction of the Confederate Navy Department's records accompanying the evacuation of Richmond late in the war. Many scholars concluded that the lack of such archives would render a comprehensive analysis of the Confederate navy fruitless. Just as important, argues Luraghi, was a conceptual error, based upon the assumption that Confederate naval strategy was based solely upon breaking the Union blockade. Since the blockade was not broken, the navy must have failed. "And who wants to study the story of a failure?" he explains (p. xi).

Carefully argued and exhaustively researched, *A History of the Confederate Navy* demonstrates not only that surviving primary documents can support a legitimate historical analysis of the war on the seas, but that Confederate naval strategy was more comprehensive than once assumed. Not content with breaking the blockade, the Confederates hoped to take advantage of recent technological developments to seize control of the seas. In the process, Luraghi challenges the very notion that the Confederate navy failed at all.

Luraghi gives Secretary of the Navy Stephen Mallory high marks. Bright, farsighted, innovative, a good judge of character, and able to get along with President Jefferson Davis, Mallory immediately seized upon the opportunities wrought by recent naval developments. Although the South possessed no navy and insufficient capacity to match Northern shipbuilding resources, steam engines, screw propellers, more powerful naval ordnance, armored ships, and submarine warfare might allow Confederate quality to overcome Union quantity. That is, immediate action might allow a small but modern Rebel fleet to defeat a larger, but older, Yankee armada.

Luraghi acknowledges that Mallory initially placed too much faith in his new armored vessels. In one instance, for example, the secretary suggested that his first craft, the C.S.S. *Virginia,* might singlehandedly destroy New York City and end the war. But Mallory soon adjusted to the war's realities. Indeed, the growing Union amphibious threat, which by summer 1862 had taken Cape Hatteras and Roanoke Island (North Carolina), Port Royal (South Carolina), and New Orleans, convinced him of the inextricable connection between coastal defense and naval success.

Thus a second phase of Confederate naval strategy emerged.

Stephen Mallory.
LIBRARY OF CONGRESS

Domestic construction sites for future ironclads would be relocated further inland, where they would be safer from Yankee amphibious assaults. Undersea warfare, featuring new underwater mines (known as torpedoes during the Civil War) as well as submarines, would help to protect remaining Confederate ports. The Navy Department would produce heavier rifled guns that would enable coastal forts to keep even the best Union ships at bay.

Efforts to purchase vessels from Europe would be redoubled. Finally, government-sponsored commerce raiding, which Mallory had envisioned at the war's outset, would be continued in earnest, diverting Union naval resources from more threatening offensive amphibious operations to less productive searches for elusive Rebel raiders.

The new strategy, concludes Luraghi, worked remarkably well. By mid-1864 the Confederate Navy "reached its peak" (p. 287). Commerce raiders were wreaking havoc among the Union merchant marine. Heavy guns and torpedoes had buttressed Southern coastal defenses, and the submarine *Hunley* had sunk the powerful U.S.S. *Housatonic*. A dozen home-built ironclads threatened any potential Union amphibious assaults; spearheaded by the C. S. S. *Albemarle,* a Confederate counteroffensive had recaptured the naval base at Plymouth, North Carolina. And the Navy Department had constructed twenty shipyards, a rolling mill for producing armor plate, two engine plants, a heavy gun foundry, powderworks, three artillery plants, two laboratories, a bakery, two food packing plants, a distillery, two shoe and clothing factories, several hospitals, and four warehouses.

But in the end Union industrial superiority overwhelmed even these "astonishing" (p. 348) Confederate naval accomplishments. The individual feats of brilliance fostered by the agricultural South, Luraghi explains, could not match the collective power of the industrialized North. "The North," he writes, "had the advantage of a strong, modern, rational, and efficient industrial concern, enjoying a wide array of skilled workmen, technicians, and engineers; in the South industry was a work of *bricoleurs,* of a few men endowed with genius but children of a bygone technical era." He concludes: "From this viewpoint, the South had lost the war even before a single cannon shot had been fired" (p. 347).

I disagree with Luraghi's contention about the war's inevitability, and historians still debate the effectiveness of the Union blockade. American readers might find the author's florid language somewhat hyperbolic, and one needs a fair amount of background knowledge to fully appreciate Luraghi's wide-ranging forays into diplomacy, bureaucracy, technology, and naval history. But these are matters of interpretation, not quality. By demonstrating the interconnection between naval and land action, accenting the importance of amphibious operations, and showing that Confederate strategy was more far-reaching than the blockade itself, *A History of the Confederate Navy* represents a much-needed contribution to our understanding of the Civil War.

47.

Lee's Tarnished Lieutenant: James Longstreet and His Place in Southern History

by William Garrett Piston

I've included this book for two reasons. First, it provides a concise summary of the life of one of the Confederacy's ablest generals, James Longstreet. Second, *Lee's Tarnished Lieutenant* (1987) describes the importance of postbellum affairs in shaping our understanding of not only Longstreet, but the war itself.

William G. Piston contends that Longstreet's first brush with the enemy during the Civil War made a lasting impression on his tactical thinking. At Blackburn's Ford, Virginia (July 18, 1861), Longstreet initially assumed a defensive stance. Following an unsuccessful enemy attack, he counterattacked, a move stymied in this instance only by unsuitable terrain. "Longstreet would attempt to repeat this pattern," argues Piston, "first receiving an attack, then counterattacking, on several other occasions during the war" (p. 14). Defensive tactics were never more successful than in the fighting at Fredericksburg, where the Confederates repulsed several enemy assaults and caused heavy casualties. Here, Longstreet had improved an already excellent defensive position by having his men erect fieldworks and dig entrenchments. In Piston's view, these latter steps explain why Longstreet's casualties were half of those suffered by the command of his more celebrated corps commander, Stonewall Jackson, even though both faced "the most intense assault the war had yet seen" (p. 34).

Piston acknowledges that Longstreet made mistakes. In 1862 a series of blunders at the Battle of Seven Pines, Virginia, marked "the lowest point in Longstreet's military career" (p. 19). While temporarily detached from Robert E. Lee's Army of Northern Virginia in late 1863, Longstreet failed to get along with his irascible commander, Braxton Bragg, and did not foresee the impending disaster which befell the latter's army at Chattanooga. Longstreet also sometimes played favorites among his subordinates, allowing personal loyalties to interfere with his professional judgment.

Still, Piston believes Longstreet to have been one of the war's best generals, even far superior to the more popularly acclaimed Stonewall Jackson. Longstreet was energetic, hardworking, and a fine administrator, and he conducted the crucial assault during the battle of Chickamauga with a skill no other Southern officer could have matched. Piston vigorously defends his subject's oft-criticized conduct at Gettysburg. Longstreet had supported the decision to invade the North that summer, in part swayed by his expectation that Lee would fight a defensive battle. But when fighting broke out at Gettysburg, Lee attacked, despite his trusted subordinate's strenuous objections. Piston argues that even in the face of this disagreement, Longstreet was not guilty of the delays his critics would later accuse him of, but carried out his orders to the best of his ability during this disastrous Confederate defeat. Piston portrays Longstreet's repeated efforts to secure a transfer out of Lee's command as naturally stemming from his belief "that the main peril lay in the western theater, necessitating a reinforcement of the armies there with men from Virginia" (p. 41). According to Piston, Longstreet's strategic plans, which in early 1864 recognized that the South might still win the war if Lincoln were not reelected, "showed remarkable breadth of vision" (p. 86).

Why, then, has Longstreet not been acknowledged his rightful place as the best corps commander of the war? Piston believes the answer lies in postbellum politics and bickering among former comrades-in-arms. When the war ended Longstreet preached reconciliation between white Southerners and the Republican Party. He believed such a course was the only alternative to black rule or

James Longstreet.
LIBRARY OF CONGRESS

another civil war. Attacks against his character by white conservatives increased as he accepted lucrative positions from Republican administrations at both state and federal levels.

In defense of his reputation, Longstreet struck back in a series of letters, articles, and eventually his own book-length account of the war, *From Manassas to Appomattox* (1896). In these writings, he exaggerated his own importance and dared to criticize Lee.

This proved a terrible blunder. An "anti-Longstreet faction emerged" (p. 129), led by Jubal Early and several of Lee's former staff officers. In the war of words that followed, critics made Longstreet the scapegoat for the Gettysburg defeat. Longstreet's delays in launching the Confederate attacks during the second day of that fateful battle, they charged, squandered an excellent opportunity to crush the Federals. Longstreet's ill-conceived verbal and written counterattacks merely added fuel to the fire. "Through needless exaggeration and a general tone of arrogance," explains Piston, "Longstreet gave reason to suspect that self-advancement, not self-defense, was the motive for his writings. . . . Because of his Republican affiliation, not one Southerner in a thousand was likely to concede Longstreet the right to criticize *any* soldier who had remained 'true' to the cause, much less the saintly Lee" (pp. 132–33).

I'm not convinced that Longstreet's actual wartime Civil War record merits the high ranking Piston suggests. And few would agree with Longstreet's belief that Joseph Johnston was a better commander than Lee. Further, Longstreet's February 1864 proposal that he mount his two infantry divisions on horses and mules and launch a gigantic raid into Kentucky verges on the fantastic—where was the Confederacy to secure a large quantity of mounts this late in the war? Finally, Longstreet was not present at Chancellorsville, the site of Lee's greatest victory. If Longstreet was so important, how did the Army of Northern Virginia succeed without him? Despite my misgivings, *Lee's Tarnished Lieutenant* establishes the importance of the postbellum war of words in shaping our understanding of the Civil War. Piston clearly establishes that Longstreet's politics, his clumsy attempts at self-defense, and the calculated public campaign to venerate Lee by his opponents fundamentally altered Longstreet's place in history.

48.

Rebel Brass: The Confederate Command System

by Frank E. Vandiver

The many works of Frank Vandiver, a noted lecturer whose rich, booming voice transforms an auditorium into a veritable Civil War battlefield, include a solid biography, *Ploughshares into Swords: Josiah Gorgas and Confederate Ordnance* (1952). His *Mighty Stonewall* (1957) was for years the standard biography of Thomas J. Jackson, but recently it has been superseded by James I. Robertson's *Stonewall Jackson: The Man, the Soldier, the Legend* [20]. Thus instead of Vandiver's work on Jackson, I've selected his *Rebel Brass* (1956), a concise assessment of the Confederate command system and the men who directed it. It is not a comprehensive history; instead, it is a clearly written, evocative critique which argues that Confederate leaders never recognized the true nature of the Civil War.

Vandiver points out that this long conflict was different from previous American experience, both in terms of the high numbers of casualties it claimed and the involvement of all citizens it demanded. The Confederacy lost, he argues, in large part because its leaders never recognized the need to effectively mobilize and use their region's national resources against a more powerful enemy. "The cause may have been lost," he concludes, "because there was not wisdom enough to recognize the beginning of a new era and not enough understanding of total war to evolve a command and logistical system adequate to the job at hand" (p. 125).

Geography, philosophy, and tradition worked against Confederate leaders. The mountains and rivers that divided the South offered convenient invasion routes to the enemy compounded the difficulty of directing the war from Richmond. Further, the Confederate States of America was born out of states' rights and government decentralization, thus making a unified war effort problematic. The conscription bureau failed to draft enough men or ensure that skilled workers remained where they would be most useful to the war effort. Ironically, argues Vandiver, the South's cadre of trained, professional officers might have worked against Confederate chances for victory. Reminding us of the success of the amateur Nathan Bedford Forrest, whose fearsome raids struck fear into many Northern hearts, he notes that professionals might have been "slower than many untrained men to see war as a changed business" (p. 12). Scarce industrial bases and natural resources had to be defended, thus reinforcing the Confederate tendency to fight a defensive war instead of engaging in "the correct strategy of eliminating enemy armies" (pp. 16–17).

The Confederacy was effectively splintered. "Bits and dribbles of the manpower reserve were siphoned off here and there to hold first one spot and then another" (p. 20), explains Vandiver. Rather than seeing the war in its entirety, leaders took a piecemeal, departmentalized approach. President Jefferson Davis, who was an excellent secretary of war during the 1850s, compounded the dilemma. Although suited by training, experience, and personality to handle the administrative puzzles of a War Department, Davis never grew out of this more limited role to become a revolutionary leader. He knew the traditional patterns of conducting war too well, just like he knew the Constitution too well. "The great paradox of the Confederacy was clearly reflected by Davis' dilemma," writes Vandiver, "he was a leader of a revolution, and yet he had a legal mind. Revolution and strict legality were somehow incompatible" (p. 27). In Vandiver's view, even able men, such as war secretaries George W. Randolph and James A. Seddon and navy secretary Stephen Mallory, could not escape their pasts. "Trained in the tradition of small government," explains Vandiver, "they could not see war as a full national effort for some time. Caught in

Lee and his generals.
NATIONAL ARCHIVES

the tradition of an agrarian economy, they could not see the war as a big business" (p. 78).

The Confederacy's efforts to resolve its logistical problems exemplified its failure to understand the nature of the Civil War. Traditionally the moving, housing, feeding, and arming of troops had been handled by separate staff bureaus. But the scale of the war rendered such a structure obsolete. Swamped by high inflation, most private contractors eventually sold out to government agencies. In turn, the individual agency then assumed more responsibility for production. Central direction, which might have overseen all government contracts and established priorities for producing scarce materials, was absent. "The trouble was that centralization did not go far enough," writes Vandiver. "While each bureau was forced to centralize, the War Department itself remained generally decentralized" (p. 96).

Vandiver suggests several steps Confederates might have taken to rectify these problems. A general staff could have provided direction and followed a more uniform strategy. A chief of logistics could have coordinated the efforts of the various bureaus within the War Department, using the Confederacy's successful blockade-running operations as a model. Desperately needing materials from abroad, in 1864 the government created the Bureau of

Foreign Supplies. Armed with the power to allot shipping space and cotton to the neediest bureaus and to oversee foreign purchases, the bureau proved remarkably effective. Because of this coordination, blockade-running served war efforts beyond all realistic expectations.

The central problem, as Vandiver sees it, was that "small thinking and small organizations were as outdated as small war" (p. 121). He continues: "Had all of the economic and human resources of the South been managed for a total war effort, the Rebels could have won the war" (p. 123). But neither Davis nor the Confederacy could escape their past training. The bonds of localism and tradition proved too strong.

Rebel Brass is an excellent introductory critique of the Confederacy's inability (or unwillingness) to fully mobilize its resources. For more thorough analyses of Confederate command and strategy, readers should consult *Jefferson Davis and His Generals* [24] or *The Politics of Command* [25]. However, Vandiver's *Rebel Brass* remains a provocative and highly readable assessment of fundamental problems within the Confederate war-making system.

49.

The Congressman's Civil War

by Allan G. Bogue

During the Civil War the U.S. Congress passed some of the most sweeping domestic legislation in American history. A higher tariff protected Northern manufacturers from European competition. A system of national banks was created and slavery was excluded from the territories. The Morrill Land Grant Act offered federal support for higher education by reserving public lands for state colleges. The Homestead Act granted free land to western settlers. The Pacific Railroad Act provided the economic basis for what would eventually become a transcontinental railroad. Given the importance of these measures, Civil War enthusiasts need to understand the inner workings of Congress, and Allan G. Bogue's *Congressman's Civil War* (1989) nicely fills this void.

The backgrounds of mid-nineteenth-century congressmen will probably surprise modern readers. Bogue bases this aspect of his study upon the eighty-three legislators who died while serving between 1844 and 1865 and who were eulogized by their surviving colleagues. (The eulogies provide the author with a convenient and thorough set of data.) Over half of his sample group had a college education and nearly two-thirds boasted some form of legal training. Only one in three had previously held local political office, but sixty-eight had served in state legislatures or state constitutional conventions before being elected to Congress. Their median age upon entering the House of Representatives was

The interior of the Senate chambers.
NATIONAL ARCHIVES

forty-three. Typically, they remained in Congress only briefly; the median length of service for representatives of the 1850s and 1860s was only two years. Pragmatic men stood for Congress not with the assumption that they would have long congressional careers, concludes Bogue, but as a means through which they might enhance their local reputations, acquaint themselves with the rich and powerful, and perhaps earn a subsequent patronage position, such as a judgeship or territorial office.

In an era devoid of civil service examinations, patronage was vital to the typical congressman. And the Civil War, with its massive expansion of the government and the armed forces, offered patronage opportunities as yet unparalleled in American history. Not only did congressmen expect to be able to reward their friends and supporters with federal jobs, they hoped to be favored with such posts themselves when they left Congress. In these matters they frequently turned to President Abraham Lincoln, who as leader of the Republican Party and commander in chief was the ultimate source of patronage. Lincoln "was most important in the eyes of the representatives and senators . . . as the general director of the system by which federal patronage was dispensed, and as an intervenor who could influence subordinate government officers in their behalf" (p. 144), Bogue points out.

This is not to suggest that ideology was absent or lacking. Rather, congressmen were simply playing the game as they knew it. Even though it held a majority in Congress, the Republican Party was sufficiently split between conservatives, moderates, and radicals to demand that the president attend carefully to coalition building. Republican congressmen proved quite ready to challenge Lincoln's policies, and on his two most significant efforts to shape Southern society—eliminating slavery and formulating a plan for readmitting formerly rebellious states into the Union—the Republican-controlled Congress refused to back the president.

Congress was involved in a great deal of investigative activity during the Civil War, another demonstration of its independence, notes Bogue. Six standing committees undertook some form of investigation, as did fifteen of the thirty-five select committees. In addition to discussing the activities of the best-known special committee, the Joint Committee on the Conduct of the War, Bogue assesses the work of several less well-known groups in an effort to shed light on the activities of the average congressman. The most intriguing of these was the Select Committee on the Loyalty of Clerks and Other Persons Employed by the Government, a five-member body headed by John F. "Bowie Knife" Potter (R—Wisconsin). At the insistence of their chair, this group met through the summer recess of 1861, interviewing 450 witnesses and assembling evidence regarding the suspected disloyalty of 550 government employees. Potter apparently displayed too much enthusiasm for rooting out suspected Southern sympathizers for the comfort of his fellow congressmen; they refused to reconstitute the group during the next Congress. Potter's exhortations also failed to impress his constituents, who turned him out of office.

Attempting to lead these diverse and independent-minded legislatures were Galusha A. Grow (R—Pennsylvania; thirty-seventh Congress) and Schuyler Colfax (R—Indiana; thirty-eighth Congress). Both were "competent men" (p. 146), according to Bogue, but they neither used his position as Speaker of the House to impose strict party discipline. Frustrated elements within the party, especially the radicals, called for frequent Republican Party caucuses in an effort to impose order. As Bogue concludes, however, "apparently these efforts were more successful in providing occasions for therapeutic expressions of irritation than in mobilizing support for radical measures or in devising means of energizing the administration" (p. 147).

The Congressman's Civil War is based on the Carl Becker Lectures presented by the author at Cornell University in 1986. Although intended for an academic audience, at its manageable length (148 pages of text, plus endnotes and bibliography), it offers general readers a fascinating look at the workings of Congress during the Civil War.

50.

John Brown's Body
by Stephen Vincent Benét

Poetry and fiction can provide extraordinary insights into our past. Readers of this volume are already aware of my admiration for Michael Shaara's *Killer Angels* [10] and Stephen Crane's *Red Badge of Courage* [45]. Stephen Vincent Benét, whose father and grandfather were both professional soldiers, was already an accomplished novelist when he received a Guggenheim fellowship in 1926. The award allowed him to complete his 15,000-line epic poem on the Civil War, *John Brown's Body* (1927), which received the Pulitzer Prize in 1929.

"It was a remarkable time," remembered Benét in the foreword to the 1941 edition, "and it summoned forth great men and small, strong figures and weak ones. . . . What I was trying to do was to show certain realities, legends, ideas, landscapes, ways of living, faces of men that were ours, that did not belong to any other country" (p. xxxi). And so he did, blending historical and fictional characters as well as various poetic styles. John Brown, Abraham Lincoln, Ulysses Grant, William Sherman, Robert E. Lee, Jefferson Davis, and a host of other historical figures grace the poem's pages, as do a series of memorable fictional characters—Jack Ellyat, the homesick, Connecticut-born Yankee wounded during the fighting at Gettysburg; Clay Wingate, heir to a Georgia plantation which is destroyed during Sherman's March to the Sea; Luke Breckinridge, Tennessee mountain man who knows lit-

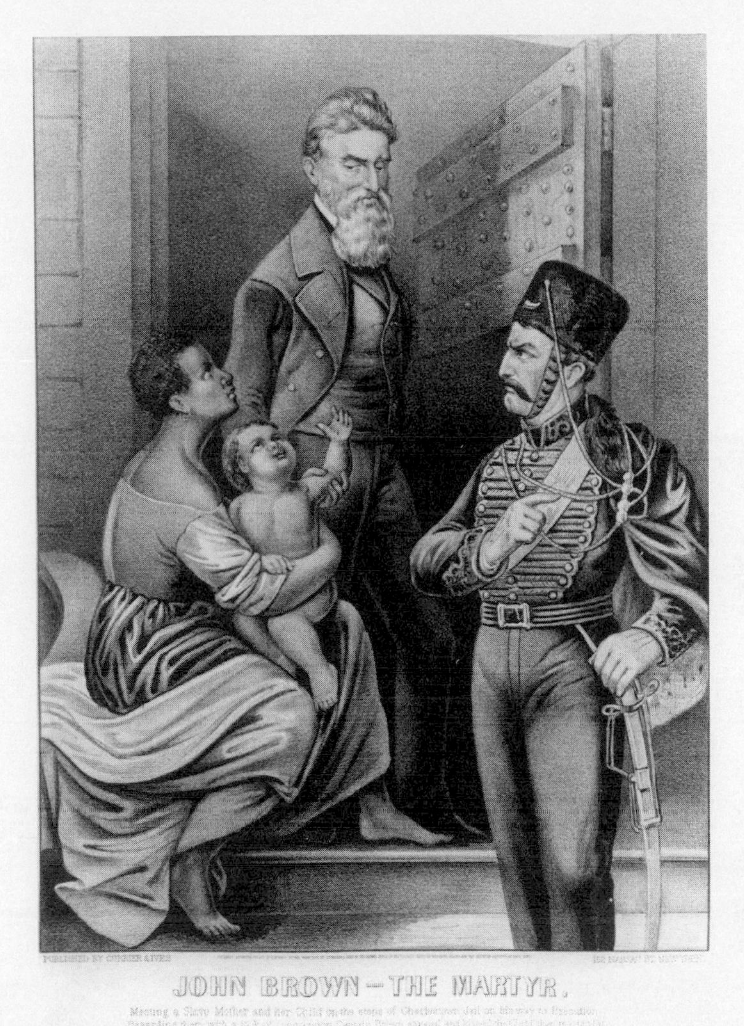

Courier and Ives lithograph entitled "John Brown—the Martyr."
LIBRARY OF CONGRESS

tle about what the war is about, other than "it don't rightly matter / Long as the Kelceys take the other side" (p. 82).

Through his range of fictional characters, Benét examines the wartime experiences of all Americans. Especially gripping are the stories of Curly Hatton, a plump young Virginian in love with Lucy Weatherby, his ardently secessionist fiancée. The good-natured Curly's "Butterball-legs under a butterball-body" make him something of a joke among his regiment of Virginia volunteers. He wonders about the necessity of secession and "knew a lot of Yankees that he liked," but has been convinced to join the army by Lucy, "the most porcelain belle of the world." Feeling himself made whole by Lucy's love, he "was ready to march to the world's end / And fight ten million Yanks to keep it so" (pp. 85–86). Curly is killed at the First Battle of Bull Run; Lucy evolves into the "Dixie Angel," for whom countless other Southerners would die. As she prayed to her pillow at night:

Pillow, tell me I'm pretty, tell me I'm lovely,
Tell me I'm nicer than anybody you know,
Tell me that nice new boy is thinking about me,
Tell me that Sally girl couldn't wear my blue,
Tell me the war won't end till we've whipped the Yankees,
Tell me I'll never get wrinkles and always have beaus.
(pp. 165–166)

Benét also offers marvelous characterizations of major Civil War scenes and figures. The Confederate Army of Northern Virginia, "Strange army of ragged individualists," was a "Praying Army, / Full of revivals, as full of salty jests, / Who debated on God and Darwin and Victor Hugo, / Decided that evolution might do for Yankees / But that Lee never came from anything with a tail" (pp. 182–83). The men of the Army of the Potomac also come alive: "Rocks from New England and hickory-chunks from the West, / Bowery boy and clogging Irish adventurer, / Germans who learnt their English under the shells / Or didn't have time to learn it before they died" (pp. 176–77). Abraham Lincoln's homespun humor also comes alive. Here Lincoln describes how he handles his feuding cabinet members, Secretary of State William Seward and Secretary of the Treasury Salmon P. Chase:

When I was a boy
I remember figuring out when I went to town
That if I had just one pumpkin to bump in a sack

It was hard to carry, but once you could get two pumpkins,
One in each end of the sack, it balanced things up.
Seward and Chase'll do for my pair of pumpkins.
(p. 69).

Lincoln's mental exhaustion is brilliantly rendered when a fictitious veteran of the Army of the Potomac describes his chance meeting with the weary president: "I never saw nobody look quite as sad as that / . . . He was glad to see us but you could tell all the same / This war's plumb killin' him. You can tell by his face" (p. 252).

Benét's emotional and impressionistic work bursts with a poet's sensitive imagery about the physical and psychological experiences of Americans during the Civil War. I had known about it for years, but admit that I had never really paid it proper notice until I began writing this book. It came to my attention again as I was reading Robert Brent Toplin's anthology, *Ken Burns's* The Civil War: *Historians Respond* [43], which traces the preparation of and controversy surrounding Ken Burns's popularly acclaimed public television documentary. When Burns requested input about important Civil War books from C. Vann Woodward, editor of *Mary Chestnut's Civil War* [45], Woodward suggested that *John Brown's Body* might be a good place to start. I wouldn't go quite that far in recommending it to a general audience, but Benét's contribution still retains its epic appeal.

HONORABLE MENTIONS

The list of excellent books about the American Civil War is indeed a long one, and fifty is an arbitrary place to stop. I very nearly included several other fine works in *The Civil War Bookshelf,* so they deserve at least a brief special mention here. They are listed in no particular order.

Fredericksburg and Chancellorsville: The Dare Mark Campaign (1998)
BY DONALD E. SUTHERLAND

The more I think about this book, the more dubious I am about my decision not to include it. In vivid and original terms, Donald E. Sutherland, author of several other books about the Civil War, describes the Fredericksburg and Chancellorsville campaigns of 1862 to 1863. The success of these campaigns depended on Union efforts—first by Ambrose E. Burnside and second by Joseph Hooker—to cross the Rappahannock River. One Confederate soldier called this river the "Dare Mark," because Robert E. Lee seemed to have drawn a line here, beyond which any Federal movement would guarantee a fight. Sutherland points out that during these campaigns, the Lincoln administration's strategy changed. Previously, Union efforts had centered on Richmond; here, along the banks of the Rappahannock, the focus shifted to Lee's army itself.

Like virtually everyone else, Sutherland criticizes the bumbling Burnside, but he reverses recent trends to exonerate Hooker by blaming him squarely for the Federal loss at Chancellorsville. Not surprisingly he also gives high praise to Lee, whose improvisation allowed him to take advantage of good fortune when it arose. "Luck favored pluck & skill," wrote one Confederate (p. 192), an analysis that still seems appropriate nearly one hundred and forty years later.

America's Civil War (1996)
BY BROOKS D. SIMPSON

Shorter by nearly two-thirds than James McPherson's *Battle Cry of Freedom* [1], Simpson's excellent survey is designed for use in college classrooms but is very well suited to general readers as well. It incorporates much of the latest scholarship and effectively interweaves military events with social, intellectual, economic, and political trends.

Incorporating the broad concepts reflected in McPherson's contingency thesis (which holds that the Confederacy could have won the war on several occasions had military events turned out differently), Simpson attributes Northern victory to better leadership, political as well as military. President Abraham Lincoln held the Union together, while Ulysses S. Grant implemented a strategy which mobilized Northern resources and used them in a coordinated manner. Grant, argues Simpson, "cashed in on his successes, while [Robert E.] Lee's victories came at so dear a cost that he was unable to capitalize upon them" (pp. 213–14). *America's Civil War* does not match McPherson's rhetorical brilliance, however, and is in my view a bit too critical of Lee, so I've relegated it to the "near miss" category.

An American Illiad: The Story of the Civil War (1991)
BY CHARLES P. ROLAND

Superior in its analysis of military events, Charles Roland's survey is another good choice for those seeking a brief overview of the war. Though largely a descriptive story of the great saga, *An American Illiad* also contains a short, insightful essay offering the author's observations on the reasons behind the North's victory. The North, argues Roland, did enjoy greater resources, but it also boasted more modern political and social systems. This allowed the Union to develop "a more effective national strategy than the Confederacy, a strategy that skillfully combined domestic and diplomatic policies and resources behind the war effort" (p. 258). Roland thus stresses the superiority of Northern political leadership.

An American Illiad is certainly a fitting culmination of Roland's distinguished career as historian and editor. My concern that *The Civil War Bookshelf* already contained too many good books on military affairs worked against my inclusion of Roland's book as a main selection.

A Great Civil War: A Military and Political History, 1861–1865 (2000)
BY RUSSELL F. WEIGLEY

A pre-eminent military historian whose previous works have included surveys of the United States army, American military policy, and the Napoleonic Wars, Weigley's latest book is a detailed history of the Civil War. Lengthy discussions on slavery, emancipation, reconstruction, and society give the book greater depth than the title might suggest. As in his earlier works, Weigley admires Robert E. Lee's tactical brilliance, but argues that his propensity for accepting heavy losses in hopes of a climatic battlefield victory hurt the Confederacy badly. "The most Napoleonic general of the war," he argues, "Lee was a Napoleon come to warfare too late" (p. 134). Weigley believes the war's intensity and destructiveness resulted from "deficiencies in strategic thinking," "limited operational thinking," and governments "too inchoate" to restrain the ever-expanding conflict (pp. xxi–xxiv). The result is a fine, readable book; its absence from my top fifty is a testament to the extremely high quality of Civil War scholarship.

Attack and Die: Civil War Military Tactics and the Southern Heritage (1982)
BY GRADY MCWHINEY AND PERRY D. JAMIESON

At the outset, I should say that I disagree with this book's provocative thesis, which attributes the Confederate propensity to assume the tactical offensive to the Celtic heritage shared by many Southerners. The Rebels, argue McWhiney and Jamieson, "favored offensive warfare because the Celtic charge was an integral part of their heritage" (p. xv). Had the Confederates learned from their mistakes and adopted defensive tactics, they very well might have won the war, the authors contend. As I've noted earlier, I'm not so convinced this would have been the case. But in pointing out the horrific casualties even the great Robert E. Lee suffered in many of his victories, McWhiney and Jamieson have made an important contribution.

Religion and the American Civil War (1998)
ED. BY RANDALL M. MILLER, HARRY S. STOUT, AND CHARLES REAGAN WILSON

The role of religion in the American Civil War has attracted surprisingly little attention from serious scholars. This anthology, the product of a 1994 conference held at the Louisville Presbyterian Theological Seminary, begins to fill this gap. Boasting a splendid introduction by the editors, an insightful overview essay by Phillip Shaw Paludan [13], and a brief afterword by James M. McPherson [1, 7], the book explores "religion's fundamental place in the war" (p. 18). Fifteen essays by distinguished historians and theologians comment on matters ranging from the Bible and slavery to the complex interplay between Irish Catholics, the Church, and wartime notions of Americanism. It merits serious attention; only my own difficulties in persuading reluctant undergraduates to grapple with the conflicting interpretations and conclusions inherent in such an anthology convinced me to relegate this important work to Honorable Mention status in a book designed for a broad readership.

From Cape Charles to Cape Fear: The North Atlantic Blockading Squadron During the Civil War (1993)
BY ROBERT M. BROWNING, JR.

This intriguing book offers a detailed examination of the Union navy's amphibious and riverine operations along the Virginia and North Carolina coasts, as well as an analysis of the North Atlantic Blockading Squadron's efforts to isolate the Confederacy. Browning gives the squadron mixed reviews, pointing out that although the North missed several excellent opportunities to exploit its early naval superiority on the central Atlantic coast, the blockade played a major role in the Confederate defeat. Rather than gauging the blockade's success solely on the tonnage of contraband goods imported and cotton bales exported, he frames his analysis within the broader context of the Confederacy's war overall war effort. The blockade, Browning contends, prevented the South from importing railroad supplies, marine engines, and manufacturing equipment. And by depriving the Confederacy of much of its normal river and sea traffic, it overloaded the creaky southern railroad system. Although somewhat narrowly focused and a bit too much resembling a dissertation in style, *From Cape Charles to Cape Fear* poses an interesting counterpoint to Raimondo Luraghi's *History of the Confederate Navy* [46].

Ulysses S. Grant: Memoirs and Selected Letters
BY ULYSSES S. GRANT
(Library of America edition, 1990)

The writing of Ulysses S. Grant's *Personal Memoirs* (1885–86) is one of the Civil War era's most compelling stories. Bankrupted by several disastrous investments, the former general-in-chief and ex-president agreed in 1884 to complete his memoirs for publication. Although he had quit smoking his trademark cigars, on February 21, 1885, doctors diagnosed him as terminally ill with throat cancer. In agonizing pain as he labored to complete the task that he hoped would ensure his family's financial well-being, he completed what would emerge as a two-volume, twelve-hundred-page tome on July16. He died of cancer a week later.

Personal Memoirs of U. S. Grant was a smashing success. His wife, Julia, received more than $400,000 in royalties, and the work is generally acknowledged as one of the best autobiographies written by a Civil War veteran. Unlike most of his peers, Grant pulled few punches. George H. Thomas, who caused frustrating delays as commander of the Army of the Cumberland around Nashville in late 1864, "was not as good . . . in pursuit [of the enemy] as he was in action" (p. 762). Confederate general Albert Sidney Johnston "was over-estimated" (p. 242); Joseph E. Johnston's tactics during the Atlanta campaign "were right" (p. 505). And although he admired Robert E. Lee, Grant did not stand in awe of him, as had many of his predecessors in the Army of the Potomac. "I had known him personally," noted Grant, "and knew that he was mortal" (p. 129).

Civil War readers need to explore this classic autobiography. *Ulysses S. Grant: Memoirs and Selected Letters,* published by the Library of America in 1990, combines the two volumes of the *Personal Memoirs* with explanatory notes by Mary Drake McFeely and William S. McFeely, the latter a Pulizter Prize winning biographer of Grant. This edition also includes selected letters by Grant and his Notes to the Doctor, scratched out in June and July 1885. The notes describe the dying man's heroic struggle to avoid becoming dependent upon morphine and cocaine to relieve his pain while he completed his memoirs. "I do not sleep though I sometimes dose [*sic*] off a little. If up I am talked to and in my efforts to answer cause pain. The fact is I think I am a verb instead of a personal pronoun. A verb is anything that signifies to be; to do; or to suffer. I signify all three" (p. 1120).

Emancipation and Reconstruction, 1862-1879 (1987)
BY MICHAEL PERMAN

Rounding out my list of very near misses is yet another survey. Like Brooks Simpson's *America's Civil War*, Perman's book is designed for use in college classes, but offers an incisive synthesis of emancipation and reconstruction during and after the Civil War. Perman's explanations of difficult and complex issues are subtle yet convincing. He sees reconstruction, which would have required strong federal support in order to truly succeed, as a radical departure from American tradition. I did not include *Emancipation and Reconstruction* in *The Civil War Bookshelf* for two reasons. First, as a book marketed largely to university orders, I'm not sure how available it is for general readers, although one could surely special order it through any decent bookstore. Second, I already had selected three other excellent books on the subjects it deals with: Kenneth M. Stampp's *Era of Reconstruction, 1865–1877* [11]; Leon F. Litwack's *Been in the Storm So Long: The Aftermath of Slavery* [26]; and Willie Lee Rose's *Rehearsal for Reconstruction: The Port Royal Experiment* [36].

LOCATING THE BOOKS

Almost all of the fifty books included in *The Civil War Bookshelf* should be easy to find. Only three are out of print as of the time I completed this manuscript. Any good-sized public or university library should have many of the books I've included. Others can easily be secured via interlibrary loan, which most librarians will be happy to help you with.

Those who would like to purchase one of the fifty books included in *The Civil War Bookshelf* may rely on the bibliographic information for the edition I used. If any of the publishing information for a paperback edition is different from that of the version I used, I have provided it. I have also tried to find the most current suggested retail price for the book, if it is in print. Whenever possible, the price refers to the paperback edition.

Purchasing books is now remarkably easy. If they are not in stock at your local bookstore, most booksellers will be glad to order them for you. And there's also the electronic option. Although I am not convinced that the Internet will solve all (or even very many) of the world's problems, it has certainly made it much easier for the Civil War enthusiast to buy books. A quick check of some of the leading Internet booksellers, such as amazon.com or barnesandnoble.com, reveals that these giants have many of these books in stock or available for shipment in two or three days from the time of order.

I've tried to provide accurate information, but am forced to conclude with this caveat: prices change, books are sometimes allowed to go out of print, and publishers and bookstores consolidate.

1. JAMES M. MCPHERSON. *Battle Cry of Freedom: The Civil War Era*. New York: Oxford University Press, 1988. Paperback, 1989, $18.
2. BRUCE CATTON. *A Stillness at Appomattox*. Garden City, N.Y.: Doubleday, 1953. Paperback, Anchor Books, 1953, $14.95.
3. DAVID HERBERT DONALD. ed. *Why the North Won the Civil War*. Baton Rouge: Louisiana State University Press, 1960. Reprint, New York: Collier Books, 1962. Paperback, Touchstone Books, 1996, $10.
4. DOUGLAS SOUTHALL FREEMAN. *Lee's Lieutenants: A Study in Command*. New York: Scribner's, 1942–44. Abridged in one volume by Stephen W. Sears, New York: Scribner's, 1998, $65.
5. GARY W. GALLAGHER. *The Confederate War*. Cambridge, Mass.: Harvard University Press, 1997. Paperback, 1999, $24.95.
6. DAVID HERBERT DONALD. *Lincoln*. New York: Simon and Schuster, 1995. Paperback, Touchstone Books, 1996, $17.
7. JAMES M. MCPHERSON. *For Cause and Comrades: Why Men Fought in the Civil War*. New York: Oxford University Press, 1997. Paperback, 1998, $13.95.
8. T. HARRY WILLIAMS. *Lincoln and His Generals*. New York: Vintage Books, 1952. Paperback, 1976, $12.75.
9. EMORY M. THOMAS. *Robert E. Lee: A Biography*. New York: Norton, 1995. Paperback, 1997, $14.95.
10. MICHAEL SHAARA, *The Killer Angels: A Novel*. New York: McKay, 1974. Reprint, New York: Ballantine, 1975. Paperback, $12.
11. KENNETH M. STAMPP. *The Era of Reconstruction, 1865–1877*. New York: Random House, 1967. Paperback, $11.95.
12. DAVID M. POTTER. *The Impending Crisis, 1848–1861*, completed and edited by Don E. Fehrenbacher. New York: Harper and Row, 1977. Paperback, HarperCollins, $17.
13. PHILLIP SHAW PALUDAN. *"A People's Contest": The Union and the Civil War, 1861–1865*. New York: Harper and Row, 1988. Second edition, with a new preface, Lincoln: University Press of Kansas, 1996. Paperback, $16.95.
14. STEPHEN W. SEARS. *Landscape Turned Red: The Battle of*

Antietam. New York: Ticknor & Fields, 1983. Reprint, New York: Warner Books, 1985. Paperback, Ticknor & Fields, 1993, $16.

15. DREW GILPIN FAUST. *Mothers of Invention: Women of the Slaveholding South in the American Civil War*. Chapel Hill: University of North Carolina Press, 1996. Reprint, New York: Vintage Books, 1997. Paperback, $15.
16. WILLIAM C. DAVIS. *Jefferson Davis: The Man and His Hour*. New York: HarperCollins, 1991. Paperback, Louisiana State University Press, 1996, $22.95.
17. SHELBY FOOTE. *The Civil War: A Narrative—Fredericksburg to Meridian*. New York: Random House, 1963. Paperback, 1986, $24.
18. BELL IRVIN WILEY. *The Life of Johnny Reb: The Common Soldier of the Confederacy*. Indianapolis: Bobbs-Merrill, 1943. Reprint, Baton Rouge: Louisiana State University Press, 1978. Paperback, 1989, $14.95.
19. KENNETH M. STAMPP. *And the War Came: The North and the Secession Crisis, 1860–61*. Baton Rouge: Louisiana State University Press, 1950. Paperback, $18.
20. JAMES I. ROBERTSON, JR. *Stonewall Jackson: The Man, the Soldier, the Legend*. New York: Macmillan, 1997. Paperback, $19.95.
21. CHARLES ROYSTER. *The Destructive War: William Tecumseh Sherman, Stonewall Jackson, and the Americans*. New York: Knopf, 1991. Paperback, Vintage Books, 1999, $17.
22. JOSEPH T. GLATTHAAR. *The March to the Sea and Beyond: Sherman's Troops in the Savannah and Carolinas Campaigns*. New York: New York University Press, 1985. Paperback, Louisiana State University Press 1995, $16.95.
23. ALVIN M. JOSEPHY, JR. *The Civil War in the American West*. New York: Knopf, 1991. Paperback, Vintage Books, 1993, $16.
24. STEVEN E. WOODWORTH. *Jefferson Davis and His Generals: The Failure of Confederate Command in the West*. Lawrence: University Press of Kansas, 1990. Paperback, 1992, $14.95.
25. THOMAS L. CONNELLY and ARCHER JONES. *The Politics of*

Command: Factions and Ideas in Confederate Strategy. Baton Rouge: Louisiana State University Press, 1973. Paperback, 1998, $14.95.

26. LEON F. LITWACK. *Been in the Storm So Long: The Aftermath of Slavery.* New York: Knopf, 1979. Paperback, Vintage Books, 1989, $21.75.
27. JOHN G. WAUGH. *The Class of 1846, From West Point to Appomattox: Stonewall Jackson, George McClellan and Their Brothers*. New York: Warner Books, 1994. Paperback, Ballantine, 1999, $14.95.
28. MARK E. NEELY, JR. *The Fate of Liberty: Abraham Lincoln and Civil Liberties*. New York: Oxford University Press, 1992. Paperback, $17.95.
29. RICHARD E. BERINGER, HERMAN HATTAWAY, ARCHER JONES and WILLIAM N. STILL, JR. *Why the South Lost the Civil War*. Athens: University of Georgia Press, 1986. Paperback, 1991, $22.95.
30. HOWARD JONES. *Union in Peril: The Crisis Over British Intervention in the Civil War*. Chapel Hill: University of North Carolina Press, 1992. Reprint, Lincoln: University of Nebraska Press, 1997. Paperback, $14.95.
31. ERIC FONER. *Free Soil, Free Labor, Free Men: The Ideology of the Republican Party Before the Civil War*. New York: Oxford University Press, 1970. Paperback, 1995, $16.95.
32. ROBERT V. BRUCE. *Lincoln and the Tools of War*. Indianapolis: Bobbs-Merrill, 1956. Paperback, University of Illinois Press, 1989, $14.95.
33. JAMES ARTHUR LYON FREMANTLE. *The Fremantle Diary: Three Months in the Southern States,* edited by Gary Gallagher. 1864. Reprint, Lincoln: University of Nebraska Press Press, 1991. Paperback, $13.95.
34. DAVID HERBERT DONALD, JEAN H. BAKER, and MICHAEL F. HOLT. *The Civil War and Reconstruction.* New York: Norton, 2001. Paperback, $43.75.
35. BROOKS D. SIMPSON. *Ulysses S. Grant: Triumph over Adversity, 1822–1865.* Boston: Houghton-Mifflin, 2000. $35.
36. WILLIE LEE ROSE. *Rehearsal for Reconstruction: The Port Royal*

Experiment. Indianapolis: Bobbs-Merrill, 1964. Paperback, University of Georgia, 1999, $16.95.

37. GABOR S. BORITT, ed. *Lincoln, the War President: The Gettysburg Lectures*. New York: Oxford University Press, 1992. Paperback, $12.95.
38. JOHN F. MARSZALEK. *Sherman: A Soldier's Passion for Order*. New York: Free Press, 1993. Paperback, Vintage Books, 1994, $18.
39. WILLIAM M. FOWLER, JR. *Under Two Flags: The American Navy in the Civil War*. New York: Norton, 1990. Out of print. Paperback edition scheduled for 2001 by Naval Institute Press.
40. WILLIAM L. BARNEY. *The Secessionist Impulse: Alabama and Mississippi in 1860*. Princeton, N.J.: Princeton University Press, 1974. Out of print.
41. RICHARD M. MCMURRY. *Two Great Rebel Armies: An Essay in Confederate Military History*. Chapel Hill: University of North Carolina Press, 1989. Paperback, 1996, $16.95.
42. GEOFFREY C. WARD with RIC BURNS and KEN BURNS. *The Civil War: An Illustrated History*. New York: Knopf, 1990. Paperback, 1992, $39.95.
43. ROBERT BRENT TOPLIN, ed. *Ken Burns's* The Civil War: *Historians Respond*. New York: Oxford University Press, 1996. Paperback, $13.95.
44. *Mary Chestnut's Civil War*, edited by C. Vann Woodward. New Haven: Yale University Press, 1981. Paperback, 1983, $22.50.
45. STEPHEN CRANE. *The Red Badge of Courage*. 1895. Reprint, New York: Norton, 1982. Paperback, Tor Books, 1997, $2.99.
46. RAIMONDO LURAGHI. *A History of the Confederate Navy,* trans. Paolo E. Coletta. Washington, D.C.: Naval Institute Press, 1996. $45.
47. WILLIAM GARRETT PISTON. *Lee's Tarnished Lieutenant: James Longstreet and His Place in Southern History*. Athens: University of Georgia Press, 1987. Paperback, 1990, $14.95.
48. FRANK E. VANDIVER. *Rebel Brass: The Confederate Command System*. Baton Rouge: Louisiana State University Press,

1956. Reprint, Westport, Conn.: Greenwood Press, 1969. Paperback, Louisiana State University Press, 1993, $12.95.

49. ALLAN G. BOGUE. *The Congressman's Civil War*. New York: Cambridge University Press, 1989. Paperback, $22.95.
50. STEPHEN VINCENT BENÉT. *John Brown's Body*. Garden City, NJ: Doubleday, Doran and Co., 1927. Paperback, Chicago: Ivan R. Dee, 1990, $14.95.

FOR FURTHER STUDY

Annotated bibliographies and other sources for Civil War related books and articles

For those seeking additional guides to Civil War literature, I highly recommend several sources. In a class of its own is David J. Eicher's *The Civil War in Books: An Annotated Bibliography* (1997). In a monumental feat, Eicher has included bibliographic information and short annotations for no less than eleven hundred books about the American Civil War. Divided into five broad headings (battles and campaigns, Confederate biographies, Union biographies, general works, and unit histories), *The Civil War in Books* is a remarkably thorough survey of Civil War literature. Civil War devotees need to be familiar with it.

Of a somewhat different intent, but equally valuable, is *Writing the Civil War: The Quest to Understand*, edited by James McPherson and William J. Cooper (1998). Boasting twelve essays written by prominent Civil War scholars, this book traces the history of writing about the war. Subjects include strategy, tactics, soldiers, presidents, politics, society, women, and slaves. In contrast to Eicher's annotated bibliography, *Writing the Civil War* is meant to be read, not simply consulted. Here readers will find excellent surveys that trace how our understanding and analysis of Civil War issues have changed over time.

Several other separate publications merit at least a brief note. A Civil War veteran himself, John Page Nicholson compiled a massive study of the literature about the war: *Catalogue of the Library of Brevet Lieutenant-Colonel John Page Nicholson Relating to the War of the Rebellion, 1861–1866* (1914). Unfortunately, only three hundred copies were printed, so the book is out of the reach of most

Civil War enthusiasts except in major libraries. Thomas Pressly, *Americans Interpret Their Civil War* (1957; rpt. 1962) is geared largely for professional historians, but gives a good indication of the changing interpretative trends. Still very useful is Allan Nevins, Bell I. Wiley, and James I. Robertson, eds., *Civil War Books: A Critical Bibliography* (two vols., 1967-69), although the annotations are much shorter than those found in Eicher. Edmund Wilson's *Patriotic Gore: Studies in the Literature of the American Civil War* (1962) is a controversial examination of how writers have grappled with the conflict.

Several of the survey texts on the Civil War include lengthy bibliographies of use to general readers. That found in *The Civil War and Reconstruction*, by James G. Randall and David Donald, [34], was considered from the 1950s through the 1970s to be a standard place to begin research. Comprehensive and easily accessible, it stood unchallenged for years. The annotated bibliography in James McPherson's *Ordeal by Fire: The Civil War and Reconstruction* (1982), is also exceptionally good on books and articles published before 1980, superseding even the bibliography in Randall and Donald. It is divided into subject areas and includes brief insights about the literature from the war's preeminent scholar. McPherson's bibliographical essay in *Battle Cry of Freedom: The Civil War Era* [1] is less exhaustive, but more current. Among the books included in *The Civil War Bookshelf*, its bibliography is clearly superior.

Useful reference books

Although I excluded reference books from *The Civil War Bookshelf*, Civil War enthusiasts should have several of these tools within easy reach, either at home or in their nearest library. The five-volume *Encyclopedia of the American Civil War: A Political, Social, and Military History* (ed. David S. and Jeanne T. Hadler, 2000) is now a starting point for those needing reference materials. Still a staple about the conflict is *The Civil War Dictionary*, by Mark M. Boatner III (1959). Reprinted many times, Boatner's one-volume dictionary includes short descriptions of the war's key individuals, battles, campaigns, armies, and terms. I own two copies—one for home and the other for my office. Almost as good is *Historical Times Illustrated Encyclopedia of the Civil War*, edited by Patricia L. Faust (1986), which has the virtue of incorporating more recent scholarship. E. B. Long's *The Civil War Day by Day: An Almanac, 1861–1865* (1971), is also quite useful in tracking the war's events. William G. Thomas and Alice E. Carter, *The Civil War on the Web: A Guide to the Very Best Sites* (2001), offers Civil War enthusiasts an excellent survey of notable Internet sites.

Hundreds of more specialized works are available, but the following stand out. *The Abraham Lincoln Encyclopedia* by Mark E. Neely, Jr. (1982), has always had everything I wanted to know about things and people associated with our sixteenth president. The four-volume *Encyclopedia of the Confederacy*, edited by Richard N. Current (1993), is another very useful source. For detailed compilations of numerical strength, organization, and casualties of Civil War armies, see Thomas L. Livermore's *Numbers and Losses in the Civil War in America, 1861–1865* (1901) and William F. Fox's *Regimental Losses in the American Civil War, 1861–1865* (1880). Although each has undergone several editions, Livermore and Fox are still fairly difficult to purchase, so a reader's best bet is probably to consult a copy in a library.

Maps and illustrations

One can't understand the American Civil War without an encyclopedic knowledge of geography or a good map. The most affordable collection of Civil War battle and campaign maps is the *Atlas for the American Civil War* (1986; series editor Thomas E. Griess). More expensive but magnificently conceived is Vincent J. Esposito's *West Point Atlas of American Wars* (1959; vol. I). *The Atlas of the Civil War*, edited by James McPherson (1994), has beautifully drawn maps, fine accompanying illustrations, and helpful text. Sadly, the maps are centered across the crease of the book, rendering them difficult to use.

The Civil War saw the first wartime photography in American history. Incredible for the time of its original publication was a ten-volume series edited by Francis T. Miller, *The Photographic History of the Civil War* (1911; rpt. 1957). Thanks to improved printing technologies, the reproductions in *The Image of War 1861–1865*, edited by William C. Davis (1981-84; six volumes) are splendid, as is the accompanying text. The multivolume Time-Life Books series, *The Civil War* (1983–87) is also profusely illustrated, often in color. The accompanying texts are sometimes uneven, although the series includes contributions by noted Civil War scholars like Alvin M. Josephy, William C. Davis, James I. Robertson, and Steven A. Channing. The University of Arkansas Press' *Portraits in Conflict* series (individual volumes on Arkansas, Georgia, Louisiana, Mississippi, North Carolina, South Carolina have been published to date) is also quite good.

Several profusely illustrated one-volume historians of the war are geared for the general reader. My favorite is *The Civil War: An Illustrated History* [42], by Geoffrey C. Ward, with Ric Burns and Ken Burns. Rivaling it is *The American Heritage New History of the Civil War*, originally written by Bruce Catton, but revised by James McPherson and Noah Trudeau (1996). Both are magnificently designed and have beautiful maps. A third book worthy of mention for its combination of high-quality text and illustrations is William C. Davis's *Fighting Men of the Civil War* (1989). The latter has particularly good pictorial exhibits of wartime ordnance and period uniforms. All of these illustrated surveys are available in affordable paperback editions.

Seeing the battlefields

To really understand the Civil War, visiting some of the battlefields is a must. Fortunately, the United States has done a much better job than most other nations in preserving its military heritage. In part because of the constant vigil of Civil War enthusiasts, segments of most of the major Civil War battlefields are in the care of the National Park Service, which usually maintains a museum on site. If you can only go to one, I strongly recommend the battlefield at Antietam, Maryland. Near the quiet little hamlet of Sharpsburg, the site is open enough to afford excellent views of the area where the bloodiest single day of fighting in American history took place. The museum is excellent, and there is a well-marked tour route that can easily be explored in a day, by automobile or bicycle. The sights there—the Cornfield, the West Woods, Bloody Lane, Burnside's Bridge, the national cemetery—are truly hallowed places for Civil War enthusiasts. Although it's less than two hours by car from Washington, D.C., the site remains very much like it was when the battle was fought.

Number two on my list of favorite Civil War battlefields is the one at Vicksburg, Mississippi. Restored artillery pieces and earthworks offer grim reminders of the six-week siege that took place here in 1863. Once again, excellent park service roads, trails, markers, and museums make the battlefield easily accessible, and the relatively open nature of the country gives the visitor superb views of the surrounding terrain.

Guides to these and other battlefield parks could take up an entire bookshelf. *The U.S. Army War College Guides to Civil War Battles* series has some splendidly detailed guides to the battlefields at Antietam, Chancellorsville and Fredericksburg, Gettysburg, Chickamauga, Shiloh, and Vicksburg. Although published too late for my review, a new series, *This Hallowed Ground*, also promises to offer readers book-length guides to individual battlefields. The best of the one-volume guides includes *The Civil War Battlefield Guide* by the Conservation Fund (1998); *National Geographic Guide to the Civil War National Battlefield Parks,* by A. Wilson Greene (1993); *Civil War Battlefields: A Touring Guide*, by David J. Eicher (1995); or *Smithsonian's Great Battles & Battlefields of the Civil War,* by Jay Wertz and Edwin C. Bearss (1997). Individual preferences and cost will determine which one best serves your needs.

The official records of the rebellion

Every Civil War enthusiast should be familiar with the existence of two of the most remarkable primary source documents in existence: *The War of the Rebellion: A Compilation of the Official Records of the Union and Confederate Armies* (seventy volumes published in 128 books), and the *Official Records of the Union and Confederate Navies in the War of the Rebellion* (twenty-seven volumes). Published by the United States government between 1881 and 1927, these comprehensively indexed collections provide the foundation for all serious research about military events during the American Civil War.

Usually referred to as the *Official Records* (or even simply the *O.R.*), these volumes offer researchers incredibly easy access to a wide variety of original materials related to the war. They are not, however, comprehensive. Some documents were not located or simply not included. The Confederacy's record-keeping was erratic even in the best of times, and innumerable documents were lost or destroyed as the war concluded. The editors of these volumes decided to exclude materials related to the service of individual soldiers. And some documents might very well have been tampered with after the war, particularly in attempts to reconstruct lost Southern archives.

Within these constraints, you can find an amazing amount of raw material in the *Official Records*. Action reports by officers, military (and often political) correspondence, orders, circulars, and tabular data on army sizes and organizations is here in abundance. Army records are divided into four series. The first (fifty-three volumes in 111 books), which covers the military operations themselves, is organized by campaigns, or by materials encompassing a particular geographic area within a particular time period. Series two is reserved for materials relating to prisoners. The third (Federal) and fourth (Confederate) series include records not included in the other two series, often related to mobilization and supply. The naval records are divided into two series, with the first (consisting of twenty-seven volumes) relating to operations, and the second dealing with construction, ships, and prisoners.

The government originally published twelve thousand copies of the *Official Records*, and privately published reprints are also available. Many libraries have copies. Recently, the *Official Records* have been put on compact disks, making it possible for even the shelf-starved Civil War enthusiast to procure a copy of this invaluable research tool. Remarkably, the Broadfoot Publishing Company (Wilmington, North Carolina) has begun publishing a *Supplement to the Official Records.* Consisting of three parts and 95 volumes as this book went to press, the *Supplement* contains additional wartime records and correspondence.

TABLES

TABLE 1. Facts About the Books in *The Civil War Bookshelf*

WHEN WERE THEY ORIGINALLY PUBLISHED?

Before 1950	4
1950–59	5
1960–69	4
1970–79	5
1980–89	11
1990–99	19
2000–01	2

WHAT ARE THE SUBJECTS?

Individual biographies	7
Behind the lines	5
General surveys of the war	4
Army histories	4
Antebellum period	4
Anthologies	3
Confederate military policy	3
Fiction	3
Reconstruction	3
Primary sources	2
Union military policy	2
Group biographies	2
Common soldiers	2
Regional military campaigns	2
Naval affairs	2
Specific campaigns	1
Diplomacy	1

Table 2.

PRESIDENTIAL ELECTIONS, 1848–1876

Year, candidate, and party	*Percent of popular vote*	*Electoral vote*	*Percent voter participation*
1848			72.7
Zachary Taylor (Whig)	47.4	163	
Lewis Cass (Democrat)	42.5	127	
Martin Van Buren (Free-Soil)	10.1	——	
1852			69.6
Franklin Pierce (Democrat)	50.9	254	
Winfield Scott (Whig)	44.1	42	
John P. Hale (Free-Soil)	5.0	——	
1856			78.9
James Buchanan (Democrat)	45.3	174	
John C. Frémont (Republican)	33.1	114	
Millard Fillmore (American)	21.6	8	
1860: See also Sectional Breakdown below			81.2
Abraham Lincoln (Republican)	39.8	180	
Stephen A. Douglas (Democrat)	29.5	12	
John C. Breckinridge (Democrat)	18.1	72	
John Bell (Constitutional Union)	12.6	39	

TABLE 2. (cont.)

Year, candidate, and party	*Percent of popular vote*	*Electoral vote*	*Percent voter participation*
1864			73.8
Abraham Lincoln (Republican)	55.0	212	
George B. McClellan (Democrat)	45.0	21	
1868			78.1
Ulysses S. Grant (Republican)	52.7	214	
Horatio Seymour (Democrat)	47.3	80	
1872			71.3
Ulysses S. Grant (Republican)	55.6	286	
Horace Greeley (Democrat; Liberal Republican)	43.9	66	
1876			81.8
Rutherford B. Hayes (Republican)	48.0	185*	
Samuel J. Tilden (Democrat)	51.0	184	

*Includes 20 contested electoral votes from Florida, Louisiana, Oregon, and South Carolina, all of which were awarded to Hayes by a specially appointed commission of five Senators, five representatives, and five Supreme Court justices.

THE ELECTION OF 1860: A SECTIONAL BREAKDOWN

	Percent of a candidate's votes from free states	*Percent of a candidate's votes from slave states*
Lincoln	98.6	1.2
Douglas	88.2	11.8
Breckinridge	32.8	67.2
Bell	13	87

SOURCE: George B. Tindall and David E. Shi, *America: A Narrative History*, 4th ed. (1994).

TABLE 3.

SLAVEHOLDING IN
THE UNITED STATES, 1860

	Estimated number of white families	*Total number of slaveholders (percent of total number of families)*	*Total number of slaveholders owning 5 or more slaves (percent of total number of families)*
Border States	466,292	76,335 (16%)	30,797 (7%)
Delaware	15,562	587 (4%)	111 (1%)
Kentucky	164,428	38,645 (24%)	16,619 (10%)
Maryland	94,855	13,783 (15%)	5,410 (6%)
Missouri	191,447	23,320 (12%)	8,657 (5%)
Upper South	515,299	124,779 (24%)	63,704 (12%)
Arkansas	57,208	1,149 (2%)	409 (1%)
South Carolina	119,127	34,658 (29%)	18,857 (16%)
Tennessee	148,025	36,844 (25%)	17,665 (12%)
Virginia	190,939	52,128 (27%)	26,773 (14%)
Lower South	487,503	181,521 (37%)	103,067 (21%)
Alabama	96,087	33,730 (35%)	19,326 (20%)
Florida	14,911	5,152 (35%)	2,919 (20%)
Georgia	109,283	41,084 (38%)	23,550 (22%)
Louisiana	70,994	22,033 (31%)	11,798 (17%)
Mississippi	62,882	30,943 (49%)	18,254 (29%)
South Carolina	56,695	26,701 (47%)	16,684 (29%)
Texas	76,651	21,878 (29%)	10,536 (14%)

SOURCE: J. G. Randall and David Donald, *The Civil War and Reconstruction*, p. 68.

TABLE 4.

AGRICULTURE, 1860

Agricultural asset	*North (percent of total)**	*South (percentof total)†*
Improved farmland, acres	106,171,756 (65%)	57,089,633 (35%)
Unimproved farmland, acres	106,486,777 (43%)	140,021,467 (57%)
Cash value of farms, dollars	4,779,933,587 (72%	1,870,938,920 (28%)
Cash value of improvements and machinery, dollars	163,033,703 (66%)	83,993,793 (34%)
Wheat, bushels	139,816,487 (82%)	31,366,894 (18%)
Corn, bushels	549,786,693 (66%)	280,665,014 (34%)
Rye, bushels	18,803,253 (90%)	2,173,033 (10%)
Barley, bushels	15,454,812 (99%)	180,307 (1%)
Oats, bushels	152,634,280 (88%)	19,920,408 (12%)
Rice, lbs.	38,313 (2%)	187,101,860 (98%)
Tobacco, lbs.	230,369,341 (54%)	199,021,430 (46%)
Cotton bales (400 lbs. each)	5,332 (1%)	5,192,744 (99%)
Peas and beans, bushels	3,632,317 (24%)	11,555,696 (76%)
Irish and sweet potatoes, bushels	182,960,269 (82%)	40,287,774 (18%)
Buckwheat, bushels	17,128,802 (97%)	536,112 (3%)
Value of orchard products, dollars	16,902,343 (86%)	2,857,018 (14%)
Hay, tons	18,059,845 (94%)	1,069,283 (6%)

*Includes the free states and territories as well as Delaware, the District of Columbia, Kentucky, Maryland, Missouri, and New Mexico territory

†Includes Alabama, Arkansas, Florida, Georgia, Louisiana, Mississippi, North Carolina, South Carolina, Tennessee, Texas, and Virginia

SOURCE: E. B. Long, *The Civil War Day by Day: An Almanac, 1861–1865* (1971).

TABLE 5.

LIVESTOCK, 1860

	North (percent of total)*		South (percent of total)†	
Horses	4,417,130	(72%)	1,698,328	(28%)
Mules	328,890	(29%)	800,663	(71%)
Milch cows	6,037,367	(69%)	2,691,495	(31%)
Other cattle	9,127,553	(54%)	7,783,922	(46%)
Sheep	18,304,727	(78%)	5,013,029	(22%)
Swine	17,024,709	(52%)	15,530,558	(48%)

*Includes the free states and territories as well as Delaware, the District of Columbia, Kentucky, Maryland, Missouri, and New Mexico territory

†Includes Alabama, Arkansas, Florida, Georgia, Louisiana, Mississippi, North Carolina, South Carolina, Tennessee, Texas, and Virginia

SOURCE: E. B. Long, *The Civil War Day by Day: An Almanac, 1861–1865* (1971).

TABLE 6.

TRANSPORTATION AND INDUSTRY, 1860

	*North (percent of total)**	*South (percent of total)†*
Railroads, miles	22,085 (72%)	8,541 (28%)
Industrial establishments	110,274 (85%)	19,514 (15%)
Capital investments, dollars	949,335,000 (90%)	100,665,000 (10%)
Value of annual industrial product, 1860, dollars	1,754,650,000 (92%)	145,350,000 (8%)
Value of homemade manufactures, 1860, dollars	10,055,922 (41%)	14,302,300 (59%)

*Includes the free states and territories as well as Delaware, the District of Columbia, Kentucky, Maryland, Missouri, and New Mexico territory

†Includes Alabama, Arkansas, Florida, Georgia, Louisiana, Mississippi, North Carolina, South Carolina, Tennessee, Texas, and Virginia

SOURCE: E. B. Long, *The Civil War Day by Day: An Almanac 1861–1865* (1971).

TABLE 7.

POPULATION, 1860

	North/Free States (percent of total)	*Border/Slave Areas (percent of total)**	*Seceding States (percent of total)†*
Total	19,034,434 (60.5%)	3,305,557 (10.5%)	9,103,332 (29%)
White	18,810,123 (69.6%)	2,743,728 (10.1%)	5,449,462 (20.2%)
Free black	225,973 (46.3%)	129,243 (26.5%)	132,760 (27.2%)
Slave	64 (—)	432,586 (11%)	3,521,110 (89%)

*Includes Delaware, the District of Columbia, Kentucky, Maryland, Missouri, New Mexico territory

†Includes Alabama, Arkansas, Florida, Georgia, Louisiana, Mississippi, North Carolina, South Carolina, Tennessee, Texas, and Virginia

SOURCE: E. B. Long, *The Civil War Day by Day: An Almanac, 1861–1865* (1971).

TABLE 8.

COMPARATIVE SIZES OF ARMIES

Date	*Union present*	*Union absent*	*Confederate present*	*Confederate absent*
July 1, 1861	183,588	3,163		
Dec. 31, 1861–Jan. 1, 1862	527,204	48,713	258,680	68,088
Mar.31, 1862	533,984	103,142		
June 30, 1862			224,146	103,903
Dec. 31, 1862–Jan. 1, 1863	698,802	219,389	304,015	145,424
Dec. 31, 1863–Jan. 1, 1864	611,250	249,487	277,970	186,676
June 30, 1864			194,764	121,083
Dec. 31, 1864–Jan. 1, 1865	620,924	338,536	196,016	204,771
Mar. 31, 1865	657,747	322,339		

SOURCE: E. B. Long, *The Civil War by Day: An Almanac, 1861–1865* (1971).

AN ANNOTATED CIVIL WAR CHRONOLOGY

1807	Robert E. Lee, future commander of the Confederate Army of Northern Virginia, born.
1808	Jefferson Davis, future president of the Confederate States of America, born.
1809	Abraham Lincoln, future president of the United States, born.
1820	Tecumseh (later William) Sherman, future Union general, born.
1820	Missouri Compromise—Temporary resolution to bitter debate about expansion of slavery. Missouri admitted as a slave state; Maine admitted as a free state; slavery excluded from the Louisiana Purchase lands north of 36' 30" latitude (except for Missouri). Helped avert major sectional crisis for three decades.
1821	James Longstreet, future Confederate general, born.
1822	Ulysses S. Grant, future general-in-chief of Union armies and president of the United States, born.
1824	Thomas J. (later "Stonewall") Jackson, future Confederate general, born.
1826	George McClellan, future commander of the Union Army of the Potomac, born.
1845–46	Texas annexed by the United States.
1846	United States declares war on Mexico.
	Representative David Wilmot (D—Pennsylvania) proposes that slavery be prohibited in all territory acquired in the war against Mexico (Wilmot Proviso). Congressional legislation comes to a standstill amidst the furor.
1848	Treaty of Guadalupe-Hidalgo ends the war with Mexico. Mexico recognizes independence of Texas, accepts

	the Rio Grande as that state's southern boundary, and cedes the Southwest (modern California, Utah, Colorado, New Mexico, and Utah) to the United States in return for $15 million and assumption of some public Mexican debts.
	Zachary Taylor (Whig—Louisiana) elected president.
1850	Zachary Taylor dies in office; succeeded by Millard Fillmore (Whig—New York).
	Compromise of 1850—California admitted as a free state; territories of Utah and New Mexico created using principle of popular sovereignty; slave trade abolished in Washington, D.C.; strong federal Fugitive Slave Act passed; Texas gives up western claims in return for $10 million.
1852	Harriet Beecher Stowe publishes *Uncle Tom's Cabin,* an antislavery tract that enrages Southerners and energizes abolitionists.
	Franklin Pierce (D—New Hampshire) elected president.
1853	Gadsden Purchase—United States purchases a strip of present-day Arizona and New Mexico for $10 million in hopes of encouraging a southern transcontinental railroad.
1854	Kansas-Nebraska Act—Sponsored by Sen. Stephen A. Douglas (D—Illinois), creates Kansas and Nebraska territories with the possibility of slavery there; repeal of Missouri Compromise, which had prohibited slavery in the region.
	Ostend Manifesto—Three U.S. diplomats urge the purchase of Cuba from Spain for as much as $120 million. Presumption is that Cuba would become a slaveholding territory. Infuriates antislavery elements in North.
	Destruction of Whig Party as national institution.
1854–55	Creation of Republican Party.
1855–56	"Bleeding Kansas"—Virtual civil war in Kansas between pro- and antislavery forces. Features widespread killings by both sides.
1856	James Buchanan (D—Pennsylvania) elected president.
1856	*Dred Scott* decision is delivered by Supreme Court. Majority opinion (written by Chief Justice Roger B. Taney) declares that blacks cannot bring federal suits

	because they are not citizens, and that Congress cannot deprive persons of their property in the territories.
1857	Economic depression begins.
1858	Lincoln-Douglas debates in race for Illinois senatorship; Douglas reelected.
1859	John Brown leads abortive raid against federal arsenal at Harpers Ferry, Virginia. Designed to foster a slave rebellion, the raid horrifies slaveowners and increases fear of slave insurrection.
1860 Apr.	Democratic Party convention meeting at Charleston, South Carolina, splits between northern and southern wings. Convention adjourns to meet again in Baltimore.
1860 May	New Constitutional Union Party meets at Baltimore, Maryland, and attempts to form coalition of Know-Nothings and former Whigs. John Bell (Tennessee) is nominated for president.
	Republicans, meeting at Chicago, Illinois, nominate Abraham Lincoln (Illinois) for president.
1860 June	Democrats reconvene at Baltimore, but are unable to agree upon a candidate. Northern wing nominates Stephen Douglas; southerners nominate John C. Breckinridge (Kentucky).
1860 Nov.	Abraham Lincoln (R—Illinois) elected president.
1860 Dec.	South Carolina leaves the Union. Federal troops at Charleston, South Carolina, commanded by Maj. Robert Anderson, evacuate exposed position at Fort Moultrie in favor of a more defensible position at Fort Sumter.
1861 Jan.	President Buchanan dispatches reinforcements for Fort Sumter aboard the unarmed merchant ship *Star of the West.* Confederates besieging Fort Sumter fire upon the ship as it attempts to enter Charleston harbor, forcing it to turn about without resupplying the Federal garrison. Mississippi, Florida, Alabama, Georgia, and Louisiana secede from the Union.
1861 Feb.	Texas secedes from the Union. Formation of the Confederate States of America. Fifty delegates from seven states in the lower South establish a provisional government and elect Jefferson Davis president.
	Crittenden Compromise, a last-ditch effort within Congress to avert secession by extending the old Missouri

	Compromise line (36'30") to territories "hereafter acquired," is rejected by President-elect Abraham Lincoln.
1861 Mar.	Abraham Lincoln inaugurated. Almost immediately, he receives word from Major Anderson that the Fort Sumter garrison will have to surrender if it is not resupplied.
	First Morrill Tariff establishes protective tariff on many imports. Long opposed by Southerners, who feared other nations would retaliate with tariffs of their own against U.S. agricultural exports.
1861 Apr.	Federal fleet dispatched to resupply Fort Sumter. Confederates demand surrender of Major Anderson and the garrison; when this is rejected, they begin bombarding the fort. Federals surrender.
	Lincoln proclaims the seven seceded states to be in a state of rebellion; calls for 75,000 volunteers and imposes a naval blockade.
	Pro-Southern mob attacks Massachusetts troops en route to Washington, D.C. Lincoln calls in reinforcements to occupy Maryland. Maryland legislature rejects secession.
	Virginia secedes.
	Federals abandon Norfolk Navy Yard, Virginia.
1861 May	North Carolina and Arkansas secede. Sporadic fighting begins in Missouri, where Unionists and secessionists clash over control of the state. Kentucky legislature rejects Gov. Boriah Magoffin's call for secession.
	Britain proclaims neutrality; other European governments follow suit.
	Confederate capital moved from Montgomery, Alabama, to Richmond, Virginia.
1861 June	Tennessee secedes.
	U.S. Sanitary Commission established, a Federal effort to improve military hygiene, care for the wounded, and coordinate supplies and reinforcements sent to soldiers.
	Delegates from western Virginia meet at Wheeling and begin steps toward establishing separate statehood.
	First Battle of Bull Run (Manassas), Virginia—Con-

	federate troops under P. G. T. Beauregard and Joseph E. Johnston defeat Union army commanded by Irwin McDowell. Thomas J. "Stonewall" Jackson gains national prominence for his performance during the battle.
1861 July	Missouri state convention elects pro-Union Hamilton R. Gamble governor.
1861 Aug.	Congress passes the first income tax in American history (initially 3 percent on income over $800; eventually rises to 10 percent of income over $5,000).
	Battle of Wilson's Creek, Missouri—Outnumbered Union forces under Nathaniel Lyon defeated by Confederate and Missouri state troops led by Benjamin McCulloch and Sterling Price, respectively. Much of southern Missouri is laid open to the Confederacy.
	Union armada forces capture Roanoke Island, North Carolina.
	John C. Frémont establishes martial law in Missouri.
1861 Sept.	Confederate forces under Leonidas K. Polk enter Kentucky. Ill-advised move buttresses pro-Union sentiment there and allows Union troops to enter in response.
	Albert Sidney Johnston assigned command of Confederate forces in the west.
1861 Oct.	William T. Sherman is given command of Union Department of the Cumberland.
1861 Nov.	George McClellan succeeds Winfield Scott as general-in-chief of U.S. Army.
	Confederate voters elect Davis to six-year term as president.
	Battle of Belmont, Missouri—Ulysses S. Grant, in his first Civil War command, launches indecisive attack against Confederates.
	Samuel F. Du Pont's Union fleet forces surrender of Port Royal, South Carolina.
	British merchant ship *Trent* is stopped in international waters by U.S. Navy; two Confederate diplomats aboard the British ship taken into temporary custody. Storm of international protest leads to release of the diplomats, thus averting further crisis.
	Don Carlos Buell supersedes Sherman as commander of newly formed Department of the Ohio. Sherman re-

	assigned to lesser command under Henry Halleck; some contend he has suffered nervous breakdown.
	Henry Halleck succeeds John C. Frémont as commander of the Department of the Missouri.
1861 Dec.	Henry H. Sibley launches Confederate invasion of New Mexico.
1862 Feb.	Fall of Forts Henry and Donelson in Tennessee to Union forces led by Ulysses S. Grant. Federal occupation of Nashville, home of some of the South's largest industries, follows.
	Battle of Valverde, New Mexico—Confederate victory throws open Albuquerque and Santa Fe to Rebel occupation.
	Davis inaugurated president of the permanent Confederate government.
	First Legal Tender Act authorizes what eventually totals about $450 million of paper currency to aid the finance of the Union war effort.
1862 Mar.	Battle of Pea Ridge (Elkhorn Tavern), Arkansas—Federals under Samuel R. Curtis defeat Confederate commands of Earl Van Dorn and Ben McCulloch, thus removing immediate threat to Union-occupied Missouri.
	Ironclad ram CSS *Virginia* takes on Union wooden fleet off Hampton Roads, Virginia, sinking one ship and forcing another to surrender. Federal ironclad, USS *Monitor* arrives that night, and fights *Virginia* to a draw the following day.
	Battle of Glorieta Pass, New Mexico—Union victory forces Confederates to evacuate New Mexico.
	Jackson's Shenandoah Valley campaign begins. Pins down thousands of Federal troops through forced marches and daring tactics; gains control of fertile Shenandoah Valley for Confederacy.
	Fearing the job entails too many responsibilities, Lincoln relieves McClellan as general-in-chief, but retains him as commander of the Army of the Potomac.
	McClellan begins Peninsular campaign in Virginia. McClellan hopes to strike Confederate capital at Richmond from the southeast, along the James River.
1862 Apr.	Battle of Shiloh (Pittsburg Landing), Tennessee—Con-

federate troops, commanded by Albert Sidney Johnston, attack Union forces under Grant. Johnston mortally wounded during the first day of fighting, with command devolving to Beauregard. Though surprised on the first day, Grant recovers and counterattacks on the second day, thus winning the battle.

Union forces under John Pope capture Island No. 10, thus opening the Mississippi River as far south as Fort Pillow, Tennessee.

Confederate Congress adopts conscription, granting exceptions for those in certain skilled occupations and slaveholders who own twenty or more slaves.

Union fleet, commanded by David Farragut, runs past Confederate forts guarding the Mississippi River. Farragut's fleet continues up the river and forces the surrender of New Orleans, Louisiana, the largest city in the South.

1862 May

Battle of Seven Pines, Virginia—Indecisive Confederate attack against McClellan on outskirts of Richmond. J. E. Johnston wounded.

Homestead Act offers what amounts to free public land to western settlers.

1862 June

Robert E. Lee assumes command of what will become the Confederate Army of Northern Virginia.

With an eye to an eventual offensive of his own, Lee recalls Jackson from the Shenandoah Valley.

Federals take Fort Pillow, forcing Confederates to abandon Memphis, Tennessee.

J. E. B. Stuart, commanding Confederate cavalry, makes first ride around Union Army of the Potomac.

Seven Days' Battles, Virginia—Lee launches multiple attacks against McClellan outside Richmond. McClellan saves his army, but retreats back down the peninsula.

Braxton Bragg replaces Beauregard as commander of main Confederate army in the west.

John Pope appointed commander of the newly formed Union Army of Virginia.

Davis establishes separate Trans-Mississippi Department, and gives Theophilus H. Holmes command.

1862 July	Pacific Railroad Act sets aside federal lands to help private companies build a transcontinental railroad.
	Morrill Land Grant Act sets aside federal lands to help fund higher education (30,000 acres per member of Congress), eventually leading to creation of numerous agricultural and mechanical colleges in states.
	Halleck named general-in-chief of Union armies.
	John Dahlgren appointed chief of the Naval Ordnance Bureau.
1862 Aug.	Braxton Bragg and Edward Kirby Smith begin Confederate invasion of Kentucky.
	The *Alabama* joins Confederate navy; will become most feared Rebel commerce-raider.
	Dakota Indian uprising in Minnesota. Several hundred whites killed in initial onslaught, but Federal positions at New Ulm and Fort Ridgely hold out.
	Second Battle of Bull Run (Manassas), Virginia—Lee nearly annihilates Pope just south of Washington, D.C.
1862 Sept.	Lee's first invasion of the North begins; many in Europe believe the Confederacy is on the verge of winning the war.
	Pope reassigned to command Department of the Northwest.
	McClellan returns to command the Army of the Potomac.
	Lee's Special Order No. 191, outlining his offensive movements into Maryland, falls into Union hands.
	Battle of South Mountain, Maryland—McClellan's overcaution wastes an opportunity to destroy Lee's scattered army.
	Battle of Antietam (Sharpsburg), Maryland—McClellan attacks Lee's outnumbered army, but allows battle to devolve into three separate stages. Lee's army is saved by late arrival of A. P. Hill from Harper's Ferry. Bloodiest single day in American military history.
	Lincoln proclaims his intention to free all slaves in areas not under Union control.
	Battle of Wood Lake, Minnesota—Federal troops commanded by Henry Hastings Sibley inflict demoralizing defeat on Dakotas. About two thousand Indians eventu-

	ally turn themselves in; 307 initially sentenced to be executed.
1862 Oct.	Battle of Corinth, Mississippi—Hoping to strike against Grant's supply line, Van Dorn launches unsuccessful attack against Federals holding key Corinth rail junction.
	Battle of Perryville, Kentucky—Bragg engages part of Buell's Union army; heavily outnumbered, Bragg withdraws and ends attempted invasion of Kentucky.
	William S. Rosecrans succeeds Buell in command of the Army of the Cumberland.
	Mathew Brady's photographs of the battlefield at Antietam are exhibited in New York City.
1862 Nov.	Ambrose E. Burnside replaces McClellan as head of the Army of the Potomac. McClellan eventually returns to civilian life.
	Grant begins first Vicksburg campaign.
	Confederate Army of Tennessee formed by junction of Kirby Smith's Army of Kentucky and Bragg's Army of Mississippi.
1862 Dec.	Raids by Nathan Bedford Forrest and Van Dorn cut Grant's supply lines, thus forcing him to abandon early efforts to move against Vicksburg.
	Thirty-eight Sioux Indians executed at Mankato, for their role in the Minnesota uprising against federal authority.
	Battle of Fredericksburg, Virginia—Burnside launches unsuccessful frontal assault against Lee's army. Confederate general James Longstreet especially magnificent in defense.
	Battle of Chickasaw Bluffs, Mississippi—Sherman launches unsuccessful front attack against Confederate forces near Vicksburg. Bloody repulse leads to Union retreat.
	Battle of Stones River (Murfreesboro), Tennessee—Rosecrans (Army of the Cumberland) inflicts bloody repulse of attacks by Bragg (Army of Tennessee).
1863 Jan.	Emancipation Proclamation goes into effect.
	Joseph Hooker assumes command of the Army of the Potomac.
	Grant begins second Vicksburg campaign.

Federal and state troops under Patrick E. Connor massacre inhabitants of northwestern Shoshoni village at Bear River, Idaho.

1863 Feb. National Banking Act—First of several wartime banking acts begins to bring about a more uniform national currency.

1863 Mar. Conscription officially begins in the North.

1863 Apr. Cpt. James Arthur Fremantle, British Army, lands in Mexico to begin five-month tour of the United States.

Bread riots in Richmond, Virginia.

Union gunboats run past Vicksburg batteries. Elements of Grant's army later cross the Mississippi River at Bruinsburg, south of Vicksburg.

Hooker begins offensive in the east.

1863 May Battle of Chancellorsville, Virginia—Despite facing an enemy army twice the size of his own, Lee routs Hooker and the Army of the Potomac. Battle features daring Confederate attack commanded by Jackson, which surprises Union right flank. Accidentally wounded by his own men, Jackson later dies from complications.

Grant marches north from Bruinsburg, isolating Confederate garrison at Vicksburg. Following unsuccessful attack against enemy fortifications, he settles in for a siege.

Former Ohio congressman Clement Vallandigham, an outspoken opponent of the war, exiled from the Union.

1863 June Battle of Brandy Station (Beverly Ford), Virginia—largest cavalry engagement of war. Alfred Pleasanton, commanding Union mounted forces, attacks Confederates under Stuart. Although Confederates retain field, Stuart is criticized for mediocre performance by Southern press.

Lee begins second invasion of the North.

West Virginia admitted into the Union.

George Meade takes command of the Army of the Potomac.

1863 July Battle of Gettysburg, Pennsylvania. First day—Confederate attack drives Union troops through Gettysburg to Cemetery Hill, but Jubal Early fails to press assault against Culp's Hill on Union right flank. Second day—

Longstreet directs disjointed Confederate attacks against Union left, at Little Round Top, Devil's Den, the Wheat Field, and the Peach Orchard. Federals continue to hold high ground. Third day—Confederate assault against Union center, spearheaded by George Pickett, thrown back with heavy losses.

Confederate garrison at Vicksburg, Mississippi, commanded by John Pemberton, surrenders to Grant.

Draft riots in New York City.

Unsuccessful attack by Robert Gould Shaw and the Fifty-fourth Massachusetts Colored Infantry against Fort Wagner, South Carolina.

1863 Aug. Pro-Southern guerrillas under William Quantrill sack Lawrence, Kansas.

1863 Sept. Federal troops under Burnside enter Knoxville, Tennessee, severing most direct Confederate rail link between Chattanooga and Virginia.

Battle of Sabine Pass, Texas—Four thousand-strong Federal invasion force sailing up Sabine River, led by William B. Franklin, checked by forty Confederates under Lt. Dick Dowling.

Rosecrans forces Bragg to evacuate Chattanooga, Tennessee.

Longstreet dispatched with two divisions from Army of Northern Virginia to reinforce Bragg's Army of Tennessee.

James Ripley resigns as army chief of ordnance.

Lincoln suspends writ of habeas corpus.

Battle of Chickamauga, Georgia—Bragg counterattacks Rosecrans just south of Chattanooga. During second day of fighting, Longstreet shatters Union center. Battered Union Army of the Cumberland retreats back into Chattanooga, where Bragg begins siege.

Federals begin transfer of two corps from Army of the Potomac to help relieve Rosecrans.

1863 Oct. Grant given command of most Federal troops in the west with formation of Military Division of the Mississippi (combining departments of the Ohio, the Tennessee, the Cumberland, and Arkansas). Thomas replaces Rosecrans as commander, Army of the Cumberland.

	Sherman and Hooker reinforce Chattanooga, breaking Confederate siege.
1863 Nov.	Longstreet begins unsuccessful siege of Knoxville, Tennessee.
	Lincoln delivers Gettysburg Address at dedication of new National Cemetery at Gettysburg.
	Battle of Lookout Mountain, Tennessee—Preliminary Union assaults versus Confederates holding high ground around Chattanooga.
	Battle of Missionary Ridge, Tennessee—Union attack routs Bragg's army.
1863 Dec.	Lincoln proposes the 10 percent plan for reconstruction, whereby government in a seceding state can be recognized once it has support of 10 percent of those who had voted in 1860.
	J. E. Johnston named commander of the Army of Tennessee.
	Navajo Indians begin surrendering in New Mexico after long campaign by Christopher "Kit" Carson.
1864 Mar.	Nathaniel P. Banks begins Red River campaign in Louisiana.
	Grant appointed general-in-chief of the armies of the United States; Sherman succeeds him as head of Military Division of the Mississippi. Philip Sheridan named commander of Army of the Potomac's cavalry. Grant will personally accompany the Army of the Potomac in the field, although Meade retains command.
1864 Apr.	Battle of Mansfield (Sabine Cross Roads), Louisiana—Confederates under Richard Taylor defeat Banks's Red River expedition.
	Battle of Pleasant Hill, Louisiana—Taylor's attempt to annihilate Banks's army fails, but Federal retreat continues.
	Fort Pillow, Tennessee, massacre of several dozen black soldiers by Forrest's Confederates.
1864 May	Battle of the Wilderness, Virginia—Lee inflicts major defeat upon Grant near old battlefields of Chancellorsville and Fredericksburg. Despite loss, Grant continues campaign by swinging south and east.
	Sheridan launches cavalry raid against Richmond.

	Battle of Spotsylvania, Virginia—Series of Federal attacks against Lee's positions, highlighted by near-breakthrough at what became known as Bloody Angle. Grant continues to try to swing south and east of Lee.
	Battle of Yellow Tavern, Virginia—Sheridan defeats Confederate cavalry; Stuart mortally wounded during battle.
	Sherman's Atlanta campaign begins.
1864 June	Jubal Early's Shenandoah Valley campaign begins, culminating in last Confederate threat against Washington D.C.
	Battle of Cold Harbor, Virginia—Grant launches futile frontal assault against Lee. Despite defeat, Grant continues to press south.
	Battle of Kennesaw Mountain, Georgia—Sherman makes unsuccessful assault against Johnston's Army of Tennessee.
	USS *Kearsage* sinks Confederate commerce raider *Alabama* off the coast of Cherbourg, France.
	Grant begins siege of Petersburg, Virginia.
1864 July	Lincoln pocket-vetoes Wade-Davis bill, which would have reorganized a seceded state after the majority of registered voters had taken an oath of allegiance and adopted a constitution acceptable to Congress and the president. No former Confederates would have been eligible to participate.
	With Sherman on outskirts of Atlanta, Hood replaces J. E. Johnston as commander of the Army of Tennessee. Hood launches several unsuccessful counterattacks against Federals.
1864 Aug.	Battle of Mobile Bay, Alabama—Damning the torpedoes, Farragut's fleet sails past Confederate defenses guarding entrance to Mobile Bay, effectively closing the port of Mobile.
	Sheridan given command of newly organized Army of the Shenandoah to deal with Early's continuing presence in the Valley.
	Sterling Price launches final major Confederate raid into Missouri.
	George McClellan accepts Democratic Party's presidential nomination.

1864 Sept. Atlanta falls to Sherman.

1864 Oct. Battle of Cedar Creek, Virginia—Early launches surprise attack against Federal Army of the Shenandoah. Sheridan, who had been in Washington, returns in time to launch dramatic afternoon counterattack, thus recovering the field.

Hood heads north into Tennessee, hoping to draw Sherman north by threatening his supply lines.

Cutting loose from his own supplies and dispatching reinforcements back to Tennessee to help check Hood's invasion, Sherman begins his March to the Sea.

1864 Nov. Lincoln elected for a second term as president. Andrew Johnson (D—Tennessee) replaces Hannibal Hamlin (R—Maine) as vice president in move designed to form a "Union" ticket, as the Republican Party styles itself in 1864.

Battle of Franklin, Tennessee—Hood attacks John Schofield's Army of the Ohio. Heavy Confederate losses, especially among general officers.

1864 Dec. Battle of Nashville, Tennessee—Commanding the reinforced Army of the Cumberland, George Thomas annihilates Hood's battered Army of Tennessee on the outskirts of Nashville. Ironically, Thomas had nearly been replaced before the battle for not attacking more quickly.

Sherman captures Savannah, Georgia.

Sand Creek, Colorado massacre of several hundred southern Cheyennes by John Chivington's state troops.

1865 Jan. Fort Fisher, North Carolina, falls to Union forces.

Lee given overall command of all Confederate armies.

1865 Feb. Sherman begins driving north from Savannah into the Carolinas.

Bureau of Refugees, Freedmen, and Abandoned Lands established to help freed slaves.

J. E. Johnston returns to command Confederate Army of Tennessee and Confederate forces in the Carolinas.

1865 Apr. Battle of Five Forks, Virginia—Sheridan's successful attack against strategic rail line forces Lee to begin abandoning his lines at Petersburg.

Union troops occupy Richmond, Virginia.

Battle of Sayler's Creek, Virginia—Lee's rear guard an-

	nihilated as he attempts to escape to the west and join J. E. Johnston.
	Lee surrenders at Appomattox Court House, Virginia.
	Lincoln assassinated by John Wilkes Booth.
	Johnston surrenders all Confederate forces in the Carolinas.
1865 May	Davis captured at Irwinsville, Georgia.
1865 June	Edmund Kirby Smith surrenders the Trans-Mississippi Department to Federal authorities.
Late 1865	President Andrew Johnson, hoping to win South's voluntary compliance and determined to maintain executive automony, announces general amnesty for those who take oath of future loyalty to the Union. He also demands that former Confederate states ratify the Thirteenth Amendment (abolishing slavery) and repudiate secession as conditions for reentering the Union. Former Confederate states begin forming local governments and electing representatives to Congress.
1865 Dec.	Thirteenth Amendment ratified.
1866	Former Confederate states enact Black Codes, designed to maintain social order in the South along racial lines by denying black's access to the courts, restricting their ability to assemble in public or to own land, requiring them to show deference to whites, and enacting stiff penalties for vagrancy.
	Congress refuses to allow representatives from unreconstructed former Confederate states to be seated. Republicans in Congress clash with Johnson over terms by which former Confederate states may reenter Union.
	In mid-term elections Republicans secure "veto-proof" congressional majority.
1867	Frustrated by President Johnson's opposition to reconstruction, Congress begins initial impeachment investigations.
	Reconstruction Acts—Congress sets out terms for readmission of unreconstructed former Confederate states into Union: ratification of Fourteenth (equal protection and due process) and Fifteenth (voting rights) Amendments, and congressional approval of proposed state constitutions. Until then, many former Confederates were disfranchised and local government were under military supervision in the South.

	Tenure of Office Act—Fearful of Johnson's meddling, Congress forbids President Johnson from removing certain Federal officials.
	United States purchases Alaska.
	House rejects initial vote of impeachment against President Johnson, 57 to 108.
1868	Fourteenth Amendment ratified.
	Johnson attempts to remove Secretary of War Edwin Stanton, thus violating Tenure of Office Act.
	House votes to impeach Johnson, 126 to 47. It later adopts articles of impeachment.
	Senate votes 35 to 19 on removal of Johnson from office (one vote short of two-thirds majority necessary for removal).
	Grant (R—Illinois) elected president.
1869	First transcontinental railroad completed.
	National Woman Suffrage Association formed.
	Fifteenth Amendment ratified.
1870	Lee dies.
1872	Grant reelected president.
1873	Economic Panic of 1873, sparked by the failure of the investment firm Jay Cooke and Company, leads to four-year economic depression.
1876	Disputed returns from Florida, Louisiana, Oregon, and South Carolina presidential election between Rutherford B. Hayes (R—Ohio) and Samuel J. Tilden (D—New York) leave neither presidential candidate with a majority of electoral votes.
1877	Informal Compromise of 1877 allows Hayes to become president in exchange for limiting federal involvement in former Confederate states. Conservative rule now reestablished in all Southern states.
1885	Grant dies.
	McClellan dies.
1889	Jefferson Davis dies.
1891	Sherman dies.
1904	Longstreet dies.

INDEX

ABOUT THE AUTHOR

While in graduate school, native Texan **Robert Wooster** worked as an assistant to James A. Michener on the latter's novel *Texas*. After Wooster completed his Ph.D. at the University of Texas in 1985, he joined the faculty at Texas A&M University–Corpus Christi. He has written books about the army in nineteenth-century Texas, military policy and the Indians in the late nineteenth century, a history of Fort Davis, Texas, and a biography of a general who served in the Civil War and Indian wars, Nelson A. Miles. Wooster's latest book, *The Civil War 100: A Ranking of the Most Influential People in the War Between the States* (1998), was also published by Citadel Press.

Wooster is currently Frantz Professor of History at Texas A&M University–Corpus Christi. In 1998 he was named a Piper Professor for his distinguished teaching. He lives in Corpus Christi, Texas.